Holistic Revolution

Holistic Revolution

The Essential Reader

Selected and edited with an Introduction by
WILLIAM BLOOM

ALLEN LANE
THE PENGUIN PRESS

For David Spangler

ALLEN LANE
THE PENGUIN PRESS

Published by the Penguin Group
Penguin Books Ltd, 27 Wrights Lane, London w8 5tz, England
Penguin Putnam Inc., 375 Hudson Street, New York, New York 10014, USA
Penguin Books Australia Ltd, Ringwood, Victoria, Australia
Penguin Books Canada Ltd, 10 Alcorn Avenue, Toronto, Ontario, Canada m4v 3b2
Penguin Books (NZ) Ltd, Private Bag 102902, NSMC, Auckland, New Zealand

Penguin Books Ltd, Registered Offices: Harmondsworth, Middlesex, England

First published by Allen Lane The Penguin Press 2000
10 9 8 7 6 5 4 3 2 1

The Acknowledgements on p. viii constitute an extension of this copyright page

Set in 10.5/14 pt PostScript Linotype Sabon
Typeset by Rowland Phototypesetting Ltd, Bury St Edmunds, Suffolk
Printed and bound in Great Britain by The Bath Press, Bath

A CIP catalogue record for this book is available from the British Library

ISBN 0-713-99421-5

Contents

Holistic Health and Healing

Feminism and the Goddess

The Shamanic and Magical Traditions

Mystic and Esoteric Religion

Modern Prophesy

Acknowledgements

There are many people who gave me their opinion on what should and what should not be in this Reader. At one point I emailed over one hundred colleagues for suggestions. I am grateful to all of them and I hope they forgive me for not listing them formally, but I am wary lest I forget one or more. My particular thanks to Gareth Mills of The Speaking Tree Bookshop in Glastonbury for his generosity of spirit. To Liz Puttick for setting the ball rolling on this project in the first place. And to Anna South at Penguin for some very helpful editorial advice.

Introduction

In a shrinking planet of free-flowing information, the whole nature of what we call religion is bound to change. The monolithic certainty which has defined most faiths has no choice today but to encounter all the other competing spiritual certainties. For some people this encounter stimulates defensiveness and fundamentalism. But for many others, in the spirit of open-mindedness, rigid boundaries melt or are overthrown.

Today, if people want to investigate the meaning and the wonder of life, if people want to understand who they are and how best to live their lives – inquiries that were once the strict preserve of the few established religions – there are now a thousand paths to pursue.

The change over the last hundred years has been dramatic. Before the twentieth century, people were genuinely restricted in seeking answers to their significant inquiries about meaning, wonder and identity. Sources of information were severely limited. Where could people go to discuss their questions and receive insight and informed advice? There were no local bookshops, few newspapers, no specialist journals, no mass media, no local libraries. For immediate attention there was little alternative but the local priest or wise woman. And what could be expected from these two largely depended on their education and attitude.

The seeker could perhaps travel, either to some library or centre of learning, or wander as a pilgrim from teacher to teacher. But that kind of searching path required a determined motivation. It also required literacy, not a common currency.

Access to information was geographically and culturally restricted. The very act of seeking the information could also be dangerous. Heresy could lead to death.

In the past, therefore, because of these general conditions it was easy for organized religious institutions to dominate access to information and the actual content of this information.

Today, on the other hand, someone who inquires into the purpose of life and the nature of identity can simply wander down to the local bookshop. Ever since the establishment of bookshops and public libraries, people have been able to pursue their investigations independently. But since the 1960s there has been a huge expansion in the number of books which explore these issues in an accessible way. The inquiry is no longer restricted to academics and intellectuals, but has become truly public. Bookshop managers classify this section of their shelves in various ways, but the most frequent labellings are Holistic, New Age or Mind-Body-Spirit, and they may cover for example popular philosophy, religion, new science, feminism, self-help, psychology, ecology and healing. In some of the specialist stores, there may be up to twenty thousand titles covering the field and there are usually one or two New Age titles in the paperback non-fiction bestseller lists.

Alongside these books there is available a whole new industry of lectures, courses, trainings, retreats, holidays, workshops, treatments and consultations, all of which give people first-hand experience of the new ideas and approaches. Mainstream universities and colleges are beginning to present these courses, in addition to which people in the established religions, including priests, are exploring the holistic approach in a way that they find complementary to, and supportive of, their faith.

In this anthology, for ease of approach, I have divided the whole field into eight sections, starting with what might be called the most physical and then travelling across a spectrum to the most metaphysical. These sections are New Science, Psychology, Gaia – The Living Earth, Holistic Health and Healing, Feminism and the Goddess, The Shamanic and Magical Traditions, Mystic and Esoteric Religion, ending with Modern Prophesy. In each section I present extracts which give a taste of its most influential ideas. Each section and contribution is separately introduced.

Throughout the book and in this introduction I use the two terms 'holistic' and 'New Age' interchangeably, as referring to the same general phenomenon. However, I imagine in the long-term that the phrase 'New Age' will pass out of common usage as the culture inevitably becomes less new and the significance of the term 'holistic' becomes better appreciated.

Originally perceived by many people as a passing fashion, the holistic and New Age movement can no longer be ignored. It threatens established religions; its activists and thinkers have increasing credibility; it represents the cutting edge of much science, medicine and psychology; it is a daily feature of contemporary media; and no matter how the establishment intelligentsia may judge it, millions of people are turning to it.

A recent survey by the *Journal of the American Medical Association* showed a dramatic surge in the popularity of alternative medical approaches during the 1990s. Forty-two per cent of the adult American population, or eighty-three million adults, used one or more of sixteen alternative therapies during 1997, a thirty per cent increase over 1990. Similar figures are available for Britain. What is also deeply significant here, as the journal itself points out, is the fact that many alternative health therapies are directly related to holistic and spiritual perspectives which are outside the usual scientific world-view.

There has also been a major shift in the way that the media deal with the holistic approach. In the 1970s and 1980s, journalists were almost universally hostile to the New Age phenomenon. It was considered a passing fashion that belonged to an eccentric minority and was the subject of mainly sardonic comments. But gradually during the 1990s there was a clear and discernible change. Whatever hard-nosed editors might have originally thought, the holistic movement was growing substantially. There was a market here, a market far larger than would normally be addressed by their religious, medical or scientific correspondents. Many newspapers, lowbrow and highbrow alike, began to run regular holistic sections under titles such as Holistic Health or Body and Spirit.

Television channels also ran series examining the New Age movement, and chat and magazine shows regularly included holistic approaches. (I was once invited to audition for a prime-time Saturday chat show and had my audition between a Barry Manilow impersonator and the ninety-year-old woman who created the children's programme

The Flower Pot Men. I was turned down – to both my disappointment and relief.)

The substantial growth of the holistic movement has been nothing to do with it being fashionable. It is because its various aspects are genuinely relevant to certain human needs. In the first place, for example, it is unlike mainstream religion and medicine. It actually encourages personal involvement and inquiry. Second, not only is it accessible, but it also offers new and practical strategies for addressing everyday challenges. The holistic movement continues to grow because it offers useful ways of engaging and coping with the modern world.

Originally holistic ideas may have seemed fashionable because so many celebrities were visibly associated with them. But very many prominent individuals, who have absolutely no need to be seen as fashionable, have become involved also. It was widely reported that at various moments of crisis both President and Hillary Clinton received personal, spiritual and communications skills counselling from holistic practitioners. Prince Charles and the late Diana, Princess of Wales have both been clearly aligned with New Age attitudes; the Prince with his interest in mysticism and organic farming, Diana with her interest in therapy and the self-help movement. The Queen of England uses homeopathy, a medical approach whose foundation is based primarily in understanding the whole person, and even the deeply conservative Prince Philip has given speeches extolling the virtues of tribal cultures in relation to the environment. The Prime Minister of Great Britain, Tony Blair, brought in the Chinese mystical technique of Feng Shui to harmonize the vibrations of 10 Downing Street. In the media itself it is extremely significant that its most powerful woman, Oprah Winfrey, has openly been a propagandist for holistic approaches.

What was marginal two decades ago is now increasingly mainstream.

There has been a huge shift, and commentators are only just beginning to grasp how deep and significant it is. Still thinking that it might be ephemeral, they are missing the wider context. The cultural environment has genuinely changed – and, with it, the form and culture of religion are transforming also.

The very nature of the post-modern global village – the contemporary way of researching, perceiving and interpreting – is that people do and will seek information as widely as possible. It is absolutely logical, then, that religion and religious inquiry will also begin to reflect these new circumstances. It will tend to be international, universalist, process-oriented, pluralistic, diverse, democratic, networked and decentralized. Reflecting the free-flowing accessibility of information, the new religious approach will also tend to be an open information system and not one of closed beliefs. All of this is exactly the nature of the holistic approach.

But this openness to diversity has also led to hostility and criticism. Many commentators have condemned the holistic movement as being a commercialization of spirituality, a supermarket approach to the meaning of life, a buffet of shallow choices. But this criticism wrongly assumes that the multifaceted approach is, by its very nature, an avoidance of serious inquiry. It also presupposes that serious invest-igation should always be within one tradition and school. It is easy to imagine one of those sardonic strip cartoons where, at the end of a haircut, a hairdresser might inquire, 'Anything for the weekend? Zen therapy, madam? Some quantum physics, sir? Tantric dancing?'

The holistic approach, however, celebrates the liberation from nar-row paths that have too often been over-controlling if not completely corrupt. It sees no problem in people exploring and 'tasting' many different approaches. In fact, the holistic approach encourages the widest possible inquiry precisely to avoid the pitfalls of cults and fundamentalism. The criticism that a widespread inquiry is in some way shallow misses the point that people need to start from a point of informed choice and then make their own decisions. Just because in the past people have been constrained to single religious paths is no sign that this was either good or useful. People should be free to explore meaning and reality in as many ways as are available.

I call the holistic movement 'religious' because it explores the major metaphysical questions of wonder, meaning and identity. But many people within the holistic movement are actively hostile to or suspicious of the word 'religion' precisely because of its association with hierarch-ical organizations seeking to impose uniformity of thought in the name of divine inspiration. One dictionary, for example, defines religion as 'belief in, worship of, obedience to a supernatural power considered to have control over human destiny . . . Any formal or institutionalized expression of such belief' (*Collins Concise Dictionary*, 1996). Most holists are profoundly antagonistic to such a definition. The very nature of the holistic approach is to be aware of as many levels of analysis and avenues of insight as are relevant.

Fundamentalists from all faiths are therefore hostile to the holistic approach. This is not surprising. The holistic approach openly challenges any belief system which claims exclusivity or monopoly of truth. This challenge is directed at spiritual monopolies as much as it is at materialist intellectualism.

How much the holistic approach threatens mainstream fundamentalism was clearly illustrated in my own experience at the 1998 Oslo Conference on Freedom of Religion and Belief. I was the delegate representing the New Age and Holistic approach to religion which had been given equal status alongside the major faiths.

During my presentation to the main conference I suggested that there was a natural human instinct to explore wonder and identity, and that this was in fact the source of religion. I suggested that the pursuit of this instinct be recognized as a basic human right. These two suggestions provoked the only openly hostile audience reaction in the whole four days. (The Buddhist monk representing Peking who suggested that the Dalai Lama should keep out of China's internal affairs was listened to diplomatically; as was the Zionist who claimed that Arab Palestinians had forfeited their religious rights.) The hostility to my holistic presentation came from Christian, Jewish and Islamic religious leaders whose basic theology presents religion as a gift or revelation from God and not as a natural impulse grounded in humanity. Holism directly threatens monopolistic theological hierarchies with their middle management of priests.

Religious fundamentalists are also suspicious of holism's genuine universality which they claim demonstrates a lack of discrimination and has no appreciation of the fact that people require guidance. Look at the holistic shelves in a bookshop, they say. The seeker, instead of finding a simple and pure source of spiritual information, is overwhelmed by choices: translations and commentaries on the religious scriptures from all cultures; first-hand accounts of tribal religions; books on the nature and pain of human growth and healing; the latest revelations of physics, cosmology and biology; inspirational and prophetic writings; prose and poetry on the beauty of our natural environment, and activism against thoughtlessness and pollution.

This is all too much for the average human being, comes the fundamentalist argument. What people need is the clear guidance of a historically grounded faith which has a genuine experience of life and which gives a clear set of moral guidelines.

This criticism has some sense in it, but it stands on ground that is giving way. Historically, it may be that the main faiths have brought decency and justice and beauty into barbaric cultures, but every child's history book also tells a story of the terrible brutalities enacted in the name of those self-same religions. Religious certainty is as much a source of danger and conflict as of peace and understanding.

We are in changing times and today, for many people, religious certainty does not seem such an attractive option. This is not just a matter of aesthetics. Anyone with the slightest knowledge of psychology or emotional intelligence recognizes that people with a fundamentalist certainty about their ideas – those who are not open to listening to and respecting other viewpoints – are either ignorant or insecure. Rigid conviction is no longer seen as an admirable role model for leadership. A monolithic belief system seems primitive and oppressive. It is a cultural dinosaur.

But it is not only religious fundamentalists who dislike the New Age approach. Cynics, atheists and materialistic fundamentalists are also antagonistic towards it. And this is understandable. Historically, religion has been tainted with oppression, superstition, manipulation and over-simplification. The victory in the last centuries of a scientific, democratic and humanistic approach over monarchy and religion is to be cherished and upheld. The holistic movement can look like just another spiritual confidence trick, especially at its more illogical, superstitious and self-obsessed edges.

When, however, sceptical commentators actually engage with holistic ideas – rather than just snipe from a distance – they are frequently disarmed. The only fundamentalist idea in holism is that the universe and consciousness are diverse but intimately interconnected, and that it is healthy and meaningful to explore it all. Four centuries ago Francis Bacon recognized this danger of a closed mind among scientists and philosophers when he asserted to them: 'There is a superstition in avoiding superstition.'

The accusation that the movement is shallow is also often accompanied by the assertion that, because of its diverse base, it has no clear morality. Where is its code of ethics? Post-modern relativism is all very well in art and fashion, but it cannot be applied to personal, social and spiritual behaviour. Relativism is too dangerous a morality. Holism provides no guidelines. This criticism also derives from the self-help aspect of the New Age movement which is well-publicized, commercially successful, often narcissistic and usually lacks social awareness.

There is a false supposition here that the holistic movement has, for some reason or another, ditched all the ethical guidelines which humanity has thus far found good and useful.

While the holistic movement has not generally articulated its moral guidelines, they are implicit in and fundamental to the holistic way of thinking. They derive from various sources and, certainly, the movement needs to articulate them more clearly.

One source is the insights which contemporary science and ecology have to offer. They demonstrate the delicate and absolute interdependence of our lives on this planet – and therefore our inescapable need to take full responsibility for our attitudes and actions.

Another source is the clear moral codes of the world's religions. The holistic movement is actively and warmly interested in all spiritual traditions and their ethical suggestions. It embraces them and is interested in how similar they are and how they complement each other. Here, in fact, is a clear example of how the holistic supermarket and post-modern relativism can work to everyone's benefit. The Ten Commandments are not in competition with the Sermon on the Mount or the Buddha's Eightfold Path or any of the injunctions from other faiths. They are all respected and drawn upon. They reinforce each other.

A third source for the holistic moral code is in its healing and therapeutic background. From within the holistic movement it seems only too obvious how vulnerable we and other life forms are. There is a clear recognition that human beings need safety, support and encouragement to fulfil themselves and their communities. There is also a clear sense that every human individual, like every tree or mountain or animal, is sacred and that, simply because we are alive, we deserve the space to grow and develop into our full potential.

In fact, Abraham Maslow's hierarchy of human needs has almost become a moral document for holists: unless you are fed, clothed and housed, unless you are psychologically and physically safe, you cannot get on with the real business of fulfilling and actualizing your life. We are all called therefore to behave in a manner which supports and encourages each other and the whole community of life. Holistic morality is not simply a matter of avoiding 'bad' behaviour. It is a clear call to a positive and proactive morality that has a distinct sense of psychological, ecological and social realities.

There are, however, crass and dangerous aspects of the movement. The accusations of commercialism and psychologically damaging quick-fixes are sometimes true. I am also concerned about those thoughtless New Age ideas which suggest that every individual creates their own reality, with no understanding of historical reality and with no compassion for people caught up in overwhelming circumstances.

My most severe doubts of the holistic movement, however, are put in perspective when I focus on its fundamentally redemptive and benevolent dynamic. This dynamic can be seen clearly in a historical and mythical context.

Anthropological studies show that tribal peoples have an instinctive awareness of their environment and its sacred dimensions. They have a direct and unselfconscious personal experience of the beauty and spirit of nature and the universe. It is reasonable to imagine a time when all hunter-gathering and early pastoral peoples had this natural religious experience.

But the rise of civilization, small cities and institutional religion, has had a profound impact upon this natural communion with nature and universe. Towns and cities, capitalism and technology, by their very nature – the noise, the busyness, the buildings, the pollution, the drives – tend to sabotage and obstruct the natural experience. This alienation from the natural and cosmic environment has been deepened by the great institutionalized religions which have tended actively to distrust any natural celebration of the environment. Many people have been tortured and burnt for their love of nature. To be a pagan is still dangerous in some places.

Marx protested about people's alienation from their own labour. Freud challenged us with ideas about our sexual repression and alienation. But perhaps the most serious alienation of the last millennium has been our lack of connection with the wonder of life. We are creatures of a beautiful nature and universe – yet we hardly feel it. We are of it, yet separate from it. This is a profound, unhealthy and dangerous division. It separates us from our true relationship with our true environment. It leaves us frigid and anxious for short-term gratification, individually and as a global community.

The holistic approach presents a creative and deeply hopeful answer. Without returning to or creating religious dogma or superstition, it affirms that the natural experience of life is to connect with its wonder and pursue our inquiry into identity and meaning. It affirms that there is an inner spirit to everything, including ourselves.

Historically the world's great faiths and their organizations have tended not to support such a democratic approach to spiritual experience. Their organizational structures reflect this with their hierarchical nature. At the top of the pyramid is some kind of divine revelation. At the bottom of the pyramid are the general recipients of the wisdom. In between is a curious layer of clerics and bureaucrats, patriarchs who usually distrust and repress those who do not respect their authority and status.

The holistic movement on the other hand has been created by people throughout the system. This has not necessarily been a conscious ideological act. It emerges from the nature of contemporary information. The hierarchical model of religious revelation and organization no longer has any relevance, because information flows in all directions and can *emerge* from anywhere within the system.

Holism also addresses and explains traditions that are foreign to each other. It is continually interested in new information and understandings. It has no desire to be centralized or organized. This is the very essence of the holistic revolution. From a religious standpoint, it marks the complete overthrow of the established style and structure.

If the religious impulse emerges from the basic and natural human need to explore identity, meaning and the wonder of the universe, then it is obvious that the information age provides an extraordinary array of choices. It accepts the realities of contemporary life, but it also attempts to see through and beyond them. It rejects any path which claims to be the only way. In opposition to both a reductionist scientific world-view and a monopolizing imperialist religion, the holistic approach affirms that *life does indeed have a wonder and inner dimension worthy of exploration*. And beyond that it only says, 'Look, here are a thousand different ways of exploring it.'

Editorial Note on the Selection

The anthology is divided into eight sections and I hope the way that I have created these categories is useful. It could of course have been done in other ways. It has been an enormous challenge to select the appropriate books and authors and then the appropriate passages. I have had to exclude many writers and many ideas, but that is inevitable with a project like this.

Because of the nature of the subject, there are also overlaps between the sections. Many of the extracts could fit in more than one section. This is the very nature of holism. Candace Pert's piece on endorphins, for instance, could easily have been included in three places, in the sections on Science or Psychology or Healing.

As an active observer and participant in the holistic movement for thirty years, I set myself the following guideline: every contribution has to represent an author or an idea which has made a substantial and popularly acknowledged contribution to holistic culture. Sometimes the extract is from a known core text that started a new line of thinking, such as Wilhelm Reich on orgasm, body armour and energy. Other times the extract is from an author who is not an initiating source, but best represents a particular subject, such as Richard Gerber on energy medicine.

New Science

The most important function of art and science is to awaken the cosmic religious feeling and keep it alive.

Albert Einstein

Introduction

The old science provides a logical and mechanical model of how the universe functions. In its own domain, it has been brilliant and transformative. But there is an essential problem with it: it is so different from the way in which human beings behave and experience life.

Human beings are eccentric, romantic, unpredictable – as is nature – so there has been a conflict between scientific logic on the one hand and the more humane and artistic experience of life on the other. Moreover, most science, especially as it manifests in industry and technology, has proven hostile to nature.

The environmental crisis, the general anxiety and alienation that many people feel, the mechanization of life, the disenchantment of the sacred – all of this seems to be the fault of a reductionist, mechanical and uncaring science. Worst of all, if this kind of mechanical science is used as the model for understanding human nature, it actively rejects humane and spiritual insights.

New science on the other hand has a different foundation. Subatomic and quantum physics have replaced mechanistic logic with an understanding and methodology that is far more fluid and relativistic. The new scientific world-view embraces unpredictability as a major feature of life and it recognizes that solid boundaries are, beneath their superficial appearance, plastic and permeable.

The old Newtonian model of the universe as a beautiful clock is giving way to something far more complex, in which matter and consciousness are part of the same spectrum, and in which the 'stuff' of the universe seems as interested in eccentric dancing as it is in obeying simple laws of push-pull.

The new insights in science are of course a natural progression from a more mechanical physics, but they have been particularly appreciated by people with a holistic approach who see the new scientific paradigm as revolutionary, liberating and humane. This is because the new perspective allows and encourages a new mindset in general.

The old science had far more influence than just as the source of new technology. The very way in which people did scientific thinking was considered to be the model for how thinking should always be done. This was not only a matter of intellectual style but it also absolutely excluded intuitive insights and connections. This is both harsh and stupid when faced with the beautiful emerging diversities of the human psyche, of culture and of complex ecosystems.

Today, the mentality which is only concerned with hard logic and closed to other more humane factors, is forced to open and transform. The hard mechanical model can no longer be used to understand people and the universe.

Science as Mysticism

FRITJOF CAPRA
The Tao of Physics

Originally a high-energy physicist at the University of Vienna, Fritjof Capra became fascinated by how the new concepts and descriptive language of subatomic physics were so similar to Eastern scriptures. In *The Tao of Physics* he put forward the argument that the mystical traditions of the East formed a coherent philosophical framework which can comfortably accommodate the most advanced scientific theories of the physical universe. This book was immensely influential and commercially successful. It popularized the whole understanding that physics had undergone an immense paradigm shift and that reality could no longer be explained in a purely mechanistic language.

The classical, mechanistic world-view was based on the notion of solid, indestructible particles moving in the void. Modern physics has brought about a radical revision of this picture. It has led not only to a completely new notion of 'particles', but has also transformed the classical concept of the void in a profound way. This transformation took place in the so-called field theories. It began with Einstein's idea of associating the gravitational field with the geometry of space, and became even more pronounced when quantum theory and relativity theory were combined to describe the force fields of subatomic particles. In these 'quantum field theories', the distinction between particles and the space surrounding them loses its original sharpness and the void is recognized as a dynamic quantity of paramount importance.

The field concept was introduced in the nineteenth century by Faraday and Maxwell in their description of the forces between electric charges and currents. An electric field is a condition in the space around a charged body which will produce a force on any other charge in that space. Electric fields are thus created by charged bodies and their effects can only be felt by charged bodies. Magnetic fields are produced by charges in motion, i.e. by electric currents, and the magnetic forces resulting from them can be felt by other moving charges. In classical electrodynamics, the theory constructed by Faraday and Maxwell, the fields are primary physical entities which can be studied without any reference to material bodies. Vibrating electric and magnetic fields can travel through space in the form of radio waves, light waves, or other kinds of electromagnetic radiation.

Relativity theory has made the structure of electrodynamics much more elegant by unifying the concepts of both charges and currents and electric and magnetic fields. Since all motion is relative, every charge can also appear as a current – in a frame of reference where it moves with respect to the observer – and, consequently, its electric field can also appear as a magnetic field. In the relativistic formulation of electrodynamics, the two fields are thus unified into a single electro-magnetic field.

The concept of a field has been associated not only with the electro-magnetic force, but also with that other major force in the large-scale world, the force of gravity. Gravitational fields are created and felt by all massive bodies, and the resulting forces are always forces of attraction, contrary to the electromagnetic fields which are felt only by charged bodies and which give rise to attractive and repulsive forces. The proper field theory for the gravitational field is the general theory of relativity, and in this theory the influence of a massive body on the surrounding space is more far-reaching than the corresponding influence of a charged body in electrodynamics. Again, the space around the object is 'conditioned' in such a way that another object will feel a force, but this time the conditioning affects the geometry, and thus the very structure of space.

Matter and empty space – the full and the void – were the two fundamentally distinct concepts on which the atomism of Democritus and of Newton was based. In general relativity, these two concepts can no longer be separated. Wherever there is a massive body, there will also be a gravitational field, and this field will manifest itself as the curvature of the space surrounding that body. We must not think, however, that the field fills the space and 'curves' it. The two cannot be distinguished; the field *is* the curved space! In general relativity, the gravitational field and the structure, or geometry, of space are identical.

They are represented in Einstein's field equations by one and the same mathematical quantity. In Einstein's theory, then, matter cannot be separated from its field of gravity, and the field of gravity cannot be separated from the curved space. Matter and space are thus seen to be inseparable and interdependent parts of a single whole.

Material objects not only determine the structure of the surrounding space but are, in turn, influenced by their environment in an essential way. According to the physicist and philosopher Ernst Mach, the inertia of a material object – the object's resistance against being accelerated – is not an intrinsic property of matter, but a measure of its interaction with all the rest of the universe. In Mach's view, matter only has inertia because there is other matter in the universe. When a body rotates, its inertia produces centrifugal forces (used, for example, in a spin-drier to extract water from wet laundry), but these forces appear only because the body rotates 'relative to the fixed stars', as Mach has put it. If those fixed stars were suddenly to disappear, the inertia and the centrifugal forces of the rotating body would disappear with them.

This conception of inertia, which has become known as Mach's principle, had a deep influence on Albert Einstein and was his original motivation for constructing the general theory of relativity. Due to the considerable mathematical complexity of Einstein's theory, physicists have not yet been able to agree whether it actually incorporates Mach's principle or not. Most physicists believe, however, that it should be incorporated, in one way or another, into a complete theory of gravity.

Thus modern physics shows us once again – and this time at the macroscopic level – that material objects are not distinct entities, but are inseparably linked to their environment; that their properties can only be understood in terms of their interaction with the rest of the world. According to Mach's principle, this interaction reaches out to the universe at large, to the distant stars and galaxies. The basic unity of the cosmos manifests itself, therefore, not only in the world of the very small but also in the world of the very large; a fact which is increasingly acknowledged in modern astrophysics and cosmology. In the words of the astronomer Fred Hoyle:

Present-day developments in cosmology are coming to suggest rather insistently that everyday conditions could not persist but for the distant parts of the Universe, that all our ideas of space and geometry would become entirely invalid if the distant parts of the Universe were taken away. Our everyday experience even down to the smallest details seems to be so closely integrated to the grand-scale features of the Universe that it is well-nigh impossible to contemplate the two being separated.[1]

The unity and interrelation between a material object and its environment, which is manifest on the macroscopic scale in the general theory of relativity, appears in an even more striking form at the subatomic level. Here, the ideas of classical field theory are combined with those of quantum theory to describe the interactions between subatomic particles. Such a combination has not yet been possible for the gravitational interaction because of the complicated mathematical form of Einstein's theory of gravity; but the other classical field theory, electrodynamics, has been merged with quantum theory into a theory called 'quantum electrodynamics' which describes all electromagnetic interactions between subatomic particles. This theory incorporates both quantum theory and relativity theory. It was the first 'quantum-relativistic' model of modern physics and is still the most successful.

The striking new feature of quantum electrodynamics arises from the combination of two concepts; that of the electromagnetic field, and that of photons as the particle manifestations of electromagnetic waves. Since photons are also electromagnetic waves, and since these waves are vibrating fields, the photons must be manifestations of electromagnetic fields. Hence the concept of a 'quantum field', that is, of a field which can take the form of quanta, or particles. This is indeed an entirely new concept which has been extended to describe all subatomic particles and their interactions, each type of particle corresponding to a different field. In these 'quantum field theories', the classical contrast between the solid particles and the space surrounding them is completely overcome. The quantum field is seen as the fundamental physical entity; a continuous medium which is present everywhere in space. Particles are merely local condensations of the field; concentrations of energy which come and go, thereby losing their individual character and dissolving into the underlying field. In the words of Albert Einstein:

We may therefore regard matter as being constituted by the regions of space in which the field is extremely intense . . . There is no place in this new kind of physics both for the field and matter, for the field is the only reality.[2]

The conception of physical things and phenomena as transient manifestations of an underlying fundamental entity is not only a basic element of quantum field theory, but also a basic element of the Eastern world-view. Like Einstein, the Eastern mystics consider this underlying entity as the only reality: all its phenomenal manifestations are seen as transitory and illusory. This reality of the Eastern mystic cannot be identified with the quantum field of the physicist because it is seen as the essence of *all* phenomena in this world and, consequently, is beyond all concepts and ideas. The quantum field, on the other hand, is a well-defined concept which only accounts for some of the physical phenomena. Nevertheless, the intuition behind the physicist's interpretation of the subatomic world, in terms of the quantum field, is closely paralleled by that of the Eastern mystic who interprets his or her experience of the world in terms of an ultimate underlying reality. Subsequent to the emergence of the field concept, physicists have attempted to unify the various fields into a single fundamental field which would incorporate all physical phenomena. Einstein, in particular, spent the last years of his life searching for such a unified field. The *Brahman* of the Hindus, like the *Dharmakaya* of the Buddhists and the *Tao* of the Taoists, can be seen, perhaps, as the ultimate unified field from which spring not only the phenomena studied in physics, but all other phenomena as well.

Holographic Universe

DAVID BOHM
Wholeness and the Implicate Order

Professor of Theoretical Physics at Birkbeck College, London University, David Bohm put forward an idea that caught people's imaginations and also had a certain mystic quality about it. This concept was that, in some way, everything is enfolded within everything else. Drawing, for instance, upon the example of the hologram, he pointed out that the hologram can be broken into fragments, yet any of these fragments still retains the image of the whole picture. Every fragment is capable of holding all reality within itself. The whole is enfolded within every aspect of itself. This is similar to mystic descriptions of that state of meditative consciousness in which, while retaining identity, people experience no boundaries and an intimate inner connection with everything. It is also a way of describing a deity which is both the whole universe, yet immanent within everything.

Implicate and explicate order

What is being suggested here is that the consideration of the difference between lens and hologram can play a significant part in the perception of a new order that is relevant for physical law. As Galileo noted the distinction between a viscous medium and a vacuum and saw that physical law should refer primarily to the order of motion of an object in a vacuum, so we might now note the distinction between a lens and a hologram and consider the possibility that physical law should refer primarily to an order of undivided wholeness of the content of a description similar to that indicated by the hologram rather than to an order of analysis of such content into separate parts indicated by a lens.

However, when Aristotle's ideas on movement were dropped, Galileo and those who followed him had to consider the question of how the new order of motion was to be described in adequate details. The

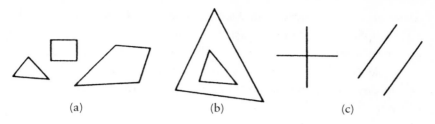

Figure 1

answer came in the form of Cartesian coordinates extended to the language of the calculus (differential equations, etc.). But this kind of description is of course appropriate only in a context in which analysis into distinct and autonomous parts is relevant, and will therefore in turn have to be dropped. What, then, will be the new kind of description appropriate to the present context?

As happened with Cartesian coordinates and the calculus, such a question cannot be answered immediately in terms of definite prescriptions as to what to do. Rather, one has to observe the new situation very broadly and tentatively and to 'feel out' what may be the relevant new features. From this, there will arise a discernment of the new order, which will articulate and unfold in a natural way (and not as a result of efforts to make it fit well-defined and preconceived notions as to what this order should be able to achieve).

We can begin such an inquiry by noting that in some subtle sense, which does not appear in ordinary vision, the interference pattern in the whole plate can distinguish different orders and measures in the whole illuminated structure. For example, the illuminated structure may contain all sorts of shapes and sizes of geometric forms (indicated in Figure 1a), as well as topological relationships, such as inside and outside (indicated in Figure 1b), and intersection and separation (indicated in Figure 1c). All of these lead to different interference patterns and it is this difference that is somehow to be described in detail.

The differences indicated above are, however, not only in the plate. Indeed, the latter is of secondary significance, in the sense that its main function is to make a relatively permanent 'written record' of the interference pattern of the light that is present in each region of space.

More generally, however, in each such region, the movement of the light implicitly contains a vast range of distinctions of order and measure, appropriate to a whole illuminated structure. Indeed, in principle, this structure extends over the whole universe and over the whole past, with implications for the whole future. Consider, for example, how on looking at the night sky, we are able to discern structures covering immense stretches of space and time, which are in some sense contained in the movements of light in the tiny space encompassed by the eye (and also how instruments, such as optical and radio telescopes, can discern more and more of this totality, contained in each region of space).

There is the germ of a new notion of order here. This order is not to be understood solely in terms of a regular arrangement of *objects* (e.g., in rows) or as a regular arrangement of *events* (e.g., in a series). Rather, a *total order* is contained, in some *implicit* sense, in each region of space and time.

Now, the word 'implicit' is based on the verb 'to implicate'. This means 'to fold inward' (as multiplication means 'folding many times'). So we may be led to explore the notion that in some sense each region contains a total structure 'enfolded' within it.

It will be useful in such an exploration to consider some further examples of enfolded or *implicate* order. Thus, in a television broadcast, the visual image is translated into a time order, which is 'carried' by the radio wave. Points that are near each other in the visual image are not necessarily 'near' in the order of the radio signal. Thus, the radio wave carries the visual image in an implicate order. The function of the receiver is then to *explicate* this order, i.e., to 'unfold' it in the form of a new visual image.

A more striking example of implicate order can be demonstrated in the laboratory, with a transparent container full of a very viscous fluid, such as treacle, and equipped with a mechanical rotator that can 'stir' the fluid very slowly but very thoroughly. If an insoluble droplet of ink is placed in the fluid and the stirring device is set in motion, the ink drop is gradually transformed into a thread that extends over the whole fluid. The latter now appears to be distributed more or less at 'random' so that it is seen as some shade of grey. But if the mechanical stirring device is now turned in the opposite direction, the transformation is reversed, and the droplet of dye suddenly appears, reconstituted.

When the dye was distributed in what appeared to be a random way, it nevertheless had *some kind* of order which is different, for example, from that arising from another droplet originally placed in a different position. But this order is *enfolded* or *implicated* in the 'grey mass' that is visible in the fluid. Indeed, one could thus 'enfold' a whole picture. Different pictures would look indistinguishable and yet have different implicate orders, which differences would be revealed when they were explicated, as the stirring device was turned in a reverse direction.

What happens here is evidently similar in certain crucial ways to what happens with the hologram. To be sure there are differences. Thus, in a fine enough analysis, one could see that the *parts* of the ink droplet remain in a one-to-one correspondence as they are stirred up and the fluid moves continuously. On the other hand, in the functioning of the hologram there is no such one-to-one correspondence. So in the hologram (as also in experiments in a 'quantum' context), there is no way ultimately to reduce the implicate order to a finer and more complex type of explicate order.

All this calls attention to the relevance of a new distinction between implicate and explicate order. Generally speaking, the laws of physics have thus far referred mainly to the explicate order. Indeed, it may be said that the principal function of Cartesian coordinates is just to give a clear and precise description of explicate order. Now, we are proposing that in the formulation of the laws of physics, primary relevance is to be given to the implicate order, while the explicate order is to have a secondary kind of significance (e.g., as happened with Aristotle's notion of movement, after the development of classical physics). Thus, it may be expected that a description in terms of Cartesian coordinates can no longer be given a primary emphasis, and that a new kind of description will indeed have to be developed for discussing the laws of physics.

The holomovement and its aspects

To indicate a new kind of description appropriate for giving primary relevance to implicate order, let us consider once again the key feature of the functioning of the hologram, i.e., in each region of space, the order of a whole illuminated structure is 'enfolded' and 'carried' in the movement of light. Something similar happens with a signal that modulates a radio wave (see Figure 2). In all cases, the content or meaning that is 'enfolded' and 'carried' is primarily an order and a measure, permitting the development of a structure. With the radio wave, this structure can be that of a verbal communication, a visual image, etc., but with the hologram far more subtle structures can be involved in this way (notably three-dimensional structures, visible from many points of view).

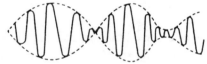

Figure 2

More generally, such order and measure can be 'enfolded' and 'carried' not only in electromagnetic waves but also in other ways (by electron beams, sound, and in other countless forms of movement). To generalize so as to emphasize undivided wholeness, we shall say that what 'carries' an implicate order is *the holomovement*, which is an unbroken and undivided totality. In certain cases, we can abstract particular aspects of the holomovement (e.g., light, electrons, sound, etc.), but more generally, all forms of the holomovement merge and are inseparable. Thus, in its totality, the holomovement is not limited in any specifiable way at all. It is not required to conform to any particular order, or to be bounded by any particular measure. Thus, *the holomovement is undefinable and immeasurable*.

To give primary significance to the undefinable and immeasurable holomovement implies that it has no meaning to talk of a *fundamental* theory, on which *all* of physics could find a *permanent* basis, or to which *all* the phenomena of physics could ultimately be reduced. Rather, each theory will abstract a certain aspect that is *relevant* only in some limited context, which is indicated by some appropriate measure.

Every particle of the world is a mirror,
In each atom lies the blazing light
  of a thousand suns.
Cleave the heart of a rain-drop,
  a hundred pure oceans will flow forth.
Look closely at a grain of sand,
  the seed of a thousand beings can be seen.
    Mahmud Shabestari 1250–1320

Chaos

JAMES GLEICK
Chaos – Making a New Science

As a *New York Times* science reporter, James Gleick wrote the first popularly accessible book on chaos theory. Chaos theory has been an important source for the holistic approach because it demonstrates several things that students of holism want to hear: it reinforces the notion that anything is capable of affecting anything else – the well-known Butterfly Effect, discovered by Edward Lorenz using computer modelling, that the flap of a butterfly's wing might, through a chain of weather events, create a storm on the other side of the globe; it clearly demonstrates that the mechanistic world-view has to give way to something far more haphazard and multi-dimensional; and it shows, too, that throughout the universe random elements emerge and self-catalyse into discernible and coherent forms which display great beauty. The last is a stunning insight which can be applied, for example, to plants, social groups and galaxies. The images of the fractals were originally the most well-known examples of this. These were first developed by Benoit Mandelbrot in his books *Fractals: Form, Chance and Dimension* and *The Fractal Geometry of Nature*.

Lorenz's discovery was an accident, one more in a line stretching back to Archimedes and his bathtub. Lorenz never was the type to shout *Eureka*. Serendipity merely led him to a place he had been all along. He was ready to explore the consequences of his discovery by working out what it must mean for the way science understood flows in all kinds of fluids.

Had he stopped with the Butterfly Effect, an image of predictability giving way to pure randomness, then Lorenz would have produced no more than a piece of very bad news. But Lorenz saw more than randomness embedded in his weather model. He saw a fine geometrical structure, order *masquerading* as randomness. He was a mathematician in meteorologist's clothing, after all, and now he began to lead a double life. He would write papers that were pure meteorology. But he would also write papers that were pure mathematics, with a slightly misleading dose of weather talk as preface. Eventually the prefaces would disappear altogether.

He turned his attention more and more to the mathematics of systems that never found a steady state, systems that almost repeated themselves but never quite succeeded. Everyone knew that the weather was such a system – aperiodic. Nature is full of others: animal populations that rise and fall almost regularly, epidemics that come and go on tantalizingly near-regular schedules. If the weather ever did reach a state exactly like one it had reached before, every gust and cloud the same, then presumably it would repeat itself forever after and the problem of forecasting would become trivial.

Lorenz saw that there must be a link between the unwillingness of the weather to repeat itself and the inability of forecasters to predict it – a link between aperiodicity and unpredictability. It was not easy to find simple equations that would produce the aperiodicity he was seeking. At first his computer tended to lock into repetitive cycles. But Lorenz tried different sorts of minor complications, and he finally succeeded when he put in an equation that varied the amount of heating from east to west, corresponding to the real-world variation between the way the sun warms the east coast of North America, for example, and the way it warms the Atlantic Ocean. The repetition disappeared.

The Butterfly Effect was no accident; it was necessary. Suppose small perturbations remained small, he reasoned, instead of cascading upward through the system. Then when the weather came arbitrarily close to a state it had passed through before, it would *stay* arbitrarily close to the patterns that followed. For practical purposes, the cycles would be predictable – and eventually uninteresting. To produce the rich repertoire of real earthly weather, the beautiful multiplicity of it, you could hardly wish for anything better than a Butterfly Effect.

The Butterfly Effect acquired a technical name: sensitive dependence on initial conditions. And sensitive dependence on initial conditions was not an altogether new notion. It had a place in folklore:

For want of a nail, the shoe was lost;
For want of a shoe, the horse was lost;
For want of a horse, the rider was lost;
For want of a rider, the battle was lost;
For want of a battle, the kingdom was lost!

In science as in life, it is well known that a chain of events can have a point of crisis that could magnify small changes. But chaos meant that such points were everywhere. They were pervasive. In systems like the weather, sensitive dependence on initial conditions was an inescapable consequence of the way small scales intertwined with large. [. . .]

One wintry afternoon in 1975, aware of the parallel currents emerging in physics, preparing his first major work for publication in book form, Mandelbrot decided he needed a name for his shapes, his dimensions, and his geometry. His son was home from school, and Mandelbrot found himself thumbing through the boy's Latin dictionary. He came across the adjective *fractus*, from the verb *frangere*, to break. The resonance of the main English cognates – *fracture* and *fraction* – seemed appropriate. Mandelbrot created the word (noun and adjective, English and French) *fractal*.

In the mind's eye, a fractal is a way of seeing infinity. Imagine a triangle, each of its sides one foot long. Now imagine a certain transformation – a particular, well-defined, easily repeated set of rules. Take the middle one-third of each side and attach a new triangle, identical in shape but one-third the size.

The result is a star of David. Instead of three one-foot segments, the outline of this shape is now twelve four-inch segments. Instead of three points, there are six.

Now take each of the twelve sides and repeat the transformation, attaching a smaller triangle on to the middle third. Now again, and so on to infinity. The outline becomes more and more detailed, just as a Cantor set becomes more and more sparse. It resembles a sort of ideal snowflake. It is known as a Koch curve – a curve being any connected line, whether straight or round – after Helge von Koch, the Swedish mathematician who first described it in 1904.

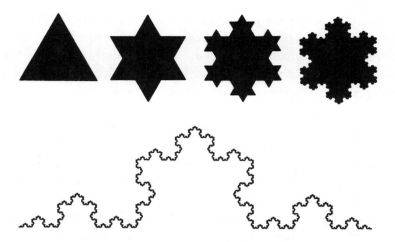

The Koch snowflake. 'A rough but vigorous model of a coastline', in Mandelbrot's words. To construct a Koch curve, begin with a triangle with sides of length 1. At the middle of each side, add a new triangle one-third the size; and so on. The length of the boundary is 3 × 4/3 × 4/3 × 4/3 – infinity. Yet the area remains less than the area of a circle drawn around the original triangle. Thus an infinitely long line surrounds a finite area.

On reflection, it becomes apparent that the Koch curve has some interesting features. For one thing, it is a continuous loop, never intersecting itself, because the new triangles on each side are always small enough to avoid bumping into each other. Each transformation adds a little area to the inside of the curve, but the total area remains finite, not much bigger than the original triangle, in fact. If you drew a circle around the original triangle, the Koch curve would never extend beyond it [...]

The mind cannot visualize the whole infinite self-embedding of complexity. But to someone with a geometer's way of thinking about form, this kind of repetition of structure on finer and finer scales can open a whole world. Exploring these shapes, pressing one's mental fingers into the rubbery edges of their possibilities, was a kind of playing, and Mandelbrot took a childlike delight in seeing variations that no one had seen or understood before. When they had no names, he named them: ropes and sheets, sponges and foams, curds and gaskets.

Fractional dimension proved to be precisely the right yardstick. In a sense, the degree of irregularity corresponded to the efficiency of the object in taking up space. A simple, Euclidean, one-dimensional line fills no space at all. But the outline of the Koch curve, with infinite length crowding into finite area, does fill space. It is more than a line, yet less than a plane. It is greater than one-dimensional, yet less than a two-dimensional form. Using techniques originated by mathematicians early in the century and then all but forgotten, Mandelbrot could characterize the fractional dimension precisely. For the Koch curve, the infinitely extended multiplication by four-thirds gives a dimension of 1.2618.

In pursuing this path, Mandelbrot had two great advantages over the few other mathematicians who had thought about such shapes. One was his access to the computing resources that go with the name of IBM. Here was another task ideally suited to the computer's particular form of high-speed idiocy. Just as meteorologists needed to perform the same few calculations at millions of neighbouring points in the atmosphere, Mandelbrot needed to perform an easily programmed transformation again and again and again and again. Ingenuity could conceive of transformations. Computers could draw them – sometimes with unexpected results. The early twentieth-century mathematicians quickly reached a barrier of hard calculation, like the barrier faced by early protobiologists without microscopes. In looking into a universe of finer and finer detail, the imagination can carry one only so far.

In Mandelbrot's words: 'There was a long hiatus of a hundred years where drawing did not play any role in mathematics because hand and pencil and ruler were exhausted. They were well understood and no longer in the forefront. And the computer did not exist.

'When I came in this game, there was a total absence of intuition. One had to create an intuition from scratch. Intuition as it was trained by the usual tools – the hand, the pencil, and the ruler – found these shapes quite monstrous and pathological. The old intuition was misleading. The first pictures were to me quite a surprise; then I would recognize some pictures from previous pictures, and so on.

'Intuition is not something that is given. I've trained my intuition to accept as obvious shapes which were initially rejected as absurd, and I find everyone else can do the same.'

Mandelbrot's other advantage was the picture of reality he had begun forming in his encounters with cotton prices, with electronic transmission noise, and with river floods. The picture was beginning to come into focus now. His studies of irregular patterns in natural processes and his exploration of infinitely complex shapes had an intellectual intersection: a quality of *self-similarity*. Above all, fractal meant self-similar.

Self-similarity is symmetry across scale. It implies recursion, pattern inside of pattern. Mandelbrot's price charts and river charts displayed self-similarity, because not only did they produce detail at finer and finer scales, they also produced detail with certain constant measurements. Monstrous shapes like the Koch curve display self-similarity because they look exactly the same even under high magnification. The self-similarity is built into the technique of constructing the curves – the same transformation is repeated at smaller and smaller scales. Self-similarity is an easily recognizable quality. Its images are every-where in the culture: in the infinitely deep reflection of a person standing between two mirrors, or in the cartoon notion of a fish eating a smaller fish eating a smaller fish eating a smaller fish. Mandelbrot likes to quote Jonathan Swift: 'So, Nat'ralists observe, a Flea/Hath smaller Fleas that on him prey,/And these have smaller Fleas to bite 'em,/And so proceed ad infinitum.'

Morphogenetic Fields

RUPERT SHELDRAKE
A New Science of Life

Rupert Sheldrake is a Cambridge-educated biochemist who, after working as a research scientist in the development of plants, lived for a year and a half at the Christian ashram of Father Bede Griffiths in south India. It was there that he developed the organismic idea that there is a field of formative causation which is responsible for the shapes and instincts of all living things, the *morphogenetic field*. Dismissed by most mainstream science as a ridiculous idea, it has nevertheless become one of the pillars of a holistic approach. Dr Sheldrake's theory, although put forward within a scientific framework, has many resonances with the mystical ideas of, for example, the Jungian school of psychology and the neo-Platonic school of philosophy, both of which suggest that there are forms and archetypal shapes which exist in a dimension beyond our normal time–space references.

The hypothesis of *formative causation* proposes that morphogenetic fields play a causal role in the development and maintenance of the forms of systems at all levels of complexity. In this context, the word 'form' is taken to include not only the shape of the outer surface or boundary of a system, but also its internal structure. This suggested causation of form by morphogenetic fields is called formative causation in order to distinguish it from the energetic type of causation with which physics already deals so thoroughly. For although morphogenetic fields can only bring about their effects in conjunction with energetic processes, they are not in themselves energetic.

The idea of non-energetic formative causation is easier to grasp with the help of an architectural analogy. In order to construct a house, bricks and other building materials are necessary; so are the builders who put the materials into place; and so is the architectural plan which determines the form of the house. The same builders doing the same total amount of work using the same quantity of building materials could produce a house of different form on the basis of a different plan. Thus the plan can be regarded as a *cause* of the specific form of the house, although of course it is not the only cause: it could never be realized without the building materials and the activity of the builders. Similarly, a specific morphogenetic field is a cause of the specific form taken up by a system, although it cannot act without suitable 'building blocks' and without the energy necessary to move them into place.

This analogy is not intended to suggest that the causative role of morphogenetic fields depends on conscious design, but only to emphasize that not all causation need be energetic, even though all processes of change involve energy. The plan of a house is not in itself a type of energy. Even when it is drawn on paper, or finally realized in the form of the house, it does not weigh anything or have any energy of its own. If the paper is burnt or the house is demolished, there is no measurable change in the total amount of mass and energy; the plan simply vanishes. Likewise, according to the hypothesis of formative causation, morphogenetic fields are not in themselves energetic; but nevertheless they play a causal role in determining the forms of the systems with which they are associated. For if a system were associated with a different morphogenetic field, it would develop differently. This hypothesis is empirically testable in cases where the morphogenetic fields acting on systems can be altered.

Morphogenetic fields can be regarded as analogous to the known fields of physics in that they are capable of ordering physical changes, even though they themselves cannot be observed directly. Gravitational and electromagnetic fields are spatial structures which are invisible, intangible, inaudible, tasteless and odourless; they are detectable only through their respective gravitational and electromagnetic effects. In order to account for the fact that physical systems influence each other at a distance without any apparent material connection between them, these hypothetical fields are endowed with the property of traversing empty space, or even actually constituting it. In one sense, they are non-material; but in another sense they are aspects of matter because they can only be known through their effects on material systems. In effect, the scientific definition of matter has simply been widened to take them into account. Similarly, morphogenetic fields are spatial structures detectable only through their morphogenetic effects on material systems; they too can be regarded as aspects of matter if the definition of matter is widened still further to include them. [. . .]

Atoms are in turn the morphogenetic germs of molecules, and small molecules the germs of larger molecules. Chemical reactions involve either the aggregation of atoms and molecules into larger molecules – for example in the formation of polymers – or the fragmentation of molecules into smaller ones, or into atoms and ions, which may then aggregate with others, for example in combustion: under the influence of external energy, molecules fragment into atoms and ions which then combine with those of oxygen to form small, simple molecules like H_2O and CO_2. These chemical changes involve the actualization of virtual forms associated with the atoms or molecules which act as morphogenetic germs.

The idea that molecules have virtual forms before they are actualized is illustrated particularly clearly by the familiar fact that entirely new compounds can first be 'designed' on the basis of empirically determined principles of chemical combination and then actually synthesized by organic chemists. These laboratory syntheses are carried out step by step; in each step a particular molecular form serves as the morphogenetic germ for the next virtual form to be synthesized, ending up with the form of the entirely new molecule.

If it seems rather artificial to think of chemical reactions as morphogenetic processes, it should be remembered that much of the effect of catalysts, both inorganic and organic, depends on their morphology. For example, enzymes, the specific catalysts of the numerous reactions of biochemistry, provide surfaces, grooves, notches or basins into which the reacting molecules fit with a specificity which is often compared to that of a lock and key. The catalytic effect of enzymes depends to a large extent on the way in which they hold reactant molecules in the appropriate relative positions for reaction to occur. (In free solution the chance collisions of the molecules occur in all possible orientations, most of which are inappropriate.)

The details of chemical morphogeneses are vague, partly because of their great rapidity, partly because the intermediate forms may be highly unstable, and also because the ultimate changes consist of probabilistic quantum jumps of electrons between the orbitals which constitute the chemical bonds. The virtual form of the molecule-to-be is outlined in the morphogenetic field associated with the atomic or molecular morphogenetic germ; when the other atom or molecule approaches in an appropriate orientation, the form of the product molecule is actualized by means of quantum jumps of electrons into orbitals which previously existed only as virtual forms; at the same time energy is released, usually as thermal motion. The role of the morphogenetic field in this process is, as it were, energetically passive, but morphologically active; it creates virtual structures which are then actualized as lower-level morphic units 'slot' or 'snap' into them, releasing energy as they do so.

Any given type of atom or molecule can take part in many different types of chemical reaction, and it is therefore the potential germ of many different morphogenetic fields. These could be thought of as possibilities 'hovering' around it. However, it may not take on its role as the germ of a particular morphogenetic field until an appropriate reagent atom or molecule approaches it, perhaps owing to specific electromagnetic or other effects of the latter upon it.

The morphogenesis of crystals differs from that of atoms and molecules in that a particular pattern of atomic or molecular arrangement is repeated indefinitely. The morphogenetic germ is provided by this pattern itself. It is well known that the addition of 'seeds' or 'nuclei' of the appropriate type of crystal greatly accelerates the crystallization of supercooled liquids or supersaturated solutions. In the absence of these seeds or nuclei, morphogenetic germs of the crystal come into being only when the atoms or molecules take up their appropriate relative positions by chance, owing to thermal agitation. Once the germ is present, the virtual forms of repetitions of the lattice structure given by the morphogenetic field extend outwards from the surfaces of the growing crystal. Appropriate free atoms or molecules which approach these surfaces are captured and 'slot' into position; again thermal energy is released as they do so. [. . .]

But then what determines the particular form of the morphogenetic field?

One possible answer is that morphogenetic fields are eternal. They are simply given, and are not explicable in terms of anything else. Thus even before this planet appeared, there already existed in a latent state the morphogenetic fields of all the chemicals, crystals, animals and plants that have ever occurred on the earth, or that will ever come into being in the future.

This answer is essentially Platonic, or even Aristotelian in so far as Aristotle believed in the eternal fixity of specific forms. It differs from the conventional physical theory in that these forms would not be predictable in terms of energetic causation; but it agrees with it in taking for granted that behind all empirical phenomena lie pre-existing principles of order.

The other possible answer is radically different. Chemical and biological forms are repeated not because they are determined by changeless laws or eternal Forms, but because of a *causal influence from previous similar forms*. This influence would require an action across space *and time* unlike any known type of physical action.

Interdependent Cosmos

FRED HOYLE and CHANDRA WICKRAMASINGHE
Cosmic Life-Force

Sir Fred Hoyle is one of the world's leading astronomers and one who, while retaining absolute logical rigour, has been prepared to think and to imagine in dramatically new ways about the universe. Chandra Wickramasinghe is Professor of Applied Mathematics and Astronomy at University College, Cardiff.

The important point about the following extract is not whether it is right or wrong, but the extraordinary field in which the discourse is happening. Here they are discussing biological molecular structures in relation to galaxies and the possibility of some creative deity. It is now impossible to distinguish between scientific cosmology and metaphysics. Holists celebrate this unity.

The position we have now reached is that the components of terrestrial life are dispersed in the form of cosmic dust particles in the most far-flung places in the universe. As a simple analogy we can regard the genetic molecular arrangements that correspond to crucial characteristics of living things as pieces of an open-ended jigsaw puzzle that could, when pieced together, give rise to an astronomically wide range of possible life-forms. Such pieces, from which all the known terrestrial life-forms might be imagined to be derived, including those coding for intelligence, are then scattered everywhere as part of the fabric of galaxies. The individual jigsaw pieces could be interpreted as informational units – e.g. the information needed to code for eyes, feathers, intelligence, and so on. All that is left to chance at any particular assembly site like the Earth is for these units to be allowed to come together in appropriate habitats, where feasible genetic combinations would be continually sorted out through the process of competition for survival in local environments.

It has often been asked by our critics whether, in arriving at this picture, we have really made any progress towards understanding the ultimate origin of life. Have we not, it is asked, merely pushed this problem back to a more remote place in the universe, and to a more distant time in the past? In some ways this comment could be seen as valid. But it should be stressed that even such a shift of venue for creation was not a matter of fanciful or arbitrary choice, but it was dictated by hard facts. If life did not emerge on the Earth in the traditional primordial soup then it becomes a matter of great scientific importance to recognize this fact. We have argued in earlier chapters that such must be the case beyond reasonable doubt. Life on Earth must have come here in the form of genetic packages that came to be progressively assembled into the multitudinous array of shapes and forms that we find today. Biological effects such as mutations, gene doublings, re-combinations, and so on, to which the whole of the evolutionary process is normally attributed, can in our view serve no more than a fine tuning to be superposed on the much greater cosmic assembly process.

The outstanding question that remains to be answered is the origin of the information content within the cosmic genetic packages that contributes to the evolution of life. This is what philosophers would regard as the quest for a First Cause. Did such information arise from a purely random assembly process, somewhere in the universe, or was the cosmic genetic system in some way deliberately created? To attempt an answer to this wider question let us turn to a group of molecules known as enzymes. Enzymes are polymers or chains of smaller units known as the amino acids. There are enzymes to assist almost every basic biochemical process and without such enzymes biology as we recognize it cannot exist. There are, for instance, enzymes to assist digestion, there are enzymes that zip apart the larger molecules of life into their component parts, and there are enzymes that assist in the assembly of the smaller molecules into long chain polymers, such as proteins and nucleic acids. In all, 2000 or more enzymes are crucial across a wide spectrum of life, ranging from simple micro-organisms all the way up to man. In general there is so much correspondence in the arrangement of amino acids within an individual enzyme, across the whole spectrum of life, that it is sometimes possible to use the enzymes of micro-organisms to serve man.

Every individual enzyme among the 2000 or more depends for its action on the way that the 20 biological amino acids are arranged along the polymer chain in question. A considerable fraction of positions in the chain have of necessity to possess a particular member of this set of 20 amino acids. Minimally, one could say that correct choices of amino acids must occur at 15 sites, while for many enzymes the number of obligatory choices is much larger than this. A simple calculation then shows that the chance of obtaining the necessary total of 2000 enzymes by randomly assembling amino acid chains is exceedingly minute. The random chance is not a million to one against, or a billion to one or even a trillion to one against, but p to 1 against, with p minimally an enormous superastronomical number equal to $10^{40,000}$ (1 followed by 40,000 zeros). The odds we have thus computed are only for the enzymes, and of course correct arrangements within many other important macromolecules of life besides enzymes must also be considered. The molecules histone-4 and cytochrome-c are two such examples, each with exceedingly small probability of being obtained by chance. If all these other relevant molecules for life are also taken account of in our calculation, the situation for conventional biology becomes doubly worse. The odds of one in $10^{40,000}$ against are horrendous enough, but that would have to be increased to a major degree. Such a number exceeds the total number of fundamental particles throughout the observed universe by very, very many orders of magnitude. So great are the odds against life being produced in a purely mechanistic way that the difficulties for an Earthbound, mechanistic biology are in our view intrinsically insuperable.

Such criticisms of this conclusion as have been voiced are, in the main, of a superficial polemical kind. By prevailing cultural standards it is usually thought that this type of conclusion is so outrageous and unacceptable that it has to be fought and condemned at all costs. Facts themselves cease to be important, and it is considered permissible to pile unlikely hypotheses, one upon another. If there remains even the slightest chance of maintaining the status quo within some type of quasi-logical framework the situation is that anything goes. The hypotheses that come to be invoked take on an extremely complex character, which appears to remain invisible to the protagonists of conventional theory.

It has been said that the enzymes themselves have 'evolved' from unknown precursor systems that were much simpler, and perhaps much more likely to form through random processes. We have no knowledge that any such precursor systems ever existed, and if they did the crucial question still arises of whether such a system could have defined a random evolutionary trend that led eventually to the 'discovery' of the present enzyme system. If one forces the logic to assert that life *must* have evolved in a purely mechanistic way, then one is led to suppose that matter has an inherent tendency to find a final highly reproducible order within the crucial life molecules. In other words, the orderings necessary for life are required to be built into the properties of matter, perhaps at a subatomic level. But the circumstance that not even the slightest hint of such a tendency has been discovered in laboratory experiments on the origins of life casts doubt on such a point of view, to say the least.

The conclusions we have reached here are derived from known, experimentally and observationally tested properties of the universe, including not least amongst them the property that living cells can replicate. The rival theory of the 'chemical evolution' of primitive life, and of the evolution of life to progressively higher levels entirely through random processes, is an uneasy combination of dogma and wishful thinking. To claim that there is evidence for chemical evolution in the fact that complex organic molecules have been discovered in meteorites or in planetary atmospheres is certainly wishful thinking. The most likely and well-tested process that could have led to meteoritic amino acids and lipids being formed must surely be biological processes operating in the body from which the meteorite was derived. [. . .]

The alternative to assembly of life by random, mindless processes is assembly through the intervention of some type of cosmic intelligence. Such a concept would be rejected out of hand by most scientists, although there is no rational argument for such a rejection. With our present knowledge, human chemists and biochemists could now perform what even ten years ago would have been thought impossible feats of genetic engineering. They could, for instance, splice bits of genes from one system to another, and work out, albeit in a limited way, the consequences of such splicings. It would not need too great a measure of extrapolation, or too great a licence of imagination, to say that a cosmic intelligence that emerged naturally in the universe may have designed and worked out all the logical consequences of our own living system. It is human arrogance and human arrogance alone that denies this logical possibility.

To suppose that a life-form based on exactly the same basic system as ours, the same complex molecular jigsaw bits, had any part in this grander scheme of things would be to beg the question of origins again. The ultimate cosmic intelligence would need to be comprised of different units from those of our own life-form, possibly also units that are intrinsically more robust than ours, with an ability perhaps to withstand much higher temperatures. The essential complexity of our own cells and of the omnipresent cosmic bacteria must be due in part to the necessity to replicate. The bare essentials for intelligence and consciousness might be separable from such fragile structures, and the ultimate cosmic intelligence built from these more robust structures could well be thought to persist for exceedingly long timescales, even for an eternity. A prime requirement is that such an intelligence be capable of computation, analysis and exploration of the universe at large. In a word it has to approximate to a condition of omniscience. Our own intelligence might be thought to be limited, ultimately, by the number of intercommunicating nerve cells that are available, and the speed of communication between them. A cosmic intelligence could be envisioned on a much more ambitious scale than the capacity of our own brains.

These considerations are admittedly vague in their detail, but such logical constructs as they generally imply cannot be denied as possible solutions of this problem. The overt rejection of logic in relation to such matters, as is apparent in the present day, can be traced back to a series of historical accidents that happened over a century ago. In the middle years of the nineteenth century the Church had become a formidable social force to be reckoned with throughout most of Western Europe. The power of the Church provoked resentment in some circles, and the only way forward to become freed of what seemed to be its repressive regime was to attack the very foundation of its beliefs. To such an end an intellectual movement was launched that culminated in the publication of Darwin's *Origin of Species*. This book has been widely acclaimed and interpreted as being a justification for abandoning the biblical ideas of creation in favour of random processes. Such processes are thought initially to operate on inorganic chemicals leading to primitive life, and thereafter on living systems themselves to produce the spectacle of life in its entirety.

This socio-scientific movement of the nineteenth century would not, we think, have gained ground but for the insistence on the side of the Church, and in particular of a few fundamentalist groups within it, that evolution itself had to be denied. To deny the fact that life evolved in a progressive and connected way from single-celled organisms to multicelled organisms to higher plants and animals, despite the well-proven facts of geology, was an invitation to disaster. Yet, even today, Christian fundamentalists insist that the biblical story of Genesis has to be regarded as literal truth, with no room for deviation, and that any science that goes against it is either deceptive or false.

The fear that Christian fundamentalism will raise its head to the detriment of science is perhaps a major reason for rejecting ideas such as are contained in the present book concerning the cosmic origins of life and intelligence. This is particularly true in the United States of America, where fundamentalists in the South are waging a battle with the Federal authorities to defend the teaching of the biblical story alongside the Darwinian explanation of evolution. Any weakening of the carefully erected Darwinian edifice, it is thought, would open the flood gates to fundamentalist dogma. If Darwinism was proven fact and all the fundamentalist dogma was proven falsehood, one might ask whether there would be any good reason for the paranoia that prevails. The truth must be that there is a lot that is basically wrong with Darwinism and a good deal that is in essence, though not in detail, right with the fundamentalist point of view.

Whatever the historical circumstances might be, there can be no justification at all for rejecting outright the concept of cosmic life and the logic of a creation.

A Quantum Model of Consciousness

DANAH ZOHAR

The Quantum Self

A graduate of M.I.T. and Harvard, Danah Zohar moved to Oxford and collaborated with Ian Marshall, her husband, on a series of books which apply the insights of subatomic physics to psychology and sociology. In *The Quantum Self* she particularly discusses what the quantum model of reality has to say about the nature of consciousness and thought. She is also not at all hesitant about discussing its relationship to mysticism and making clear claims that a holistic perspective, by its very nature, is a healthy step forward.

Who, for instance, has not had the experience of entertaining a vague train of thought only to find that the act of concentrating in order to bring it into better focus somehow changes the original sequence or 'flavour'. Like the electrons governed by Heisenberg's Uncertainty Principle, which are never the same again once they've been looked at (measured), a thought which has been highlighted through attention is different from the vague musing which preceded it. We might say the focused thought has 'position', like the particle aspect of an electron's two-sided nature, whereas the vague musing had 'momentum', like the wave aspect. We can never experience (measure) both simultaneously.

Then too, just as quantum systems are essentially unified, so are our thought processes. I can no more separate the peculiar charm of my daughter's toothless smile from the fact that she is my daughter than a physicist can separate the electron he is measuring from the instrument with which he is measuring it. The meaning of each – in the case of the electron its mode of being – depends on its place within a relationship, on its context. Thus, as Bohm says:

Thought processes and quantum systems are analogous in that they cannot be analysed too much in terms of distinct elements, because the 'intrinsic'

33

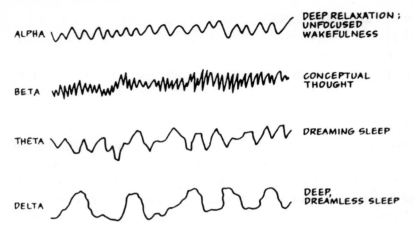

Figure 1 EEG patterns of brain activity. Could these be mirroring excitations of the Bose-Einstein condensate?

nature of each element is not a property existing separately from and independently of other elements but is, instead, a property that arises partially from its relation with other elements.[1]

And finally, there is an intriguing parallel between the way that logic helps to structure and focus our otherwise 'indeterminate', flowing thought processes and the way that the laws of classical physics make it possible to describe the everyday world of separate objects and causal relationships which overlie and are the limit of quantum-level processes. Without this classical limit there would be no solid, 'real' world; without logic there would be no way to express our thoughts clearly, no way to test them against the outside world. [...]

A quantum mechanical model of consciousness, then, gives rise to a picture of our overall mental life which is neither entirely like a computer nor entirely like a quantum system – indeed not entirely 'mental'. What we recognize as our full-blown conscious life, using 'conscious' in its common vernacular sense, is actually a complex, multi-layered dialogue between the quantum aspect (the ground state) and a whole symphony of interactions that cause patterns to develop in the ground state – interactions with our computing facilities in the cerebral cortex, with our instinctual and emotional capacities in the primitive forebrain, with our appetites and our twitches (or pains), with a whole host of activities going on in the body, and to some extent with the conscious lives of other people and creatures. It is the quality of play by the various members of this symphony which ultimately determines the overall quality and content of the music played – our conscious life.

Whether or not any existing theory, such as that applying Fröhlich's* pumped systems or Popp's† coherent photons to the problem, proves correct, the very existence of a viable quantum mechanical model of consciousness is already pregnant with far-reaching philosophical implications. The unbroken wholeness which is a prerequisite for any such model, and hence the loss of individuality of its constituent parts, bears on the whole question of personal identity and group relations.

Then, too, any quantum mechanical model is necessarily a physical model, and thus assumes that the phenomena of consciousness (awareness, perception, thought, memory, etc.), along with those of physics, chemistry and biology, belong to the order of Nature and can be experimentally investigated. This way of looking at consciousness also implies that consciousness and matter are so integrally bound up with each other that either consciousness is a property of matter (as in panpsychism), or else, as Nagel‡ suggests, that consciousness and matter arise together from the same common source – in our terms, from the world of quantum phenomena.

Either view takes consciousness out of the realm of the supernatural and makes it a proper matter for scientific inquiry. It challenges the widely held dualist assumption that consciousness and matter ('mind', or 'soul', and body) are entirely separate phenomena, each evolving in its own way and only accidentally touching one another in this imperfect world of ours. If it were to be proven that consciousness is indeed a quantum process, the long-standing claims of dualism would be challenged in a way more profound than ever before. [. . .]

---

* H. Fröhlich, 'Coherent Excitations in Active Biological Systems', in F. Gutman and H. Keyzer (eds), *Modern Bioelectrochemistry*, Plenum, 1977.
† Fritz-Albert Popp, 'On the Coherence of Ultraweak Photonemission from Living Tissue', in C. W. Kilmister (ed.), *Disequilibrium and Self-Organization*, D. Reidel Publishing Company, 1968.
‡ Thomas Nagel, *The View From Nowhere*, Oxford University Press, 1986.

The exciting realization, from the point of view of understanding consciousness, its roots and its purpose, is that one of the fields within the vacuum is thought to be a coherent Bose-Einstein condensate,[2] that is, a condensate with the same physics as the ground state of human consciousness. Further, excitations (fluctuations) of this coherent vacuum condensate appear to have the same mathematics as the excitations of our own, Fröhlich-style Bose-Einstein condensate.[3]

Understanding this might well lead us to conclude that the physics which gives us human consciousness is one of the basic potentialities within the quantum vacuum, the fundament of all reality. It might even give us some grounds to speculate that the vacuum itself (and hence the universe) is 'conscious' – that is, that it is poised towards a basic sense of direction, towards a further and greater ordered coherence. If we were looking for something that we could conceive of as God within the universe of the new physics, this ground state, coherent quantum vacuum might be a good place to start.

For some people the idea of a transcendent God who creates, and possibly controls, the universe from a vantage point outside the laws of physics, from beyond space and time, will always remain appealing. There is nothing to stop them speculating that this God precedes – and possibly caused – the Big Bang. This is a perfectly tenable position, though it leaves us with a God who Himself undergoes no creative transformation, who is not in dialogue with His world, and it must remain wholly a matter of faith. There is no way from our post-Big Bang position that we can know who or what preceded it.

But if we think of God as something embodied within, or something which uses, the laws of physics, then the relationship between the vacuum and the existing universe suggests a God who might be identified with the basic sense of direction in the unfolding universe – even, perhaps, with an evolving consciousness within the universe. The existence of such an 'immanent God' would not preclude that of a transcendent God as well, but, given our knowledge of the universe, the immanent God (or immanent aspect of God) is more accessible to us.

This immanent God would be at every moment involved in a mutually creative dialogue with His world, knowing Himself only as He knows His world. It is the concept of God proposed most strongly in this century by Teilhard de Chardin,[4] and more recently by 'process theology',[5] and it is a concept in terms of which it makes sense to speak of human beings – with our physics of consciousness which mirrors the physics of the coherent vacuum – as conceived in the image of God, or as partners in God's creation. As Teilhard puts it:

We are not only concerned with thought as participating in evolution as an anomaly or as an epiphenomenon; but with evolution as so reducible to and identifiable with a progress towards thought that the movement of our souls expresses and measures the very stages of evolution itself. Man discovers that *he is nothing else than evolution become conscious of itself*, to borrow Julian Huxley's concise expression.[6]

Like the ground state of human consciousness, which is coherent but in itself 'uninteresting' – without features – the coherent quantum vacuum contains within itself all potentiality,* but it can only realize that potentiality through the fluctuations within itself, excitations which lead to the birth of particles and their relationships. In ourselves, these excitations give birth to thoughts. Our thoughts are the 'interesting' and creative aspect of consciousness, but they purchase these qualities at the expense of splitting off from the coherent ground state. It is the same with particles.

In religious terms, this splitting off might be equated with alienation, or The Fall. It is the prerequisite of all creation (or knowledge), but it means leaving the Eden of total fusion.

We have seen, however, that the basic evolutionary drive of the universe, or at least of that aspect of the universe which results, eventually, in living systems and in human consciousness, is towards more and greater ordered coherence. Thus once particles (bosons) are split off from the vacuum's coherent ground state, there is a long, slow process of rediscovering (creatively rediscovering in partnership with fermions) a new coherence.

We human beings, with our need to form a coherent world, do a great deal to further that process of evolving coherence, first as a

---

* At least, all conscious potentiality – the world of matter may arise from an incoherent field within the vacuum.

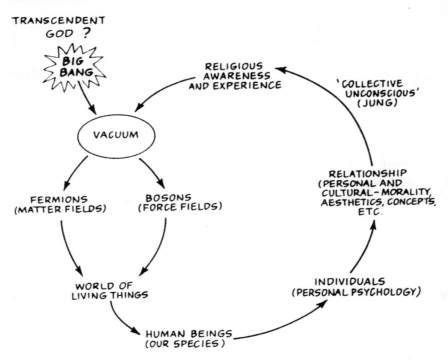

Figure 2 The chain of evolving consciousness. Things emerge as fluctuations (excitations) in the vacuum, grow towards renewed coherence, and return to the vacuum as 'enriched' fluctuations.

species, then as individuals, and finally through our relationships and our culture. Each is an advanced stage in creating greater ordered coherence, and at each stage of its evolution, it is possible to speculate, this process would itself be in dialogue with the vacuum (God?), being expressed as further fluctuations within it. Mystical experiences are sometimes described as though they might be mirroring such a dialogue (Figure 2).

Again, in religious terms, the basic drive towards greater ordered coherence might be seen as the physical basis of Grace, that which allows us, through relationship, to transcend our individuality (The Fall) and to return to unity (God). In Jewish terms, the saving relationship is The People Israel (the Law); for Christians, the Body of Christ. In broader quantum terms, it is the process of overlapping with and

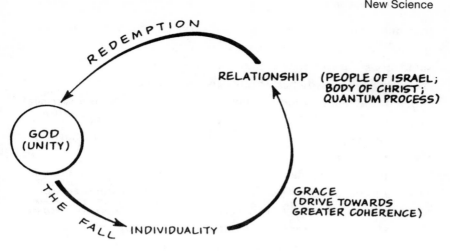

Figure 3 The evolution of consciousness seen in religious categories.

coming into non-local correlation with each other (and each other's worlds) as fellow quantum systems – seeing, feeling and becoming part of this process (Figure 3).

Jung tells the story of a belief held by America's Pueblo Indians that they are sons of the Sun, and that in this role it is their daily duty to perform a ritual which helps Father Sun to traverse the sky. They feel this duty as an awesome responsibility and feel that they carry it out for the benefit of the whole world. Jung says of this belief:

I then realized on what the 'dignity', the tranquil composure of the individual Indian, was founded. It springs from his being a son of the sun; his life is cosmologically meaningful, for he helps the father and preserver of all life in his daily rise and descent. If we set against this our own self-justifications, the meaning of our own lives as it is formulated by our reason, we cannot help but see our poverty.[7]

Understanding the basic origins of consciousness and our own place within its evolution might help to transcend that poverty.

Because the whole evolutionary process being described is a quantum process, it might be expected to have many 'virtual transitions', or probabilistic 'trial runs'. The process which leads to us as a crucial link in the circle of evolving consciousness (evolving ordered coherence) may not in the end be the one which survives. Our success or lack of it as lasting partners in the drama of evolution would be subject to the same 'constraint of the natural' as the success or lack of it of our morality or our aesthetics. If our existence leads to more and greater ordered coherence within the universe, we will succeed as a species; if not, we will fail. We are, in the meantime, a trial run, a probabilistic ripple on the pond, but even as such, we will leave our mark. 'For virtual transitions have many real effects . . .'

Stephen Hawking has said that if we were to discover a complete theory of cosmology, we might come to know the mind of God.[8] I would suggest that if we truly understand our place in the evolving universe, we might come to see ourselves as thoughts (excitations) in the mind of God. In some very important sense, each of us lives his life within a cosmic context.

The Mechanics of Consciousness

ITZHAK BENTOV
Stalking the Wild Pendulum

Originally a specialist in biomedical engineering and instrumentation, Itzhak Bentov transferred his attention to the science of consciousness. In his writings he attempted to apply the insights of the new science to the nature and function of consciousness. He was particularly interested in how subatomic physics and the new cosmologies could be applied to phenomena such as extrasensory perception and telepathy.

Our bodies are, of course, made up of many kinds of tissue. Certain tissues will interact more with one kind of vibratory energy than another. For instance, certain radiations will penetrate our skin to different depths. Ultraviolet rays will affect one layer of our skin and not another. They will not penetrate deeply. Sound waves will penetrate and reflect from certain tissues better than from others. The body as a whole will be affected by gravitational or magnetic effects. No matter how small the effect, our psyches may respond strongly to it. Just check police records on the effect of the full moon on the crime rate at your local police station or the incidents of violence in psychiatric wards in mental hospitals. In both instances, there is a great increase.

It seems that the full moon will have the stronger effect; the new moon, a lesser one, but both effects are above average. Earlier we discussed the rhythmic motion of our bodies and of our skulls, which accelerates our brains up and down. The force causing this acceleration is much stronger than the effect of the distant moon overhead. Still, the moon's gravitational influence tends to affect this force ever so slightly, and that influence seems sufficient to affect our psyches very strongly. Naturally, people do not react to the moon equally strongly. The strongest effect is found in highly emotional or emotionally unbalanced people.

Let us look now at the fields we encounter outside our bodies.

The electromagnetic and electrostatic fields making up and shaping our bodies are relatively strong and serve to hold our atoms and molecules together. They weaken as they move outside our bodies. We are surrounded and permeated by several fields:

1. The so-called isoelectric static field of the planet.
2. The electrostatic fields created by our bodies.
3. The magnetic field of the earth.
4. The electromagnetic field, which has a very wide spectrum, ranging from the very slow wave caused by disturbances in the atmosphere, through the spectrum of the visible light, and into the ultraviolet and higher frequency radiation.
5. The gravitational fields of the earth, the moon, and the neighbouring planets and the sun.
6. The electromagnetic fields created by humans; the different broadcasting fields of radio and television networks.

We shall discuss the first two of these fields. As you know, our planet is surrounded by a layer of electrically charged particles called the ionosphere. The lower layer of the ionosphere starts at about 80 km from the surface of the earth. It is a charged layer and is known to reflect radio waves. It is therefore essential to radio communication around the globe. We are interested, however, in another aspect of this layer.

Since this is a highly charged layer, it forms a so-called capacitor with the earth. This means that there is a difference in electric potential between these two, the earth being negatively and the ionosphere positively charged. This potential difference is evenly distributed along the distance between the earth and the ionosphere and comes to about 200 volts per metre. When standing on the earth, we are moving constantly within this field, which is, so to speak, very 'stiff'. It means that it behaves like a fairly rigid jelly. We have all had the experience of handling a bowl of jelly and know how sensitive it is to vibration. Visualize a few raisins embedded in this jelly. Poke one of the raisins and vibrate it; you'll soon see that all the other raisins in this jelly are vibrating, too. We can also add that the raisins are quite well *coupled* with this jelly field. By coupling we mean that there is a good connection between the raisin and the jelly, that the energy transfer between them is good. They can't make the slightest movement without the jelly transmitting it to the other raisins.

The electrostatic field of the planet is like the stiff jelly. When our bodies move and vibrate, these movements are transmitted to the environment, including all human and animal bodies on this planet. These fields not only impinge on our bodies, but they also affect the charges inside our bodies. But how effective is this coupling? Can't we make the slightest move without detection? What influences this coupling effect? The coupling is, in fact, quite good. It has been shown by our measurements that when a human body is standing on the ground under normal conditions, it is electrically grounded. It acts as a sink for the electrostatic field and will distort the force lines somewhat. But if there were a charge on our bodies, the interaction would be stronger, independent of the polarity of the charge.

It turns out that our bodies do indeed have a charge. They keep producing a field around themselves as long as they are alive. The electrostatic field of the body can nowadays be quite easily measured by commercially available static meters. We have constructed a special device in our lab to measure these fields. We can measure the disturbance produced by our bodies in the electrostatic field. The device is sensitive enough to be able to pick up this signal at 16 to 18 inches from the body. The large waves are again created mostly by the reaction of the body to the ejection of blood from the left ventricle. The strength of this signal changes with distance from the body.

We notice that as we approach the body with the sensor, there is a gradual increase in the signal. Then suddenly at about 4 inches from the body there is a sharp increase. This increase will occur within about ¼ inch movement of the sensor. The strength of this signal depends very much on the vitality of the subject. A person brimming with energy will produce a big signal, while one whose vitality is low will produce practically no signal at all.

Thus, we have an electrostatic field around the body. This field couples us well to the isoelectric field of the planet, which means that the motions of our bodies are transmitted far and wide around the planet. This is, naturally, a very weak signal.

Remember now the discussion about resonant systems in Chapter

43

1. You will recall that when we have what is called a 'tuned system', consisting of at least two oscillators of identical resonant frequencies, if one of the oscillators starts emitting, the others will be activated by this signal very soon. In other words, the coupling between them is ideal. Such systems will respond to the tiniest clues and start resonating.

Remember also the case of the pendulum clocks hanging on the wall, which rhythm entrain each other. Now, you recall that the resonant frequency of the earth – ionosphere cavity – is about 7.5 cycles per second and that the micromotion of the body is about 6.8 to 7.5 Hz. This suggests a tuned resonant system. We may say now that in deep meditation the human being and the planet system start resonating and transferring energy. This is occurring at a very long wavelength of about 40,000 km, or just about the perimeter of the planet. In other words, the signal from the movement of our bodies will travel around the world in about one-seventh of a second through the electrostatic field in which we are embedded. Such a long wavelength knows no obstacles, and its strength does not attenuate much over large distances. Naturally, it will go through just about anything: metal, concrete, water, and the fields making up our bodies. It is the ideal medium for conveying a telepathic signal.

We have said previously that when we stop breathing, the amplitude of the micromotion increases by about a factor of three because the body goes into resonance, and its movement becomes very regular. Can this resonant state be extended in some way?

Meditative states

Techniques of extending this harmonious resonant state have been known for thousands of years. These are the different meditative techniques. They slow down the metabolic rate of the body so that much less oxygen is required to keep the body going. Moreover, as one becomes proficient in meditation, the breathing becomes so gentle as not to disturb the resonant state of the aorta. It seems that an automatic process develops in which the lungs and the diaphragm regulate the heart-aorta system so as to keep them well tuned and thus extend the resonant behaviour in spite of some shallow breathing. The resonant state will naturally apply to the whole body. The skeleton and all the inner organs will move *coherently* at about 7 cycles per second. It so happens that the natural frequency of the normal body seems to lie in this range. It therefore takes very little effort on behalf of the heart-aorta system to drive the body at this rate. It is similar to pushing a swing in correct timing. The normally occurring destructive interference ceases, and the body starts acting in an increasingly coherent fashion. The resonant state of the body seems to be a very restful and beneficial state.

Psychology

Introduction

Old psychology reflects the old scientific paradigm. Put at its worst, it wants to understand people as if they are biological machines responding to fixed stimuli, rewards and punishments. Just as the behaviour of rats can be changed through new stimuli or drugs, so can that of human beings. Although this behavioural approach may be useful as one level of analysis, people generally find that it is both unattractive and crudely shallow when applied to the depths and kaleidoscope of the 'human iceberg'.

Although the psychoanalytic approach initiated by Freud is deeper, as it investigates the dynamic realms of the unconscious mind, its theoretical basis, like behaviourism, is also purely biological.

The richness of the human imagination, the spectrum from tragedy to bliss, the instinct to fulfil ourselves, the sense of connection with a universe of consciousness – none of this is touched by biological psychology. From a holistic perspective, the approach of the old psychology is less than human. Where is the complexity, the genius, the eccentricity, the soul?

The biological psychologists will answer that everything is essentially brain-based. Electric communications between brain cells and a genetic imperative to reproduce provide a full understanding of consciousness and human purpose. 'That's all there is, so be realistic!' But this answer is neither engaging nor open-minded.

Although mainstream and holistic psychology meet in their concern to provide healing, therapy and support, holists tend to perceive mainstream psychology as a cool approach to a passionate and complex subject.

From the holistic perspective, it is self-evident that consciousness, meaning and imagination are more than productions of the biological brain. To say that the brain produces all the manifestations of consciousness, is as untrue as suggesting that the inner wiring of your television set produces all the material you can see on its screen.

From a holistic perspective, psychology is the science that explores the nature of human consciousness and through understanding our consciousness, we may also understand our meaning and purpose. It is also interested in the continuum between the biological body, the emotional personality and spiritual consciousness. The holistic approach believes that comprehension comes through integrating many levels of analysis at the same time. This includes the metaphysical and physical as much as the emotional and mental.

What is beginning to emerge in the holistic field, therefore, is an understanding of the human psyche as a dynamic system in which various energies are working interdependently together. Each aspect only makes full sense when understood in reference to the others.

Dreams and Archetypes

CARL JUNG

Memories, Dreams, Reflections

Carl Jung is the psychologist most referred to in the holistic world. This is mainly due to his extensive writings which frequently connect psychology and religion. He developed a theory of the mind which he called the 'collective unconscious' – a psychic realm shared by everyone. This was combined with a theory of archetypes, a number of patterns and images which manifest universally through human dreams, ideas and behaviour. Holists appreciate him because his work suggests that human consciousness, by its very nature, is both mythic and mystic, as well as grounded in biological reality.

Towards the autumn of 1913 the pressure which I had felt was in *me* seemed to be moving outwards, as though there were something in the air. The atmosphere actually seemed to me darker than it had been. It was as though the sense of oppression no longer sprang exclusively from a psychic situation, but from concrete reality. This feeling grew more and more intense.

In October, while I was alone on a journey, I was suddenly seized by an overpowering vision: I saw a monstrous flood covering all the northern and low-lying lands between the North Sea and the Alps. When it came up to Switzerland I saw that the mountains grew higher and higher to protect our country. I realized that a frightful catastrophe was in progress. I saw the mighty yellow waves, the floating rubble of civilization, and the drowned bodies of uncounted thousands. Then the whole sea turned to blood. This vision lasted about one hour. I was perplexed and nauseated, and ashamed of my weakness.

Two weeks passed; then the vision recurred, under the same conditions, even more vividly than before, and the blood was more emphasized. An inner voice spoke. 'Look at it well; it is wholly real and it will be so. You cannot doubt it.' That winter someone asked me what I thought were the political prospects of the world in the near future. I replied that I had no thoughts on the matter, but that I saw rivers of blood.

I asked myself whether these visions pointed to a revolution, but could not really imagine anything of the sort. And so I drew the conclusion that they had to do with me myself, and decided that I was menaced by a psychosis. The idea of war did not occur to me at all.

Soon afterwards, in the spring and early summer of 1914, I had a thrice-repeated dream that in the middle of summer an Arctic cold wave descended and froze the land to ice. I saw, for example, the whole of Lorraine and its canals frozen and the entire region totally deserted by human beings. All living green things were killed by frost. This dream came in April and May, and for the last time in June, 1914.

In the third dream frightful cold had again descended from out of the cosmos. This dream, however, had an unexpected end. There stood a leaf-bearing tree, but without fruit (my tree of life, I thought), whose leaves had been transformed by the effects of the frost into sweet grapes full of healing juices. I plucked the grapes and gave them to a large, waiting crowd.

At the end of July 1914 I was invited by the British Medical Association to deliver a lecture, 'On the Importance of the Unconscious in Psychopathology', at a congress in Aberdeen. I was prepared for something to happen, for such visions and dreams are fateful. In my state of mind just then, with the fears that were pursuing me, it seemed fateful to me that I should have to talk on the importance of the unconscious at such a time!

On 1 August the world war broke out. Now my task was clear: I had to try to understand what had happened and to what extent my own experience coincided with that of mankind in general. Therefore my first obligation was to probe the depths of my own psyche. I made a beginning by writing down the fantasies which had come to me during my building game. This work took precedence over everything else. [. . .]

In order to grasp the fantasies which were stirring in me 'underground', I knew that I had to let myself plummet down into them, as it were. I felt not only violent resistance to this, but a distinct fear. For I was afraid of losing command of myself and becoming a prey to the fantasies – and as a psychiatrist I realized only too well what that meant. After prolonged hesitation, however, I saw that there was no other way out. I had to take the chance, had to try to gain power over them; for I realized that if I did not do so, I ran the risk of their gaining power over me. A cogent motive for my making the attempt was the conviction that I could not expect of my patients something I did not dare to do myself. The excuse that a helper stood at their side would not pass muster, for I was well aware that the so-called helper – that is, myself – could not help them unless he knew their fantasy material from his own direct experience, and that at present all he possessed were a few theoretical prejudices of dubious value. This idea – that I was committing myself to a dangerous enterprise not for myself alone, but also for the sake of my patients – helped me over several critical phases.

It was during Advent of the year 1913 – 12 December, to be exact – that I resolved upon the decisive step. I was sitting at my desk once more, thinking over my fears. Then I let myself drop. Suddenly it was as though the ground literally gave way beneath my feet, and I plunged down into dark depths. I could not fend off a feeling of panic. But then, abruptly, at not too great a depth, I landed on my feet in a soft, sticky mass. I felt great relief, although I was apparently in complete darkness. After a while my eyes grew accustomed to the gloom, which was rather like a deep twilight. Before me was the entrance to a dark cave, in which stood a dwarf with a leathery skin, as if he were mummified. I squeezed past him through the narrow entrance and waded knee-deep through icy water to the other end of the cave where, on a projecting rock, I saw a glowing red crystal. I grasped the stone, lifted it, and discovered a hollow underneath. At first I could make out nothing, but then I saw that there was running water. In it a corpse floated by, a youth with blond hair and a wound in the head. He was followed by a gigantic black scarab and then by a red, newborn sun, rising up out of the depths of the water. Dazzled by the light, I wanted to replace the stone upon the opening, but then a fluid welled out. It was blood. A thick jet of it leaped up, and I felt nauseated. It seemed to me that the blood continued to spurt for an unendurably long time. At last it ceased, and the vision came to an end.

I was stunned by this vision. I realized, of course, that it was a hero and solar myth, a drama of death and renewal, the rebirth symbolized by the Egyptian scarab. At the end, the dawn of the new day should have followed, but instead came that intolerable outpouring of blood – an altogether abnormal phenomenon, so it seemed to me. But then I recalled the vision of blood that I had had in the autumn of that same year, and I abandoned all further attempt to understand.

Six days later (18 December, 1913), I had the following dream. I was with an unknown, brown-skinned man, a savage, in a lonely, rocky mountain landscape. It was before dawn; the eastern sky was already bright, and the stars fading. Then I heard Siegfried's horn sounding over the mountains and I knew that we had to kill him. We were armed with rifles and lay in wait for him on a narrow path over the rocks.

Then Siegfried appeared high up on the crest of the mountain, in the first ray of the rising sun. On a chariot made of the bones of the dead he drove at furious speed down the precipitous slope. When he turned a corner, we shot at him, and he plunged down, struck dead.

Filled with disgust and remorse for having destroyed something so great and beautiful, I turned to flee, impelled by the fear that the murder might be discovered. But a tremendous downfall of rain began, and I knew that it would wipe out all traces of the dead. I had escaped the danger of discovery; life could go on, but an unbearable feeling of guilt remained.

When I awoke from the dream, I turned it over in my mind, but was unable to understand it. I tried therefore to fall asleep again, but a voice within me said, 'You *must* understand the dream, and must do so at once!' The inner urgency mounted until the terrible moment came when the voice said, 'If you do not understand the dream, you must shoot yourself!' In the drawer of my night table lay a loaded revolver, and I became frightened. Then I began pondering once again, and suddenly the meaning of the dream dawned on me. 'Why, that is the problem that is being played out in the world.' Siegfried, I thought, represents what the Germans want to achieve, heroically to impose their will, have their own way. 'Where there is a will there is a way!' I had wanted to do the same. But now that was no longer possible. The dream showed that the attitude embodied by Siegfried, the hero, no longer suited me. Therefore it had to be killed.

After the deed I felt an overpowering compassion, as though I myself had been shot: a sign of my secret identity with Siegfried, as well as of the grief a man feels when he is forced to sacrifice his ideal and his conscious attitudes. This identity and my heroic idealism had to be abandoned, for there are higher things than the ego's will, and to these one must bow.

These thoughts sufficed for the present, and I fell asleep again.

The small, brown-skinned savage who accompanied me and had actually taken the initiative in the killing was an embodiment of the primitive shadow. The rain showed that the tension between consciousness and the unconscious was being resolved. Although at the time I was not able to understand the meaning of the dream beyond these few hints, new forces were released in me which helped me to carry the experiment with the unconscious to a conclusion.

Peak-Experiences

ABRAHAM H. MASLOW
Religions, Values and Peak-Experiences

Along with Carl Rogers, Abraham Maslow is the most well-known parent of humanistic psychology. He was particularly interested in the psychology of well-being and mental health, and forcefully argued that it was inherent in human beings to fulfil and actualize themselves in order to achieve their full potential. He identified the famous hierarchy of human needs, which essentially states that you cannot get on with the business of fulfilling your psychological self unless other basic needs – food, shelter, physical and psychological safety – are first met. He also noted that fulfilled people had *peak*-experiences of enjoyment and that beyond the peak-experience was the plateau experience, an ongoing sense of connection, confidence and happiness. Maslow's psychology clearly bridges the gap between physical and spiritual experience.

The empirical fact is that self-actualizing people, our best experiencers, are also our most compassionate, our great improvers and reformers of society, our most *effective* fighters against injustice, inequality, slavery, cruelty, exploitation (and also our best fighters *for* excellence, effectiveness, competence). And it also becomes clearer and clearer that the best 'helpers' are the most fully human persons. [. . .]

Descriptively, we can see in each person his own (weak) tendencies to grow towards self-actualization; and also descriptively, we can see his various (weak) tendencies towards regressing (out of fear, hostility, or laziness). It is the task of education, therapy, marriage, and the family to ally themselves to the former, and to be conducive to individual growth. But why? How to prove this? Why is this not just a covert smuggling in of the arbitrary, concealed values of the therapist?

1. Clinical experience and also some experimental evidence teaches us that the consequences of making growth-choices are 'better' in terms of the

person's own biological values, e.g., physical health; absence of pain, discomfort, anxiety, tension, insomnia, nightmares, indigestion, constipation, etc.; longevity, lack of fear, pleasure in fully-functioning; beauty, sexual prowess, sexual attractiveness, good teeth, good hair, good feet, etc.; good pregnancy, good birth, good death; more fun, more pleasure, more happiness, more peak-experiences, etc. That is, if a person could himself see all the likely consequences of growth and all the likely consequences of coasting or of regression, and if he were allowed to choose between them, he would always (in principle, and under 'good conditions') choose the consequences of growth and reject the consequences of regression. That is, the more one knows of the actual consequences of growth-choices and regression-choices, the more attractive become the growth-choices to practically any human being. And these are the actual choices he is prone to make if conditions are good, i.e., if he is allowed truly free choice so that his organism can express its own nature.

2. The consequences of making growth-choices are more in accordance with paradic design (C. Daly King), with actual use of the capacities (instead of inhibition, atrophy, or diminution), i.e., with using the joints, the muscles, the brain, the genitalia, etc., instead of not using them, or using them in a conflicted or inefficient fashion, or in losing the use of them.

3. The consequences of growth are more in accordance with either Darwin-type survival and expansion or with Kropotkin-type survival and expansion. That is, growth has more survival value than regression and defence (under 'good' conditions). (Regression and defence sometimes have more survival value for a particular individual under 'bad' conditions, i.e., when there is not enough to go around, not enough need gratifiers, conditions of mutually exclusive interests, of hostility, divisiveness, etc. But 'bad' conditions always means that this greater survival value for some must be paid for by lesser survival value for others. The greater survival value for the individual under 'good' conditions, however, is 'free,' i.e., it doesn't cost anybody anything.)

4. Growth is more in accordance with fulfilling Hartman's definition of the 'good' human being. That is, it is a better way of achieving more of the defining characteristics of the concept 'human being'. Regression and defence, living at the safety level, is a way of giving up many of these 'higher' defining characteristics for the sake of sheer survival. ('Bad' conditions can also be defined circularly as conditions which make lower-need

gratifications possible only at the cost of giving up higher-need gratifications.)

5. The foregoing paragraph can be phrased in a somewhat different way, generating different problems and a different vocabulary. We can begin with selecting out the 'best specimen', the exemplar, the 'type specimen' of the taxonomists, i.e., the most fully developed and most fully 'characteristic' of those characteristics which define the species (e.g., the most tigerish tiger, the most leonine lion, the most canine dog, etc.), in the same way that is now done at 4-H meetings where the healthiest young man or woman is selected out. If we use this 'best specimen', in the zookeeper or taxonomist sense, as a model, then growth conduces to moving towards becoming like this model, and regression moves away from it.

6. It looks as if the non-pathological baby put into free-choice situations, with plenty of choice, tends to choose its way towards growth rather than towards regression. In the same way, a plant or an animal selects from the millions of objects in the world those which are 'right' for its nature. This is based on its own physical-chemical-biological nature, e.g., what the rootlets will let through and what they won't, what can be metabolized and what cannot, what can be digested and what cannot, whether sunshine or rain helps or hurts, etc.

7. Very important as a source of data to support the biological basis of choosing growth over regression is the experience with 'uncovering therapy' or what I have begun to call Taoistic therapy. What emerges here is the person's own nature, his own identity, his bent, his own tastes, his vocation, his species values, and his idiosyncratic values. These idiosyncratic values are so often different from the idiosyncratic values of the therapist as to constitute a validation of the point, i.e., uncovering therapy is truly uncovering rather than indoctrination.

The Human of Tomorrow

CARL ROGERS
A Way of Being

Carl Rogers was one of the most significant figures in humanistic psychology
and in the counselling movement in general. He suggested that the theoretical stance and techniques of the psychologist, psychiatrist or therapist
were unimportant compared to certain personal attitudes in the therapeutic
relationship: the realness and authenticity of the therapist; the degree of
genuine empathy; and the unconditional non-possessive liking and appreciation of the client. One could say that all these attitudes are a manifestation
of love. In the following extract, written towards the end of his life, he
demonstrates his essentially holistic attitude.

What is the meaning, the significance, of all of these current developments in modern life?

Taken together, these trends profoundly transform our concept of
the person and the world that he or she perceives. This person has
hitherto undreamed-of potential. This person's non-conscious intelligence is vastly capable. It can control many bodily functions, can heal
diseases, can create new realities. It can penetrate the future, see things
at a distance, communicate thoughts directly. This person has a new
awareness of his or her strength, abilities, and power, an awareness
of self as a process of change. This person lives in a new universe,
where all the familiar concepts have disappeared – time, space, object,
matter, cause, effect – nothing remains but vibrating energy.

In my judgement, these developments constitute a 'critical mass'
that will produce drastic social change. In the development of the
atomic bomb, temperature and other conditions were gradually heightened until a certain mass was attained. The attainment of this critical
mass brought about an explosively expanding process. These developments are of that sort, except that the process will be in persons and
social systems.

59

Another scientific analogy is the 'paradigm shift'. Our scientific view of the world, at any one time, fits into a general pattern. To be sure, there are events and phenomena that do not quite fit, but they are disregarded until they begin to pile up and can no longer be ignored. Then, a Copernicus or an Einstein provides us with a whole new pattern, a new world-view. It is not something patched on to the old paradigm, although it absorbs the old. It is a totally new conceptualization. One cannot move gradually from the old to the new. One must adopt one or the other: this is the paradigm shift. It has been pointed out that in science, most older scientists go to their graves believing in the previous paradigm, but the new generation grows up with, and lives comfortably with, the new paradigm.

What I am saying is that the many converging trends I have listed constitute a paradigm shift. We will try, of course, to live in our familiar world, just as people lived upon a flat world long after they knew it was round. But as these new ways of conceptualizing the person and the world sink in, becoming increasingly the basis of our thinking and our lives, transformation becomes inevitable. Ilya Prigogine (1980), the Belgian chemist who won the Nobel Prize in 1977 and who has contributed much to the new concepts of science, says, speaking for scientists: 'We see a new world around us. We have the impression that we are at the dawn of a new period, with all the excitement, the hopes, and also the risks which are inherent in a new start.'

The person of tomorrow

Who will be able to live in this utterly strange world? I believe it will be those who are young in mind and spirit – and that often means those who are young in body as well. As our youth grow up in a world where trends and views such as I have been describing envelop them, many will become new persons – fit to live in the world of tomorrow – and they will be joined by older folk who have absorbed the transforming concepts.

Not all young people, of course. I hear that young people today are only interested in jobs and security, that they are not persons who take risks or make innovations, just conservatives looking out for 'number one'. Possibly that is so, but it certainly is not true of the young people with whom I come in contact. But I am sure that some will continue to live in our present world; many, however, will dwell in this new world of tomorrow.

Where will they come from? It is my observation that they already exist. Where have I found them? I find them among corporation executives who have given up the grey-flannel rat race, the lure of high salaries and stock options, to live a simpler new life. I find them among young men and women in blue jeans who are defying most of the values of today's culture to live in new ways. I find them among priests and nuns and ministers who have left behind the dogmas of their institutions to live in a way that has more meaning. I find them among women who are vigorously rising above the limitations that society has placed on their personhood. I find them among blacks and Chicanos and other minority members who are pushing out from generations of passivity into an assertive, positive life. I find them among those who have experienced encounter groups, who are finding a place for feelings as well as thoughts in their lives. I find them among creative school drop-outs who are thrusting into higher reaches than their sterile schooling permits. I realize, too, that I saw something of this person in my years as a psychotherapist, when clients were choosing a freer, richer, more self-directed kind of life for themselves. These are a few of the places in which I have found persons who may be able to live in this transformed world.

The qualities of the person of tomorrow

As I have experienced these individuals, I find they have certain traits in common. Perhaps no one person possesses all of these qualities, but I believe that ability to live in this utterly revolutionized world of tomorrow is marked by certain characteristics. I will very briefly describe some as I have seen and experienced them.

1. *Openness*. These persons have an openness to the world – both inner and outer. They are open to experience, to new ways of seeing, new ways of being, new ideas and concepts.

2. *Desire for authenticity.* I find that these persons value communication as a means of telling it the way it is. They reject the hypocrisy, deceit, and double-talk of our culture. They are open, for example, about their sexual relationships, rather than leading a secretive or double life.

3. *Scepticism regarding science and technology.* They have a deep distrust of our current science and the technology that is used to conquer the world of nature and to control the world's people. On the other hand, when science – such as biofeedback – is used to enhance self-awareness and control of the person by the person, they are eager supporters.

4. *Desire for wholeness.* These persons do not like to live in a compartmentalized world – body and mind, health and illness, intellect and feeling, science and common sense, individual and group, sane and insane, work and play. They strive rather for a wholeness of life, with thought, feeling, physical energy, psychic energy, healing energy, all being integrated in experience.

5. *The wish for intimacy.* They are seeking new forms of closeness, of intimacy, of shared purpose. They are seeking new forms of communication in such a community – verbal as well as non-verbal, feelingful as well as intellectual.

6. *Process persons.* They are keenly aware that the one certainty of life is change – that they are always in process, always changing. They welcome this risk-taking way of being and are vitally alive in the way they face change.

7. *Caring.* These persons are caring, eager to be of help to others when the need is real. It is a gentle, subtle, non-moralistic, non-judgemental caring. They are suspicious of the professional 'helpers'.

8. *Attitude towards nature.* They feel a closeness to, and a caring for, elemental nature. They are ecologically minded, and they get their pleasure from an alliance with the forces of nature, rather than in the conquest of nature.

9. *Anti-institutional.* These individuals have an antipathy for any highly structured, inflexible, bureaucratic institution. They believe that institutions should exist for people, not the reverse.

10. *The authority within.* These persons have a trust in their own experience and a profound distrust of external authority. They make their own moral judgements, even openly disobeying laws that they consider unjust.

11. *The unimportance of material things.* These individuals are fundamentally

indifferent to material comforts and rewards. Money and material status symbols are not their goal. They can live with affluence, but it is in no way necessary to them.

12. *A yearning for the spiritual.* These persons of tomorrow are seekers. They wish to find a meaning and purpose in life that is greater than the individual. Some are led into cults, but more are examining all the ways by which humankind has found values and forces that extend beyond the individual. They wish to live a life of inner peace. Their heroes are spiritual persons – Mahatma Gandhi, Martin Luther King, Teilhard de Chardin. Sometimes, in altered states of consciousness, they experience the unity and harmony of the universe.

These are some of the characteristics I see in the person of tomorrow. I am well aware that few individuals possess all of these characteristics, and I know that I am describing a small minority of the population as a whole.

The striking thing is that persons with these characteristics will be at home in a world that consists only of vibrating energy, a world with no solid base, a world of process and change, a world in which the mind, in its larger sense, is both aware of, and creates, the new reality. They will be able to make the paradigm shift.

The Transpersonal Self

ROBERTO ASSAGIOLI
Psychosynthesis

Roberto Assagioli, an Italian psychiatrist, developed the approach known as psychosynthesis. Psychosynthesis was the first modern psychological approach explicitly to draw a map of the psyche which named the 'transpersonal' or 'higher' self. In his writings as a psychiatrist he avoided defining the meaning and purpose of this transpersonal self, but the therapeutic strategies of psychosynthesis recognize that, for general psychological health, the transpersonal self – the soul – needs to be the driving force. Assagioli was also a student of the Tibetan teacher Dhwahl Kuhl and the theosophist, Alice Bailey. His understanding, therefore, of the transpersonal self was based in a clear mystical map.

Let us examine *whether* and *how* it is possible to solve this central problem of human life, to heal this fundamental infirmity of man. Let us see how he may free himself from this enslavement and achieve an harmonious inner integration, true Self-realization, and right relationships with others.

The task is certainly neither easy nor simple, but that it can be accomplished has been demonstrated by the success of those who have used adequate and appropriate means.

The stages for the attainment of this goal may be tabulated as follows:

1. Thorough knowledge of one's personality.
2. Control of its various elements.
3. Realization of one's true Self – the discovery or creation of a unifying centre.
4. Psychosynthesis: the formation or reconstruction of the personality around the new centre.

Let us examine each of these stages.

1. *Thorough knowledge of one's personality.*

We have recognized that in order really to know ourselves it is not enough to make an inventory of the elements that form our conscious being. An extensive exploration of the vast regions of our unconscious must also be undertaken. We have first to penetrate courageously into the pit of our lower unconscious in order to discover the dark forces that ensnare and menace us – the 'phantasms', the ancestral or childish images that obsess or silently dominate us, the fears that paralyse us, the conflicts that waste our energies. It is possible to do this by the use of the methods of psychoanalysis.

This search can be undertaken by oneself but it is accomplished more easily with the help of another. In any case the methods must be employed in a genuinely scientific manner, with the greatest objectivity and impartiality; without preconceived theories and without allowing ourselves to be deterred or led astray by the covert or violent resistance of our fears, our desires, our emotional attachments.

Psychoanalysis generally stops here; but this limitation is not justified. The regions of the middle and higher unconscious should likewise be explored. In that way we shall discover in ourselves hitherto unknown abilities, our true vocations, our higher potentialities which seek to express themselves, but which we often repel and repress through lack of understanding, through prejudice or fear. We shall also discover the immense reserve of undifferentiated psychic energy latent in every one of us; that is, the plastic part of our unconscious which lies at our disposal, empowering us with an unlimited capacity to learn and to create.

2. *Control of the various elements of the personality.*

After having discovered all these elements, we have to take possession of them and acquire control over them. The most effective method by which we can achieve this is that of dis-identification. This is based on a fundamental psychological principle which may be formulated as follows:

We are dominated by everything with which our self becomes identified. We can dominate and control everything from which we dis-identify ourselves.

In this principle lies the secret of our enslavement or of our liberty. Every time we 'identify' ourselves with a weakness, a fault, a fear or any personal emotion or drive, we limit and paralyse ourselves. Every time we admit 'I am discouraged' or 'I am irritated', we become more and more dominated by depression or anger. We have accepted those limitations; we have ourselves put on our chains. If, instead, in the same situation we say, 'A wave of discouragement is *trying* to submerge me' or 'An impulse of anger is *attempting* to overpower me', the situation is very different. Then there are two forces confronting each other; on one side our vigilant self and on the other the discouragement or the anger. And the vigilant self does not submit to that invasion: it can objectively and critically survey those impulses of discouragement or anger; it can look for their origin, foresee their deleterious effects, and realize their unfoundedness. This is often sufficient to withstand an attack of such forces and win the battle. [. . .]

3. Realization of one's true Self – the discovery or creation of a unifying centre.

On the basis of what we have said about the nature and power of the Self, it is not difficult to point out *theoretically* how to reach this aim. What has to be achieved is to expand the personal consciousness into that of the Self; to reach up, following the thread or ray (see diagram 1) to the star; to unite the lower with the higher Self. But this, which is so easily expressed in words, is in reality a tremendous undertaking. It constitutes a magnificent endeavour, but certainly a long and arduous one, and not everybody is ready for it. But between the starting point in the lowlands of our ordinary consciousness and the shining peak of Self-realization there are intermediate phases, plateaus at various altitudes on which a man may rest or even make his abode, if his lack of strength precludes or his will does not choose a further ascent.

In favourable cases the ascent takes place to some extent spontaneously through a process of natural inner growth, fostered by the manifold experiences of life; but often the process is very slow. In all cases, however, it can be considerably accelerated by our deliberate conscious action and by the use of appropriate active techniques.

The intermediate stages imply new identifications. The men and women who cannot reach their true Self in its pure essence can create a picture and an ideal of perfected personality adequate to their calibre, their stage of development and their psychological type, and therefore can make this ideal practicable in actual life.

For some it may be the ideal of the artist who realizes and expresses himself as the creator of beautiful forms, who makes art the most vital interest and the animating principle of his existence, pouring into it all his best energies. For others it may be the ideal of the seeker after Truth, the philosopher, the scientist. For yet others it is a more limited and personal ideal, that of the good father or mother. [. . .]

This outward projection of one's own centre, this excentricity (in the etymological sense of the word) should not be underrated. While it does not represent the most direct way or the highest achievement, it may, despite appearances, constitute for the time being a satisfactory form of indirect self-realization. In the best instances the individual does not really lose himself in the external object, but frees himself in that way from selfish interests and personal limitations; he realizes himself *through* the external ideal or being. The latter thus becomes an indirect but true link, a point of connection between the personal man and his higher Self, which is reflected and symbolized in that object.

4. Psychosynthesis: the formation or reconstruction of the personality around the new centre.

When the unifying centre has been found or created, we are in a position to build around it a new personality – coherent, organized, and unified.

This is the actual *psychosynthesis*, which also has several stages. The first essential is to decide the plan of action, to formulate the 'inner programme'. We must visualize the purpose to be achieved – that is,

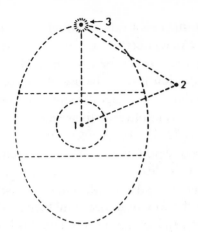

Diagram 1.
1. Conscious self or 'I'
2. External Unifying Centre
3. Higher Self

the new personality to be developed – and have a clear realization of the various tasks it entails.

Some people have a distinct vision of their aim from the outset. They are capable of forming a clear picture of themselves as they can and intend to become. This picture should be realistic and 'authentic', that is, in line with the natural development of the given individual and therefore capable – at least in some measure – of realization, and should not be a neurotic, unreal 'idealized image' in the sense of Karen Horney. A genuine 'ideal model' has a dynamic creative power; it facilitates the task by eliminating uncertainties and mistakes; it concentrates the energies and utilizes the great suggestive and creative power of images.

Other individuals of a more plastic psychological constitution, who live spontaneously, following indications and intuitions rather than definite plans, find it difficult to formulate such a programme, to build according to a pattern; they may even positively dislike such a method. Their tendency is to let themselves be led by the Spirit within or by the will of God, leaving Him to choose what they should become. They feel that they can best reach the goal by eliminating, as much as possible, the obstacles and resistances inherent in their personality; by widening the channel of communication with the higher Self through aspiration and devotion and then letting the creative power of the Spirit act, trusting and obeying it. Some take a similar attitude but express it in a different way; they speak of tuning in with the cosmic order, with the universal harmony, of letting Life act in and through them (the Wu-Wei of Taoists).

Both methods are effective, and each is appropriate to the corresponding type. But it is well to know, to appreciate and to use both to some extent in order to avoid the limitations and the exaggerations of each by correcting and enriching the one with elements taken from the other.

Thus, those who follow the first method should be careful to avoid making their 'ideal picture' too rigid; they should be ready to modify or to enlarge it – and even to change it altogether as later experiences, fresh outlooks or new clarifications indicate and demand this change.

On the other hand, those who follow the second method should guard against becoming too passive and negative, accepting as intuitions and higher inspirations certain promptings which are, in reality, determined by unconscious forces, wishes and desires. Moreover, they must develop the ability to stand steady during the inevitable phases of inner aridity and darkness, when conscious communion with the spiritual Centre is interrupted, and the personality feels itself abandoned.

The 'ideal models' or images that one can create are many, but they can be divided into two principal groups. The first is formed of images representing harmonious development, an all-round personal or spiritual perfection. This kind of ideal is aimed at chiefly by introverts. The second group represents specialized efficiency. The purpose here is the utmost development of an ability or quality corresponding to the particular line of self-expression and the social role or roles which the individual has chosen. This is the ideal of the artist, the teacher, the advocate of a good cause, etc. Such models are generally preferred by extroverts.

Orgasm and Body Armour

WILHELM REICH
The Function of the Orgasm

An Austrian medical doctor and close follower of Freud, Reich pioneered an integrative approach to psychoanalysis, sex and body therapy. His ideas shocked many of his colleagues, but several decades later in a more permissive and liberal climate, his ideas make substantial common sense and are the basis of many therapeutic approaches which work with direct intervention on the physical body.

His basic premise is that psychological wounding and trauma anchor into the physical body as tension and armouring, preventing a healthy flow of libido and vitality. He further suggests that libidinous energy is quantifiable, as 'orgones', and that there is a flow between the human body and the orgones that circulate in nature and the cosmos. Fulfilled orgasm, then, is a metaphor and a reality for a healthy psyche which is connected with self, with libido and with the cosmos.

The more precisely my patients described their behaviour and experiences in the sexual act, the more firm I became in my clinically substantiated conviction that *all patients, without exception, are severely disturbed in their genital function*. Most disturbed of all were those men who liked to boast and make a big show of their masculinity, men who possessed or conquered as many women as possible, who could 'do it' again and again in one night. It became quite clear that, though they were erectively very potent, such men experienced no or very little pleasure at the moment of ejaculation, or they experienced the exact opposite, disgust and unpleasure. The precise analysis of fantasies during the sexual act revealed that the men usually had sadistic or conceited attitudes and that the women were afraid, inhibited, or imagined themselves to be men. For the ostensibly potent man, sexual intercourse means the piercing, overpowering, or conquering of the woman. He merely wants to prove his potency or to be admired for his erective endurance. This 'potency' can be easily undermined by uncovering its motives. Severe disturbances of erection and ejaculation are concealed in it. In none of these cases is there the slightest trace of *involuntary behaviour or loss of conscious activity in the act*. Gradually, groping my way ahead step by step, I acquired a knowledge of the characteristics of *orgastic impotence*. It took me a decade to gain a full understanding of this disturbance; to describe it and to learn the correct technique for eliminating it.

Orgastic impotence has always been in the forefront of sex-economic research, and all of its details are still not known. Its role in sex-economy is similar to the role of the Oedipus complex in psychoanalysis. Whoever does not have a precise understanding of it cannot be considered a sex-economist. He will never really grasp its ramifications. He will not understand the difference between health and sickness, nor will he comprehend human pleasure anxiety or the pathological nature of the parent–child conflict and the misery of marriage. It is even possible that he will endeavour to bring about sexual reforms, but he will never touch upon the core of sexual misery. He might admire the bion experiments, even imitate them perhaps, but he will never really conduct research in the field of sex-economy. He will never comprehend religious ecstasy, nor have the least insight into fascist irrationalism. Because he lacks the most important fundamentals, he will of necessity adhere to the antithesis between nature and culture, instinct and morality, sexuality and achievement. He will not be able to really solve a single pedagogic problem. He will never understand the identity between sexual process and life process. Nor, consequently, will he be able to grasp the sex-economic theory of cancer. He will mistake sickness for health and health for sickness. He will end up misinterpreting man's fear of happiness. In short, he might be anything, but he will never be a sex-economist, who knows that man is the sole biological species that has destroyed its own natural sexual function and is sick as a consequence of this.

Instead of a systematic presentation, I want to describe the theory of the orgasm in the way in which it developed. This will enable the reader to grasp more easily its inner logic. It will be seen that no human brain could have invented these relationships.

Until 1923, the year the orgasm theory was born, only ejaculative

71

and erective potency were known to sexology and psychoanalysis. Without the inclusion of the functional, economic, and experiential components, the concept of sexual potency has no meaning. Erective and ejaculative potency are merely indispensable preconditions for orgastic potency. *Orgastic potency is the capacity to surrender to the flow of biological energy, free of any inhibitions; the capacity to discharge completely the dammed-up sexual excitation through involuntary, pleasurable convulsions of the body.* Not a single neurotic is orgastically potent, and the character structures of the overwhelming majority of men and women are neurotic. [. . .]

Some sixty years of sexology, forty years of psychoanalysis, and almost twenty years of my own work on the orgasm theory still had not succeeded in providing the clinician (who was supposed to cure human sexual disturbances, i.e., neuroses) with an answer to this question. Let us recall the point of departure of the orgasm theory. Neuroses and functional psychoses are sustained by surplus, inadequately discharged sexual energy. Initially it was called 'psychic energy'. No one knew what it really was. Psychic illnesses were undoubtedly rooted 'in the body'. Hence, there was good reason to assume that the psychic proliferations were nourished by an energy stasis. Only the elimination of this energy source of the neurosis through the establishment of full orgastic potency seemed to make the patient immune against a relapse. There could be no thought of preventing psychic illnesses on a mass scale without a knowledge of the biological foundation of these illnesses. The premise 'given gratifying sexuality, there are no neurotic disturbances' was unassailable. Naturally, this contention had individual as well as social implications. The significance of the sexual question is obvious. Yet, in spite of Freud, official science wanted to know nothing about the implication of sexuality. Psychoanalysis itself showed an increasing tendency to shrink away from the question. In addition, the question was imbued with the outpourings of a pathological, distorted, somehow always pornographically tinged 'sexuality', i.e., with the sexuality which governs human life. The clear-cut distinction between 'natural' sexual expression and pathological, culturally anchored sexual expression, between the 'primary' drives and the 'secondary' drives, made it possible to persist and to pursue the problem to its core. Reflection alone would not have produced a solution, nor would the collation of the many brilliant insights in modern physiological literature that, from about 1925, appeared in increasing abundance and were condensed and compiled in Müller's *Die Lebensnerven*.

Once again clinical observation provided the correct line of approach. In Copenhagen, in 1933, I treated a man who offered considerable resistance to the uncovering of his passive homosexual fantasies. This resistance was overtly expressed in the extremely stiff attitude of his throat and neck ('stiff-necked'). A concentrated attack on his defence finally caused him to yield, though in an alarming way. For three days, he was shaken by acute manifestations of vegetative shock. The pallor of his face changed rapidly from white to yellow to blue. His skin was spotted and motley. He experienced violent pains in the neck and back of the head. His heartbeat was rapid and pounding. He had diarrhoea, felt tired, and seemed to have lost control. I was uneasy. True, I had often seen similar symptoms, but never in such violent form. Something had happened here that, while somehow a legitimate part of the work, was not immediately intelligible. *Affects had broken through somatically after the patient had relinquished his attitude of psychic defence.* Apparently, the stiff neck, which emphasized austere masculinity, had bound vegetative energies which now broke loose in an uncontrolled and chaotic manner. A person with an ordered sexual economy is not capable of such a reaction. Only continuous inhibition and damming-up of biological energy can produce it. The musculature had served the function of inhibition. When the neck muscles relaxed, powerful impulses, as if unleashed from a taut coil, broke through. The alternating pallor and flushing of the face could be nothing other than the flowing back and forth of body fluids, i.e., the contraction and dilation of the blood vessels. This fits in extremely well with my earlier described views on the functioning of biological energy. The direction, 'out of the self towards the world', alternated rapidly and continuously with the opposite direction, 'away from the world – back into the self'.

By means of tensions, the musculature can obstruct the flow of blood, in other words can reduce the movement of body fluids to a minimum. I checked a number of other patients to see whether this observation held true in their cases, too, and I also thought about

73

patients whom I had treated earlier. All observations confirmed this phenomenon. In a short time, I had a profusion of facts at my disposal. They reduced themselves to a concise formulation: *sexual life energy can be bound by chronic muscular tensions. Anger and anxiety can also be blocked by muscular tensions.* From now on, I found that whenever I dissolved a muscular tension, one of the three basic biological excitations of the body, anxiety, hate, or sexual excitation, broke through. I had, of course, succeeded in doing this before through the loosening of purely characterological inhibitions and attitudes. But now the breakthroughs of vegetative energy were more complete, more forceful, experienced more affectively, and occurred more rapidly. In the process, the characterological inhibitions were loosened spontaneously. These findings, made in 1933, were published in an incomplete form in 1935. In 1937, I published them in more detail.[1] Quite rapidly, a number of decisive questions pertaining to the relationship between mind and body were clarified.

Character armourings were now seen to be functionally identical with muscular hypertonia. The concept, 'functional identity', which I had to introduce, means nothing more than that muscular attitudes and character attitudes have the same function in the psychic mechanism: they can replace one another and can be influenced by one another. Basically, they cannot be separated. They are identical in their function.

Postulations resulting from the connecting of facts immediately lead to further findings. If the character armour could be expressed through the muscular armour, and vice versa, then the unity of psychic and somatic functioning had been grasped in principle, and could be influenced in a practical way. From that time on, I was able to make practical use of this unity whenever necessary. If a character inhibition did not respond to psychic influencing, I resorted to the corresponding somatic attitude. Conversely, if I had difficulty in getting at a disturbing somatic attitude, I worked on its expression in the patient's character and was able to loosen it. I was now able to eliminate a typical friendly smile which obstructed the analytic work, either by describing the expression or by directly disturbing the muscular attitude, e.g., pulling up the chin. This was an enormous step forward. It took another six years to develop this technique into the vegetotherapy of today.

The loosening of the rigid muscular attitudes produced peculiar body sensations in the patients: involuntary trembling and twitching of the muscles, sensations of cold and hot, itching, the feeling of pins and needles, prickling sensations, the feeling of having the jitters, and somatic perceptions of anxiety, anger, and pleasure. I had to break with all the old ideas about the mind-body relationship, if I wanted to grasp these phenomena. They were not 'results', 'causes', 'accompanying manifestations' of 'psychic processes'; they were simply these phenomena themselves in the somatic realm. I categorized as 'vegetative currents' all somatic phenomena which, in contrast to rigid muscular armourings, are characterized by movement. Immediately the question arose: are the vegetative currents merely the movements of fluid or are they more than that? I could not be satisfied with the explanation that these currents were merely mechanical movements of fluid. While purely mechanical movements could account for the hot and cold sensations, pallor, and blushing, the 'simmering of the blood', etc., they could not explain the feeling of pins and needles, the sensation of prickling, shuddering, the sweet preorgastic sensations of pleasure, etc. The crucial problem of orgastic impotence was still unsolved: it is possible for the genital organs to be filled with blood without a trace of excitation. Hence, sexual excitation can certainly not be identical with, nor be the expression of the flow of blood. There are anxiety states without any particular pallor of the face or skin. The feeling of 'tightness' in the chest ('angustiae', anxiety), the feeling of 'constriction', could not be traced back solely to a congestion of blood in the central organs. If this were so, one would have to feel anxiety after a good meal, when the blood is concentrated in the stomach. In addition to the flow of the blood, there must be something else which, depending upon its biological function, causes anxiety, anger, or pleasure. In this process, the flow of blood merely represents an essential means. Perhaps this unknown 'something' does not occur when the movement of the body fluids is hindered.

THE ORGASM FORMULA:

TENSION → CHARGE → DISCHARGE → RELAXATION

The unknown 'something' I was looking for could be nothing other than *bioelectricity*. This occurred to me one day when I tried to

75

understand the physiology of the process of friction which takes place between the penis and the walls of the vaginal mucous membrane in the sexual act. Sexual friction is a fundamental biological process. It is found throughout the animal kingdom wherever reproduction takes place in the union of the two sexes. Two surfaces of the body rub against one another. In this process, *biological excitation* occurs, together with congestion, expansion, 'erection'. On the basis of pioneer experiments, the Berlin internist Kraus ascertained that the body is governed by electrical processes. It is made up of countless 'border surfaces' between membranes and electrolytic fluids, having various densities and compositions. According to a well-known law of physics, electrical tensions develop at the borders between conducting fluids and membranes. Since the concentrations and structure of the membranes are not homogeneous, differences develop in the tensions at the border surfaces, and, simultaneously, differences in potential of varying intensity. These differences of potential may be likened to the energy differences of two bodies at different heights. The body having the higher elevation is capable of performing more work as it drops than the body having the lower elevation. A weight of one kilogram will drive a stake deeper into the earth when it is dropped from a height of three metres than when it is dropped from a height of one metre. The 'potential energy of position' is higher, and, therefore, the 'kinetic energy' which is generated will also be greater when this potential energy is released. The principle of 'potential difference' can be easily applied to the difference in electrical tensions. If I attach a wire from a highly charged body to a less highly charged one, a current will flow from the first to the second. In this process, static electrical energy is converted into current energy. Moreover, an equalization takes place between the two charges, in the same way that the water level in two vessels becomes the same if I connect the two by means of a pipe. The equalization of energy presupposes a difference in potential energy. Our body consists of billions of such potential surfaces having various potential energies. Consequently, the energy in the body is in constant motion from places of higher to places of lower potential.

Self and Non-Self

KEN WILBER
The Atman-Project

Ken Wilber is the most rigorous scholar and theoretician of the transpersonal psychologists and philosophers. His conceptual roots certainly derive from the mystic traditions, particularly those of the East, and although his approach is multifaceted and diverse, he is also fiercely critical of flaky and inconsistent thinking in the transpersonal and holistic movements. People with an academic bent, and who are looking for some intellectual support for their mystic and holistic disposition, love Ken Wilber because he is a scholastic thinker.

We have seen that psychological development in humans has the same goal as natural evolution: the production of ever-higher unities. And since the ultimate Unity is Buddha, God, or Atman (to use those terms in their broadest sense as 'ultimate reality'), it follows that psychological growth aims at Atman. And that is part of what we call the Atman-project.

We saw that the individual being, from the very start, contains all the deep structures of consciousness enfolded and enwrapped in his own being. And in particular, he contains or participates in prior Atman-consciousness – *from the start*. The infant is not enlightened, obviously. But just as obviously, the infant is not without Atman. 'All sentient beings,' says the *Nirvana Sutra*, 'possess the Buddha Nature.' 'Wherever there is consciousness,' proclaims the *Tibetan Book of the Dead*, 'there is Dharmakaya.' *Anima Naturaliter Christiana*, said Tertullian, by which he meant that 'The soul is endowed *from the outset* with the knowledge of God and that whatever God imparts in this manner can at most be obscured, but never entirely extinguished.' Likewise, 'This is what the Jewish midrash means when it ascribes knowledge to the unborn babe in the womb, saying that over its head there burns a light in which it sees all the ends of the world.' From the outset, the soul intuits this Atman-nature, and seeks, from the start, to *actualize* it as a reality and not just an enfolded potential. That drive to actualize Atman is part of the Atman-project.

But it is only part, because – even though each stage of psychological growth is a step closer to God – each stage is *still* only a stage. That is, each stage towards God is still not itself God. Each stage is a search for God which occurs under conditions which fall short of God. The soul must seek Unity through the constraints of the present stage, which is not yet Unity. And *that* is the other side of the Atman-project: each individual wants only Atman, but wants it under conditions which prevent it. Only at the end of psychological growth is there final enlightenment and liberation in and as God, but that is the *only* thing that is desired from the beginning. But notice: since at every stage of growth the soul wants only Unity or Atman, but since each stage is less than Atman, then each stage tends to become, in effect, a compromise and a *substitute* for Atman – and this occurs consciously or unconsciously. It occurs at every level, from the lowest to the highest, as a simple reflex of manifestation.

The point is that each stage or level of growth seeks absolute Unity, but in ways or under constraints that necessarily prevent it and allow only compromises: substitute unities and substitute gratifications. The more primitive the level, the more primitive the substitute unity. Each successive stage achieves a higher-order unity, and this continues until there is *only* Unity. The Atman-project continues until there is only Atman. There is the dynamic, and there the goal, of evolution and development.

If we look carefully at that definition of the Atman-project, we can see that it has three different strands. 'Each stage or level of growth seeks absolute Unity' – that we call the Atman-trend or Atman-telos. 'But in ways or under conditions that necessarily prevent it' – that we call the Atman-constraint or Atman-denial or contraction. 'And allow only substitute unities and substitute gratifications' – that is the Atman-project proper, a compromise formation between the Atman-trend and the Atman-constraint. Because I don't want to be over-technical about this, I will usually just refer to the whole complex as the Atman-project. The interested reader will be able to tell, from the context, which of these three strands I intend.

Variations on the Atman-Project

What I would like to do in this section, simply, is describe the nature of the Atman-project from several different angles, in the abstract, so that we may better grasp its general and overall structure. Then, in the succeeding chapters, we will examine the stage-specific forms of the Atman-project which appear throughout development.

According to the perennial philosophy, the ultimate nature of reality is *sunyata* or *nirguna*, which is usually translated as 'emptiness', 'voidness', or 'nothingness'. But *sunyata* does *not* mean blankness or vacant absence. The 'void', as R. H. Blyth remarked, does not mean featureless, but *seamless* – 'the seamless coat of the universe', as Whitehead put it. *Sunyata* simply means that, just as the arms and legs and fingers are quite different entities but also are parts of *one* body, so all things and events in the universe are aspects of one fundamental Whole, the very source and suchness which is the Real itself. This holds, obviously, for men and women as well. The ultimate psychology is a psychology of fundamental Wholeness, or the superconscious All. At any rate, let us simply note that this Wholeness, according to the perennial psychology, is *what* is real and *all* that is real. A radically separate, isolated and bounded entity does not exist anywhere. There are no seams in the world, in things, in people or in God.

It follows, then, that to erect a self boundary or barrier, and hold a separate-identity feeling *against* the prior Wholeness, not only involves *illusion*, it requires a constant expenditure of energy, a perpetual *contracting* or restricting activity. This, of course, obscures the prior Wholeness itself, and this – as I have elsewhere suggested – is the primal repression. It is the illusory repression of universal consciousness and its projection as an inside-self vs. an outside-world, a subject vs. an object.

Let us note, then, that a separate-subject or self-identity, such as most normal individuals possess, is based upon the superimposition of an illusory *boundary* upon prior Wholeness. That prior Wholeness then *appears* as a subject-in-here vs. a world-out-there. There is a boundary; and thus there is a subject vs. an object – and if this boundary is exclusively executed, it obscures (but does not destroy) the prior Wholeness of Atman.

According to the perennial philosophy, the re-discovery of this infinite and eternal Wholeness is men and women's single greatest need and want. For not only is Atman the basic nature of all souls, each soul or each subject knows or intuits that this is so. Every individual – every sentient being – constantly intuits that his prior Nature *is* the infinite and eternal, All and Whole – he is possessed, that is, with a true Atman-intuition. *Anima Naturaliter Christiana.*

But, at the same time, the subject is terrified of real transcendence, because transcendence entails the 'death' of his isolated and separate-self sense. The subject can find the prior Whole only by letting go of the *boundary* between subject and object – that is, by dying to the exclusive subject. And the subject, obviously, is terrified of this. And because he can't or won't let go of and die to his separate self, he cannot find true and real transcendence, he cannot find that larger fulfilment as the Whole. Holding on to himself, his subjectivity, he shuts out Atman; grasping only his own ego, he denies the rest of the All.

Yet, notice immediately that men and women are faced with a truly fundamental dilemma: above all else, each person wants true transcendence, Atman-consciousness, and the Whole; but, above all else, each person fears the loss of the separate self, the 'death' of the isolated ego or subject. All a person wants is Wholeness, but all he does is fear and resist it (since that would entail the death of his separate self). Atman-telos vs. Atman-restraint. And there is the fundamental double-bind in the face of eternity, the ultimate knot in the heart of the separate self.

Because man wants real transcendence above all else, but because he cannot or will not accept the necessary death of his separate-self sense, he goes about seeking transcendence in ways, or through structures, that *actually prevent* it and *force symbolic substitutes*. And these substitutes come in all varieties: sex, food, money, fame, knowledge, power – all are ultimately substitute gratifications, simple substitutes for true release in Wholeness. As Gilson put it, 'Even in the midst of the lowest pleasures, the most abandoned voluptuary is still seeking God.' That can now be said with absolute assurance. And that is why human desire is insatiable, why all joys yearn for infinity – all a person wants is Atman; all he finds are symbolic substitutes for it. This attempt to regain Atman consciousness in ways or under conditions that prevent it and force symbolic substitutes – this is the Atman-project.

The subjective wing

Even an individual's feeling of being a separate, isolated, and bounded self is a mere substitute for one's own true Nature, a substitute for the transcendent Self of the ultimate Whole. Every individual *correctly* intuits that he is of one nature with Atman, but he *distorts* that intuition by applying it to his separate self. He feels his separate self is immortal, all-embracing, central to the cosmos, all-significant. That is, he *substitutes* his ego for Atman. Then, instead of finding actual and timeless wholeness, he merely substitutes the wish to live for ever; instead of being one with the cosmos, he substitutes the desire to possess the cosmos; instead of being one with God, he tries himself to play God.

This is what we call the *subjective wing* of the Atman-project. Since the Atman-project is created by the split between subject and object, the Atman-project can be played out through a manipulation of both the subjective and objective sides of awareness (we will return to the objective wing shortly). The subjective wing of the Atman-project is the *impossible* desire that the individual self be immortal, cosmocentric, and all-important, but based on the *correct* intuition that one's real Nature is indeed infinite and eternal. Not that his deepest nature is *already* God, but that his ego *should* be God – immortal, cosmocentric, death-defying and all-powerful – there is his Atman-project. And there is either Atman, or there is the Atman-project.

Hubert Benoit has an exquisite quote on the nature of the subjective wing of the Atman-project. 'One should ask oneself,' he begins, 'how this thing can be, how [any person] can come to believe that he accepts his temporal state, this limited and mortal state [of being only a separate self and not the Whole] which is in reality affectively inacceptable, how can he live this way?' That is, how can one live without Atman? The answer, of course, is to create substitutes for that Estate: to create an Atman-project by (consciously or unconsciously) making the separate self *appear* to be Atman-like – cosmocentric, immortal, deified, central to all that is and the prime mover of all that is. And so, says Benoit, how does this soul live with this inacceptable situation of not realizing Atman? 'He arrives at it, essentially, through the play of his imagination, through the faculty which his mentality possesses of recreating a *subjective world* whose unique motor principle this time he is. The man would never resign himself to not being the unique motive-power of the real universe [i.e., to not being Atman] if he had not this consoling faculty of creating a universe for himself, a universe which he creates all alone.' And that is part, the subjective part, of the Atman-project.

Life and death

Once this false, individual, and separate self sense is created out of prior Wholeness, then that self is faced with two major drives: the perpetuation of its own existence (Eros) and the avoidance of all that threatens its dissolution (Thanatos). This inward, isolated, pseudo-self is fiercely defended against death, dissolution, and transcendence (Thanatos), on the one hand, while aspiring and pretending to cosmocentricity, omnipotence, and immortality on the other (Eros). These are simply *the positive and negative sides* of the Atman-project: Life and Death, Eros and Thanatos, Vishnu and Shiva.

Thus, arising as a function of the subject vs. object boundary, are the two major dynamic factors: Eros and Thanatos, Life and Death. Eros ultimately is the desire to recapture that prior Wholeness which was obscured when the boundary between self and other was constructed. But to actually gain a true re-union of subject and object, self and other, requires the death and dissolution of the exclusively separate self – and this is precisely what is resisted. Thus Eros cannot find true union, real Wholeness, but is instead driven to find symbolic substitutes for the lost Whole, and these substitutes, in order to work, must *present as fulfilled* the wish for prior Unity. Eros, then, is the underlying power of seeking, grasping, wishing, desiring, perpetuating, loving, living, willing, and so on. And it is *never* satisfied because it finds only substitutes. Eros is ontological hunger.

We come, then, to Thanatos. Thanatos – death and the fear of death. What has been so very difficult for Western psychology to grasp is that there are at least two major but quite different forms of fear and anxiety. One form is pathological or neurotic terror: any type of anxiety that can legitimately be traced to 'mental illness', pathological defence mechanisms, or neurotic guilt. But the other form of terror is not due to a mental aberration or neurotic illness but to a perception of the *truth* – it is a basic, unavoidable, inescapable terror *inherent* in the separate self sense. Man's prior Nature is the Whole, but once he splits that Nature into a separate self vs. an external other, then that separate self necessarily is faced with an awareness of death and the terror of death. It is existential, given, inherent (as long as the boundary exists between subject and object) – and the perception of this terror is a perception of the truth of the situation, not a perception of mental illness.

The Upanishads put this fact beautifully: 'Wherever there is other, there is fear.' That has been perfectly obvious to the East for at least 3000 years. But fortunately, the existential psychologists in the West have finally – after decades of orthodox psychiatry's trying to reduce existential dread to neurotic guilt – exposed and explained this essential point with such clarity that it can only be overlooked by exposing one's ignorance.

Out of the Body Experiences

SYLVAN MULDOON and HEREWARD CARRINGTON
The Phenomena of Astral Projection

At the age of twelve Sylvan Muldoon found himself out of his physical body and yet still conscious. His physical body remained in one place, while he entered into another, separate, vehicle of consciousness. These spontaneous experiences continued and he kept silent about them until he read Hereward Carrington's *Modern Psychical Phenomena*, and discovered that many other people also found themselves out of the body. Together Muldoon and Carrington carried out extensive research and published three classic books in the field.

These books, along with many other similar descriptions, make a powerful case for the fact that human consciousness can exist beyond the physical brain. This is obviously very challenging to mainstream orthodoxy.

The belief that man possesses a 'double' or spiritual body of some kind dates back to the veriest antiquity. In the Egyptian *Book of the Dead*, this idea is already fully developed, and illustrated in considerable detail, where the Ka is shown returning to its mummified body. In China and Tibet the same doctrine held sway from time immemorial, and ancient Chinese prints show the emergence of such a body, when a victim is being subjected to torture. The ancient writings of Tibet enter into the question at great length. Among primitives, this belief has always been held – that a man, during his sleep, leaves his physical body and wanders far afield. Anthropologists, of course (such as Tyler, in his *Primitive Culture*), have invariably attributed such beliefs to the realm of fantasy – contending that *dreams* would have given rise to such beliefs in primitive minds. But then, anthropologists as a class refuse to acknowledge the reality of *any* genuine psychic phenomena believed in by 'savages', despite the absurdity of such an attitude, as pointed out by Andrew Lang and other competent critics. The general attitude seems to be that, just *because* primitive peoples believe in certain unusual phenomena, that *therefore* these beliefs of theirs are erroneous, and that such phenomena do not occur! But, of course, few if any anthropologists accept the reality of psychic phenomena. If they did, they might see that these beliefs are based upon *actual experiences*, and that, when primitive peoples contended that they actually left their bodies at night, and visited distant places, they actually did so – as proved by subsequent verification of their statements, which turned out to be true. Such verifications have as a rule either been ignored, or treated as 'coincidences'. The unscientific character of this attitude should be obvious to any serious student of these problems.

The belief in some sort of spiritual body has doubtless been maintained and fortified, throughout history, by constantly reported cases of *apparitions*; or, more popularly speaking, 'ghosts'. It is perhaps hardly necessary to emphasize the fact that such cases have been recounted from the earliest times, and from every country in the world. Until our own times, 'ghosts' were unceremoniously classified under one of two categories: they were dismissed as hallucinations and the disordered imaginations of credulous minds, *or* they were accepted as real, outstanding entities – that is, space-occupying forms. Holding such diametrically opposite views, it is small wonder that believers and disbelievers could find no common ground on which to meet. Such ground was only provided by the progress of psychic science, and the later and more rational interpretation of the majority of such phantoms.

Briefly, the modern view is that the majority of apparitions are indeed subjective, rather than objective, but that, in many instances, they are more than this. If the appearance of the phantom coincides with the death or illness of its originator, we seem forced to the conclusion that some causal connection exists between the death and the appearance of the phantasm; and this factor is now thought to be *telepathy*. Accordingly, such cases are now generally regarded, for the most part, as 'telepathic hallucinations'. The mind of the dying person has in some manner influenced the mind of the seer, causing it to conjure up the visual picture of that person, which becomes 'externalized' in the form of a hallucination. In some such way, doubtless, the vast majority of 'apparitions of the dying' may be explained.

But not all of them! Obstinate cases keep cropping up which seemingly cannot be accounted for in this simple manner. Some 'ghosts' are reported to have opened and closed doors, or pulled aside curtains, or produced raps, or been seen by animals, or by several people at the same time. Occasionally, such 'ghosts' have been photographed. A hallucination cannot snuff a candle or open a door, or affect the emulsion on a photographic plate! That requires some semi-material body, capable of influencing matter. It was cases such as these which forced Mr Andrew Lang to write, in his *Cock Lane and Common Sense* (p. 206): '*Some* apparitions are "ghosts" – real objective entities, filling space.' Thus the traditional 'ghost' comes into his own again: the majority of them may be subjective, but a small minority of them seem to be objective in the most literal sense of the term: they are space-occupying phantoms. If this be true, we can see that (as usual) both sides in this dispute were right, and both of them were wrong! Their fault lay in trying to classify and explain *all* such phenomena in one way, and place them under a single heading.

It is not the province of this book to deal with apparitions of the subjective type; this subject has already been covered in several excellent works, of which Frank Podmore's *Apparitions and Thought Transference* may serve as an example. We desire to deal with those rare cases where there seems to be evidence of the objectivity of the phantom observed; or, more specifically, of those instances in which the projector has not only been *seen* – but has *been* the phantom! These are the cases of so-called 'astral projection', in which the subject is actually conscious of his presence, and aware of the fact that he has left his physical body. In such cases, he does not *see* the ghost, he *is* the ghost! [...]

THE LANDA CASE
Saw self being operated upon

Dr Herman Wolf, of Amsterdam, Holland, a member of the National Board of Education, originally recorded this case just as it had been furnished to him by the subject, B. Landa, who was a school janitor. As the result of an accident, Landa was forced to seek the services of a surgeon, and during the operation had the following experience:

I found that I was fearfully nervous up to the time that I was anaesthetized for the operation . . . For some time, I do not know how long, I was unconscious . . . Suddenly a violent reaction, which was combined with violent inner resistance – as if I were being torn apart – gripped me . . . Just as suddenly and as briefly as the reaction, calmness came.

I saw myself – my physical self – lying there. I saw a sharply outlined view of the operating table. I myself, freely hovering and looking downward from above, saw my physical body, lying on the operating table. I could see the wound of the operation on the right side of my body, see the doctor with an instrument in his hand, which I cannot more closely describe.

All this I observed very clearly. I tried to hinder it all. It was so real, I can still hear the words I kept calling out: 'Stop it – what are you doing there?'

As suddenly as this picture which I have just described was seen and experienced by me, it also vanished again . . . but to me the experience will never be forgotten. [. . .]

THE JOHNSON CASE
Pain induces projection

Mr M. J. Johnson of Stockport, England, furnishes me with the following case:

One night I awakened with severe cramps in my legs. I got out of bed, but, do what I would, I could not ease the pain. It was so intense that I fear I must have fallen to the floor, unconscious.

The noise of the fall awakened my wife who called out to my two daughters in the next room . . . Now this is the peculiar part – while my corporeal body was lying prone, and my wife and daughters were trying to raise me, *my conscious self was looking on at them from over the shoulder of my wife*! And I was smiling at their apparent ineffectual efforts!

In a little while the two bodies seemed to unite or merge again, and soon I was able to speak, move, and arise, but I was terribly weak. I told my wife and daughters what had happened, but, of course, they could not understand anything like that occurring . . .

I asked Mr Johnson if it would be possible for him to furnish me with any corroborative evidence for his case, in the way of dates, etc., to which he replied (9 March, 1938):

I am unable to recall the exact date of the experience, other than to say that it was early in 1933. At that time I had absolutely no knowledge of this subject, and only thought of the occurrence as very curious and out of reason. While I knew *it happened*, it was not until I read of a similar experience, described by Sir Arthur Conan Doyle, that I realized what the explanation was.

At my request, Mr Johnson's two daughters furnished a statement to verify the incident:

I remember the occasion when my father fell unconscious on the bedroom floor and I assisted him. He did tell us of a queer experience he had at the time, of being outside his body and watching us over Mother's shoulder. I could not understand what he meant.

Past Lives

ROGER WOOLGER
Other Lives, Other Selves

With degrees in psychology, philosophy, literature and comparative religion, Roger Woolger trained as a psychotherapist at the Jung Institute. Originally sceptical of past lives, a series of experiences led him to accept their reality and develop a practical therapeutic framework for working with them.

Recent surveys in Britain and the United States show that nearly half the population believe in past lives. In the East, in Hinduism and Buddhism for instance, past lives and their reincarnational effects are taken for granted. If reincarnation is indeed a reality, it has substantial ramifications for how we understand psychology and human purpose.

What I have evolved in my own practice over the years is a personal blending of a number of therapeutic techniques and perspectives: Freudian, Jungian, Reichian, Gestalt, and more. I have absorbed from these schools a number of disciplines and attitudes which call upon sub-personalities, body language, psychodramatic role playing, trance work, catharsis, symbol awareness, and meditation. If there is a dominant metaphor to my approach to the unconscious, and especially past lives, that holds all these approaches together, it is probably the story. It seems to me, from the many cases I've treated, that the unconscious mind strongly resembles the figure of the Ancient Mariner – it wants to tell its story.

As I sit and listen to each client's elaboration of worries about career, money, relationships, sex, family, or whatever, I have trained my awareness to listen for the other stories – the stories behind or beneath the story presented. By letting my intuitive imagination cast a wider net, I have learned that behind every personal complaint – compulsive eating, fear of flying, impotence, money worries, depression, and so on – there lurk older, fuller stories with events often far more devastating and cataclysmic than the surface fears my clients find themselves enumerating.

Nothing illustrates the power of this approach more than the case of a professional woman in her early forties, whom I shall call Elizabeth.

A major issue in Elizabeth's life was her anxiety about the three cats who lived with her in her city apartment. What she felt was that she could never leave them for very long – so much so that she was virtually unable to take vacations. Once she had asked an acquaintance to feed them so she could get away, and one of the cats somehow got stuck in a closet for nearly a week and almost died. This, of course, confirmed her worst fears.

The more I probed, there seemed to be all sorts of relationships with animals in her life that were surrounded by disasters of one sort or another: a dog that was killed when she was a child, a cat she had rescued that was later killed, and more.

What was it that made her certain of further disasters to her pets? As our interview proceeded I became aware of two strongly related thoughts running through the various animal sagas she related: 'I can't leave them, because something will happen to them' and 'It's all my fault, I didn't do enough for them.'

As soon as we had passed through the preliminary focusing that put her in touch with the past life level of her unconscious, she began, with tears in her eyes, to tell the following story:

I'm an old woman living in a large bleak stone house. It's northern, maybe Scotland. There's a storm outside. I've been fighting with my husband. He says I don't care about the children. Perhaps he's right. I swore I'd never have children because I don't want to take care of them. But we've got two now, three and four years. He's outside screaming. I'm not letting him in. Let him take them if he knows better. I'm not letting them in.

The storm's getting worse but he has stopped screaming now. It's quiet for a while, an hour or so. Now it's knocking, it sounds like my little boy. Oh, no he won't, he's not doing that one. He's just sent the boy because he thinks I'll relent. Well, I'll show him. They're not coming in.

Now it's morning. The storm's over. They didn't come back. I'll bet they went to the inn. But I don't want to go to the door. Something's wrong.

I go to the door finally; it won't open. Oh, my dear lord. It's the children blocking it! My little girl is dead. My boy is unconscious, my husband's nowhere to be seen. [She weeps bitterly.]

It's all my fault! It's all my fault! They must have been so scared out there, so weak and helpless! [deep sobbing and remorse]

The rest of the story emerged slowly and painfully. The little boy died within hours. The poor woman in Elizabeth's unconscious was later to learn that her husband had loaded the children on to a handcart and while heading for the inn at the height of the storm had collapsed and died of a heart attack. The children had come back to the house to tell their mother, only to be shut out by her. In the extremity of her shame and remorse, the woman never tells her neighbours, letting them think that her husband was responsible. Her guilt torments her for the rest of her life and she dies with the thought, 'I don't trust myself to take care of anyone.'

This, then, was the appalling story that lay behind the fear of leaving her cats. The catharsis and insight gained brought her enormous relief. Most encouraging of all was that shortly after the session Elizabeth took a two-week vacation, leaving a friend to feed her cats. She sent me a card afterwards. 'I had a wonderful time,' she wrote. 'I never thought once about the cats.'

Authentic and inauthentic suffering

Had we stayed at the reality level of the story of Elizabeth's cats we might have gone nowhere. Any outside observer could easily suggest half a dozen ways for Elizabeth to get her cats taken care of, but that would not have relieved the residual guilt that would have ruined her vacation with worry. Most of us would tend to be impatient with her complaints as neurotic over-attachment of some sort.

For the therapist, what is important is not the literal truth of a story but its psychological truth. Jung once remarked that neurotic suffering is inauthentic suffering, implying, so it seems to me, that the pain experienced is out of proportion to the supposed event that apparently occasions it. We all know of cases of inauthentic, neurotic suffering: the clinging and hysterical wife who finds all kinds of reasons why she cannot take a job in the world; the lower-echelon administrator who complains endlessly about his bullying superior and yet who tyrannizes others in his own charge; the fiercely independent man or woman who labours in the woods in a half-built cabin with frozen pipes all winter. These are all dramas of inauthentic suffering, feeble cries for help or sympathy that, as the uninvolved listener, we often turn a deaf ear to. Somehow we know the situation is transparently phony, a set-up, and that these intense and intractable situations are what Eric Berne calls 'games people play'.

In taking the perspective of past lives in therapy I listen intently to these neurotic life patterns with the unvoiced question 'What is the authentic suffering behind this?' What is the deeper, archaic, lurking fear or trauma *beneath* this displaced surface story?

Using the various methods I shall describe below, past-life therapy probes to a deeper layer of the complex, where things are more raw, more extreme, and where, in the controlled, safe environment of therapy, the authentic pain at the heart of the complex can emerge and be released.

Behind the fears of a clinging housewife, for example, we may find a historical story of a black slave life complete with auction, humiliation, sexual brutality, and maybe even suicide, all adding up in her unconscious fantasy to a terror of the market place which she is now acting out by refusing to go out into the world.

Beneath an administrator's petty tyrannies may lie a feudal story of land dispossessed and an unsatisfied longing for revenge, so that the unfinished story of power, control, and defeat is played out again and again in this man's work life.

At the back of a young man's or woman's retreat into the woods we may find an old story of a native American tribe where a young child ran into the woods to escape massacre only to return to find the mutilated corpses of his parents and villagers. So present life becomes structured around the fear of being fully in the world, and although it is seemingly safe and protected in the woods, he or she puts out desperate but ambivalent messages about being helpless and alone.

So the purpose of telling the past-life story is to return the individual's neurotic suffering to its authentic psychic roots so that it may be detached from the contemporary situations to which it does not properly belong. As in the case of Elizabeth's cats, once seen in a new, truthful perspective the anxiety usually is resolved and disappears, leaving the client free to live his or her current life unfettered.

The body tells its story too

Freud has shown how hysterical symptoms like a paralysed arm may be an arrested symbolic expression about some painfully repressed story to do with touching or embracing. More recently, popular psychology has accustomed us to the notion of body language and psychosomatic complaints.

When I listen to my client's story I also watch and empathize with his or her body language as well as carefully take a history of his or her physical illnesses, noting especially what each coincided with in my client's life. I have learned that for every chronic physical symptom – particularly those that resist conventional treatment, e.g., back pain, premature ejaculation, asthma – buried in the symptom is an older story of disaster, deprivation, or violent death. Back pains produce images of stabbing, beating, crushing, being broken, burdens; premature ejaculation evokes memories of shame, humiliation, sexual torment; asthma brings with it fears of drowning, asphyxiation, death from smothering, and so on.

The body and its various aches, pains, and dysfunctions is a living psychic history book when read correctly. My therapeutic approach is very simple. All I do is ask my client 'What is your pain *like?*' In the search for a fitting word to describe it, my client will focus on the embodied complex and find metaphors that swiftly begin to reveal the elements of a story. A pain may be strikingly specific: 'It's as though it goes through my left eye and out of the side of my neck,' one client said. In seconds the image of an arrow sprang to his mind and he was suddenly on a battlefield struck down by enemy fire. 'My arm feels as though it's being pulled, wrenched,' another client said. 'What's pulling it?' I asked. 'Oh, help! It's an animal, a lion. I'm in an arena. They are tearing me apart.' In no time at all the grisly end of a Christian martyr was re-enacted with the amazing release and relief of chronic aches and pains that had before been quite unrelated to each other as physical symptoms.

Even though the physical ailment may have very specific origins in a person's current life, I have found more and more that there are several layers to every major syndrome of physical illness, accident, or weakness. If Freud's observation was that behind every slip of the tongue there lies a buried complex, why not behind every slip on the ice, every car accident, every illness that strikes us out of the blue? If there is a buried complex behind each accident in this life, could there possibly be an old past-life injury behind the complex?

The existence of a past-life level of physical problems has been confirmed over and over again in the cases I have seen. So much so that I have learned when taking a psychological case history to ensure that we include all major illnesses, accidents, and chronic ailments and especially the chronological ages at which they occur.

Working with a woman client in her early forties named Jane, for instance, I helped her relive an unfulfilled life as a woman in pioneer days which ended tragically when a horse and trap overturned and she broke her back and died. In the regression I had not thought to ask her age until our session was almost completed. 'How old were you?' I asked. 'Twenty-seven,' she said with certainty. 'Does twenty-seven remind you of anything in this life?' I queried. Suddenly a look of astonishment came over her. 'My goodness,' she exclaimed, 'it was at twenty-seven that I was in the hospital with a very serious kidney infection they couldn't properly diagnose. I nearly died.' She reached down the left side of her back. 'The pain was terrible, just here, *exactly* in the place where I broke my back as that pioneer woman.' As we talked further it was clear that twenty-seven was a crisis point both in this life and the past life. Gnawing self-doubt about the direction of her life and her failure to marry had surfaced at this juncture in the past life and it had taken a fatal turn. When similar issues emerged in her current life it was as though her body had started to repeat and re-enact the old story.

I am not a mechanism, an assembly of various sections.
And it is not because the mechanism is working wrongly, that I am ill.
I am ill because of wounds to the soul, to the deep emotional self
and the wounds to the soul take a long, long time, only time can help
and patience, and a certain difficult repentance,
long, difficult repentance, realization of life's mistake, and the freeing oneself
from the endless repetition of the mistake
which mankind at large has chosen to sanctify.

D. H. Lawrence

Gaia – The Living Earth

I will sing well of well-founded Gaia, Mother of All, eldest of all beings, she feeds all creatures that are in the world, all that go upon the goodly land and all that are in the paths of the sea, and all that fly: these are fed of her store.

Homeric Hymn, seventh century BC

Introduction

The destruction of forests, the pollution of the soil and the oceans, the disappearance of natural habitats and wilderness – all of this, as we know, is not just a matter of aesthetic concern. As biological creatures we are dependent upon our environment and it has become increasingly obvious that we are threatening our own survival. We have been forced into looking at the effects that modernization and industrialization are having on the planet. It is a simple fact that we cannot abuse her without, in the end, abusing ourselves. The silver lining is that, in the most blunt way, we have been forced back into a relationship with nature.

There are two other reasons why we have also been led back into a respectful relationship. One of them is that environmental science and systems theories in general both demonstrate the delicate and intimate interdependence of all life. The other is that many people are beginning once again to respect the spirit and life in every aspect of nature and ecology.

Holistic people believe that it is normal and healthy for us to experience a deep sense of companionship with Earth and nature. Our physical bodies are essentially of the same matter and, whatever the particular history, we emerged together out of the same cosmic origin. In most people there is an instinctive understanding that nature is alive, that she has integrity and beauty and meaning, and that she deserves respect, awe and positive loving cooperation. Almost without exception when people allow themselves time in nature, they find themselves nurtured, relaxed and entranced by her. This is not romance. It is a return to understanding and above all experiencing humanity's place within nature and the cosmos.

This appreciation of nature brings the environmental campaigner into alliance with the lyrical lovers of landscape, and with the animist tribal religions and pagans and feminists, who honour every aspect of the planet as being sacred and alive.

But this mystic understanding is obviously worthless if our lifestyles remain selfish and harmful. Holistic culture has begun to grasp this challenge and to look at the whole issue of right livelihood.

Chief Seattle's Speech

CHIEF SEATTLE

Address Given in January, 1854

This famous speech, given by Chief Seattle in January of 1854, is the subject of historical debate and the reality is that there is no verbatim script in existence. It is believed to be the response of a Duwamish or Suquamish chieftain to white imperialism and the monetary offers from the President of the United States. The first version appeared in the *Seattle Sunday Star* on 29 October 1887, but there are several other versions of it in circulation including those of the poet William Arrowsmith dating from the late 1960s and Texas professor Ted Perry from some time around 1970. I downloaded the version reproduced here from Ben & Jerry's website.

How can you buy or sell the sky, the warmth of the land? The idea is strange to us. If we do not own the freshness of the air and sparkle of the water, how can you buy them? Every part of this earth is sacred to my people. Every shining pine needle, every sandy shore, every mist in the dark woods, every clearing and humming insect is holy in the memory and experience of my people.

The sap which courses through the trees carries the memories of the red man. The white man's dead forget the country of their birth when they go to walk among the stars. Our dead never forget this beautiful earth, for it is the mother of the red man. We are part of the earth and it is part of us. The perfumed flowers are our sisters; the deer, the horse, the great eagle, these are our brothers. The rocky crests, the juices in the meadows, the body heat of the pony, and man – all belong to the same family.

So, when the Great Chief in Washington sends word that he wishes to buy land, he asks much of us. The Great Chief sends word he will reserve us a place so that we can live comfortably among ourselves. He will be our father and we will be his children. So we will consider your offer to buy our land. But it will not be easy. For this land is sacred to us. This shining water that moves in the streams and rivers is not just water but the blood of our ancestors.

If we sell you land, you must remember that it is sacred, and you must teach your children that it is sacred and that each ghostly reflection in the clear water of the lakes tells of events and memories in the life of my people. The water's murmur is the voice of my father's father. The rivers are our brothers, they quench our thirst. The rivers carry our canoes, and feed our children. If we sell you our land, you must remember, and teach your children, that the rivers are our brothers, and yours, and you must henceforth give the rivers the kindness you would give any brother.

We know that the white man does not understand our ways. One portion of land is the same to him as the next, for he is a stranger who comes in the night and takes from the land whatever he needs. The earth is not his brother, but his enemy, and when he has conquered it, he moves on. He leaves his father's graves behind, and he does not care. He kidnaps the earth from his children, and he does not care. His father's grave, and his children's birthright, are forgotten. He treats his mother, the earth, and his brother, the sky, as things to be bought, plundered, sold like sheep or bright beads. His appetite will devour the earth and leave behind only a desert. I do not know.

Our ways are different from your ways. The sight of your cities pains the eyes of the red man. But perhaps it is because the red man is a savage and does not understand. There is no quiet place in the white man's cities. No place to hear the unfurling of leaves in spring, or the rustle of an insect's wings. But perhaps it is because I am a savage and do not understand. The clatter only seems to insult the ears. And what is there to life if a man cannot hear the lonely cry of the whippoorwill or the arguments of the frogs around a pond at night? I am a red man and do not understand.

The Indian prefers the soft sound of the wind darting over the face of a pond, and the smell of the wind itself, cleaned by a midday rain, or scented with the pinion pine. The air is precious to the red man, for all things share the same breath – the beast, the tree, the man, they all share the same breath. The white man does not seem to notice the air he breathes. Like a man dying for many days, he is numb to the stench. But if we sell you our land, you must remember that the air is precious to us, that the air shares its spirit with all the life it supports. The wind that gave our grandfather his first breath also receives his last sigh. And if we sell you our land, you must keep it apart and sacred, as a place where even the white man can go to taste the wind that is sweetened by the meadow's flowers.

So we will consider your offer to buy our land. If we decide to accept, I will make one condition: the white man must treat the beasts of this land as his brothers. I am a savage and I do not understand any other way. I've seen a thousand rotting buffaloes on the prairie, left by the white man who shot them from a passing train. I am a savage and I do not understand how the smoking iron horse can be more important than the buffalo that we kill only to stay alive. What is man without the beasts? If all the beasts were gone, man would die from a great loneliness of spirit. For whatever happens to the beasts, soon happens to man. All things are connected.

You must teach your children that the ground beneath their feet is the ashes of your grandfathers. So that they will respect the land, tell your children that the earth is rich with the lives of our kin. Teach your children what we have taught our children, that the earth is our mother. Whatever befalls the earth befalls the sons of the earth. If men spit upon the ground, they spit upon themselves. This we know: the earth does not belong to man; man belongs to the earth. This we know.

All things are connected like the blood which unites one family. All things are connected. Whatever befalls the earth befalls the sons of the earth. Man did not weave the web of life: he is merely a strand in it. Whatever he does to the web, he does to himself. Even the white man, whose God walks and talks with him as friend to friend, cannot be exempt from the common destiny. We may be brothers after all. We shall see.

One thing we know, which the white man may one day discover: our God is the same God. You may think now that you own Him as you wish to own our land; but you cannot. He is the God of man, and His compassion is equal for the red man and the white. This earth is precious to Him, and to harm the earth is to heap contempt on its Creator. The whites too shall pass; perhaps sooner than all other tribes. Contaminate your bed, and you will one night suffocate in your own waste. But in your perishing you will shine brightly, fired by the strength of God who brought you to this land and for some special purpose gave you dominion over this land and over the red man.

That destiny is a mystery to us, for we do not understand when the buffalo are all slaughtered, the wild horses are tamed, the secret corners of the forest are heavy with scent of many men, and the view of the ripe hills is blotted by talking wires.

The Gaia Hypothesis

J. E. LOVELOCK
Gaia – A New Look at Life on Earth

A specialist in gas chromatography and inventor of the electron capture detector, Jim Lovelock worked as an independent scientist researching the possibility of life on Mars for NASA. Looking at large-scale phenomena such as atmospheric gases rather than smaller individual signs of life he disappointed NASA by pronouncing Mars a lifeless planet and then turned his attention to large-scale phenomena on our own planet.

Here on Earth he detected systemic cycles and events in the biosphere which led to his suggesting that the Earth as a whole is a living being. This theory is immediately attractive to many different groups of scholars and activists. Students of systems theory and cybernetics enjoy a hypothesis that can be applied to such a large system. It also provides tantalizing evidence of a semi-mystical assumption that the whole is more than just the sum of its parts. Mystics, animists and tribal religionists are happy to have restated for them what has always been an eternal truth – that the Earth is alive.

Working in a new intellectual environment, I was able to forget Mars and to concentrate on the Earth and the nature of its atmosphere. The result of this more single-minded approach was the development of the hypothesis that the entire range of living matter on Earth, from whales to viruses, and from oaks to algae, could be regarded as constituting a single living entity, capable of manipulating the Earth's atmosphere to suit its overall needs and endowed with faculties and powers far beyond those of its constituent parts.

It is a long way from a plausible life-detection experiment to the hypothesis that the Earth's atmosphere is actively maintained and regulated by life on the surface, that is, by the biosphere. Much of this book deals with more recent evidence in support of this view. In 1967 the reasons for making the hypothetical stride were briefly these:

Life first appeared on the Earth about 3,500 million years ago. From that time until now, the presence of fossils shows that the Earth's climate has changed very little. Yet the output of heat from the sun, the surface properties of the Earth, and the composition of the atmosphere have almost certainly varied greatly over the same period.

The chemical composition of the atmosphere bears no relation to the expectations of steady-state chemical equilibrium. The presence of methane, nitrous oxide, and even nitrogen in our present oxidizing atmosphere represents violation of the rules of chemistry to be measured in tens of orders of magnitude. Disequilibria on this scale suggest that the atmosphere is not merely a biological product, but more probably a biological construction: not living, but like a cat's fur, a bird's feathers, or the paper of a wasp's nest, an extension of a living system designed to maintain a chosen environment. Thus the atmospheric concentration of gases such as oxygen and ammonia is found to be kept at an optimum value from which even small departures could have disastrous consequences for life.

The climate and the chemical properties of the Earth now and throughout its history seem always to have been optimal for life. For this to have happened by chance is as unlikely as to survive unscathed a drive blindfold through rush-hour traffic.

By now a planet-sized entity, albeit hypothetical, had been born, with properties which could not be predicted from the sum of its parts. It needed a name. Fortunately the author William Golding was a fellow-villager. Without hesitation he recommended that this creature be called Gaia, after the Greek Earth goddess also known as Ge, from which root the sciences of geography and geology derive their names. In spite of my ignorance of the classics, the suitability of this choice was obvious. It was a real four-lettered word and would thus forestall the creation of barbarous acronyms, such as Biocybernetic Universal System Tendency/Homoeostasis. I felt also that in the days of Ancient Greece the concept itself was probably a familiar aspect of life, even if not formally expressed. Scientists are usually condemned to lead urban lives, but I find that country people still living close to the earth often seem puzzled that anyone should need to make a formal proposition of anything as obvious as the Gaia hypothesis. For them it is true and always has been.

I first put forward the Gaia hypothesis at a scientific meeting about the origins of life on Earth which took place in Princeton, New Jersey, in 1969. Perhaps it was poorly presented. It certainly did not appeal to anyone except Lars Gunnar Sillen, the Swedish chemist now sadly dead, and Lynn Margulis, of Boston University, who had the task of editing our various contributions. A year later in Boston Lynn and I met again and began a most rewarding collaboration which, with her deep knowledge and insight as a life scientist, was to go far in adding substance to the wraith of Gaia, and which still happily continues.

We have since defined Gaia as a complex entity involving the Earth's biosphere, atmosphere, oceans, and soil; the totality constituting a feedback or cybernetic system which seeks an optimal physical and chemical environment for life on this planet. The maintenance of relatively constant conditions by active control may be conveniently described by the term 'homoeostasis'.

Gaia has remained a hypothesis but, like other useful hypotheses, she has already proved her theoretical value, if not her existence, by giving rise to experimental questions and answers which were profitable exercises in themselves. [. . .]

Let us now examine contemporary pollution from a Gaian rather than a human angle. So far as industrial pollution is concerned, by far the most heavily affected places are the densely populated urban areas of the north temperate zones: Japan, parts of the USA, of Western Europe and of Soviet Russia. Many of us have had a chance to view these regions from the window of an aeroplane in flight. Provided that there is enough wind to disperse the smog so that the surface is visible, the usual sight is of a green carpet lightly speckled with grey. Industrial complexes stand out, together with the close-packed housing of the workers, yet the general impression is that everywhere the natural vegetation is biding its time and waiting for some unguarded moment that will give it a chance to return and take over everything again. Some of us remember the rapid colonization by wild flowers of city areas cleared by bombing in the Second World War. Industrial regions seldom appear from above to be the denatured deserts which the professional doomsters have led us to expect. If this is true of the most polluted and populous areas of our planet, it may seem that there is no urgent cause for concern about man's activities. Unfortunately this is not necessarily so; it is merely that we have been led to look for trouble in the wrong places. [. . .]

What, then, are those activities of man which pose a threat to the Earth and the life upon it? We as a species, aided by the industries at our command, have now significantly altered some of the major chemical cycles of the planet. We have increased the carbon cycle by 20 per cent, the nitrogen cycle by 50 per cent, and the sulphur cycle by over 100 per cent. As our numbers and our use of fossil fuels increase, these perturbations will grow likewise. What are the most likely consequences? The only thing we know to have happened so far is an increase in atmospheric carbon dioxide of about 10 per cent and perhaps also, although this is debatable, an increase in the burden of haze attributable to particles of sulphate compounds and soil dust.

It has been predicted that the increase in carbon dioxide will act as a sort of gaseous blanket to keep the Earth warmer. It has also been argued that the increase in haziness of the atmosphere might produce some cooling effect. It has even been suggested that at present these two effects cancel one another out and that is why nothing significant has so far emerged from the perturbation caused by the burning of fossil fuels. If the growth projections are correct and if as time goes by our consumption of these fuels continues to double more or less with each passing decade, we shall need to be vigilant.

The parts of the Earth responsible for planetary control may still be those which carry the vast hordes of micro-organisms. The algae of the sea and of the soil surface use sunlight to perform the prime task of living chemistry, photosynthesis. They still turn over half of the Earth's supply of carbon, in co-operation with the aerobic decomposers of the soil and the seabed, together with the anaerobic microflora in the great mud zones of the continental shelves, sea bottom, marshes, and wet lands. The large animals, plants, and seaweeds may have important specialist functions, but the greater part of Gaia's self-regulating activity could still be conducted by micro-organisms.

As we shall see in the next chapter, there may be some regions of the world more vital to Gaia than others; so that however urgent is the need to match the world's increasing population with increasing food supplies, we should take special care not to disturb too drastically those regions where planetary control may be sited. The continental shelves and wetlands generally have features and properties which make them suitable candidates for this role. It may be that we can create deserts and dust bowls with comparative impunity but if we devastate the area of the continental shelves through irresponsible bad husbandry in our first attempts at sea-farming, we shall do so at our peril.

Among the relatively few firm predictions about man's future is the one that our present numbers will, within the next few decades, at least double. The problem of feeding a world population of 8,000 million without seriously damaging Gaia would seem more urgent than that of industrial pollution. It may be argued, yes, but what of the more subtle poisons? The pesticides and herbicides, to say nothing of the ozone depleters, are surely the greatest threat?

A great debt is owed to Rachel Carson for having so movingly warned us of the threat to the biosphere arising from the careless and over-lavish use of pesticides. Yet it tends to be forgotten that we do take heed. A silent spring with no bird song has not arrived, although many birds, especially the rarer birds of prey, came near to extinction in some parts of the world. George Woodwell's careful study of the distribution and fate of DDT throughout the Earth is a model of how the pharmacology and toxicology of Gaia should be handled. The accumulation of DDT was not as great as was expected and recovery from its toxic effects was quicker. There appear to be natural processes for its removal which were not anticipated when the investigation began. The period of peak concentration of DDT in the biosphere is now well past. DDT will no doubt continue to be used in its life-saving and life-enriching role as a weapon against insect-borne disease, but it will probably be more carefully and economically employed in future. Such substances are like drugs, beneficial in the proper dose but harmful or even lethal in excess. It used to be said of fire, the first of the technological weapons, that it was a good servant but a bad master. The same holds true for the newer weapons of technology.

We may well need the fierce emotional drive of the radical environmentalist to alert us to the dangers of real or potential pollution hazards, but in our response we must take care not to over-react.

The Politics of Ecology

JONATHON PORRITT
Seeing Green

As Director of Friends of the Earth and a leading member of the Ecology Party, Jonathon Porritt is possibly Great Britain's most effective environmental propagandist. A gifted campaigner, he is also a shrewd diplomat able to communicate with diverse and frequently opposing camps. He has a clearly holistic perspective about which he communicates in a style that is often embarrassed and self-deprecating. This is his way of dealing – successfully – with the scepticism that often greets a spiritual approach.

Today's dominant social paradigm offers little scope for compromise and systematically represses the articulation of alternatives. Yet with the basic needs of the majority of people on this planet still unmet, with widespread poverty still a part of almost all developed nations, with alienation an endemic feature of the way we organize ourselves, it is clear that the system has failed even in its own terms. Worse still, the 'Faustian bargain' we have made has resulted in a totally distorted set of values and a complete loss of any spiritual dimension. The cohesion of industrial society is ensured by an all-embracing alliance of vested interests, including manifestations of so-called 'opposition', subsumed within the super-ideology of industrialism. Economic values dominate the deliberations and decisions of our democracy; human, non-material values are readily sacrificed in the pursuit of material power. The future is seen to offer no more than a continuation of the present, a deterministic acceptance of a world system that is clearly breaking down.

This determinism is rooted in a particular and ominous view of human nature. When all rational argument fails, critics of the green approach desperately fall back on the old line that we're just naive idealists, that what we propose is simply not possible when confronted with the 'reality of human nature'. Human nature is held to be immutably aggressive, intolerant, self-seeking and shallow, and will therefore work against any initiatives to move towards a sustainable future. Such critics refer us back to our own analysis of the destructive, scorched-earth history of humankind, and triumphantly conclude by claiming, 'You can't change human nature.'

This little catch-phrase, the self-fulfilling prophecy of all determinists, often tells us more about their particular brand of cynicism, apathy, helplessness or alienation than about human nature! There is not a shred of evidence that we are genetically modelled to behave for ever as we do today, but the belief that it is possible to change depends upon a belief in free will and the potential in each of us to counter the deterministic programming of contemporary society. As Duane Elgin says, 'Like the seed with the potential of becoming a flower, human nature is not a static thing but a spectrum of potentials.'[1] In today's wasteland much of the human potentiality for good is inevitably thwarted, but we should never ignore the creativity, the capacity for vision and compassion and the vast resources of moral energy that are innate within each of us. There is nothing naive about realistic idealism: without it, the pattern of the future will be a sad and sorry affair. No one has expressed this more clearly than R. H. Tawney:

It is obvious that no change of system or machinery can avert those causes of social malaise which consist of egotism, greed or quarrelsomeness of human nature. What it can do is to create an environment in which those are not the qualities which are encouraged. It cannot secure that men live up to their principles. What it can do is to establish their social order upon principles to which, if they please, they can live up and not live down. It cannot control their actions. It can offer them an end on which to fix their minds. And, as their minds are, so in the long run and with exceptions, their practical activity will be.[2]

Self-interest is and will remain a fundamental characteristic of human nature; but in today's world individual interests are identified almost exclusively with the accumulation of material wealth, and few politicians are prepared to articulate a concept of social progress that is not totally dependent on increases in GNP. The problem for the future is to ensure that the interests of the individual are more in line with those of society at large and with those of the planet. The materialistic ethic of mass consumption has even managed to obscure the ultimate goal of survival, and has obscured it so successfully that survival and the pursuit of individual self-interest, in the manner prescribed by *all* politicians apart from the greens, are now mutually exclusive.

It is not so much the political process itself that will determine our fate as the values on which that process is premised. 'Values are the key to the evolution of a sustainable society not only because they influence behaviour but also because they determine a society's priorities and thus its ability to survive.'[3] That is the uncompromising message throughout Lester Brown's work, and he goes on to quote these words from US environmentalist Tom Bender: 'Values are really a complex and compact repository of survival wisdom – an expression of those feelings, attitudes, actions and relationships that we have found to be most essential to our well-being.'[4]

Wants and needs

Society's values are neither timeless nor absolute; they change according to our changing circumstances and our perception of these circumstances. The dominant values of industrialism are already under the microscope, and many will necessarily be rejected as we move towards a more sustainable society. There will, for example, be far more attention paid to the distinction between *wants* and *needs*, needs being those things that are essential to our survival and to civilized, humane existence, wants being the extras that serve to gratify our desires. We all need good food; some people want to subsist on a diet of extravagant and often harmful luxuries. We all need to get from A to B; some people insist they can manage such a feat only in the back of a Rolls-Royce. We all need clothes; some people aspire after a new outfit for every day of the year. The distinctions are not always cut and dried, and the manipulative skills of the advertising industry in converting wants into needs make it difficult to expose the excesses thrown up by mass-consumption industrialism. By today's standards, keeping up with the Joneses is a positive social virtue.

To distinguish between genuine needs and artificial needs requires an unequivocal value judgement, the distinction between the two depending on the extent to which their satisfaction *genuinely* contributes to our well-being. Is our well-being genuinely enhanced by electric toothbrushes or umpteen varieties of cat food? Indeed, is it genuinely enhanced by having 'unlimited' freedom of choice? There are no easy answers; we are merely insisting that such questions must now be put, for continued reliance on the operations of a so-called 'value-free' market amounts to no more than a cowardly and perverse refusal to face reality. That reality tells all of us, whatever our political allegiance, that we must renounce the suicidal imperative of *more* for the sustainable logic of *better*.

The work of the psychologist Abraham Maslow suggests the direction in which we should be moving. He put forward the idea of a hierarchy of needs, suggesting that once our basic survival or physiological needs are met, 'higher-order needs' become increasingly important. Once we have food, clothing and shelter, we concern ourselves more with satisfying human relationships and the ways in which we experience a sense of belonging. The next 'level' (I find it difficult to interpret the hierarchy too literally) involves the need for recognition, for status, social position and self-esteem; and finally we move on to what Maslow refers to as the need for 'self-actualization', making the most of the multifarious talents and creative resources with which we are endowed. The problem, of course, is that in our alienated, materialistic society these higher-order needs are often 'satisfied' in an alienated, materialistic fashion: people may seek to '*buy* love', to '*win* a circle of friends', to '*acquire* status', to '*gain* self-respect'. But there is no binding imperative that tells us that these needs *have* to be met materialistically; indeed, it is part of *our* understanding of human nature that they may be met both more rewardingly and more sustainably in non-materialistic ways. If we are to redirect the drives that lie behind these needs towards less materialistic and destructive goals, then many of our current symbols of success and achievement must be altered. Henryk Skolimowski quotes Denis Healey's plaintive words: 'What people want are stable prices and a secure job. These things aren't very exciting to visionaries, but they are what most people want, and it is very difficult to get them. Trying to get them is not an ignoble thing to do.'[5] Indeed not, but nor is it adequate, whether or not you see yourself as a 'visionary'. Consider, by way of contrast, the four 'consumption criteria' proposed by the Simple Living Collective of San Francisco:

1. Does what I own or buy promote activity, self-reliance and involvement, or does it induce passivity and dependence?
2. Are my consumption patterns basically satisfying, or do I buy much that serves no real need?
3. How tied is my present job and lifestyle to instalment payments, maintenance and repair costs, and the expectations of others?
4. Do I consider the impact of my consumption patterns on other people and on the Earth?[6]

I'd lay odds that many of you are now thinking, 'How naive, quite unrealistic, hardly the stuff of *real* politics.' Just remember that those, like Denis Healey's, are *value* judgements, the product of an obsolescent value system that couldn't look reality in the face even if it knew where to find it. And just remember the words of J. M. Keynes: 'The power of vested interests is vastly exaggerated compared with the gradual encroachment of ideas.'

Metaphysical reconstruction

Only now are we beginning to realize the urgency of transcending our industrial perspective, of discovering new values and new ways of relating to each other and to the planet. Schumacher referred to this as a process of 'metaphysical reconstruction', and greens today see this in terms of at least four components: the person, the people, the planet and the spirit. The rest of the chapter looks at each of these in turn, reconfirming the obvious but often neglected truth that politicians are powerless unless they move with the spirit of the times. We believe that spirit has as little in common with the weary reiteration of collectivist abstractions as it does with the mean-minded promotion of individualist self-concern.

We prefer to talk of a 'third way', of the *politics of the person*, in the belief that only a completely different approach can resolve today's paradox of scale: that things are both too big and too small at one and the same time – too big because we are all made to feel like pygmies, too small because we are incapable of adopting a genuine planetary ethic. By stressing the importance of personal responsibility, by refusing to accept that any of us are neutral in our actions or decisions, green politics enables people to determine appropriate responses in a complex and confusing world. Barry Commoner once wrote: 'Like the ecosphere itself, the peoples of the world are linked through their separate but interconnected needs to a common fate. The world will survive the environmental crisis as a whole, or not at all.'[7] The acceptance of human interdependence must be at the heart of any new ethic: in Hazel Henderson's words, 'Morality has at last become pragmatic.'

The development of that sort of planetary consciousness depends upon our being able to rediscover our links with the Earth, and to work in sympathy with rather than against the organic harmonies that make life possible. This is the most important feature of what ecologists refer to as 'holism', embracing the *totality* of something in the knowledge that it is so much greater than the sum of its component parts; things cannot be understood by the isolated examination of their parts. The wisdom of the future depends on our ability to synthesize, to bring together rather than to take apart. So often the total picture, the sense of the whole, either eludes us or is wilfully set aside. Politics has reduced the 'average voter' to an opinion-poll read-out of immediate material needs; science has reduced the planet to a quantifiable aggregate of physical resources. It is the job of ecologists to re-present the whole picture, in all its diversity, complexity and frustrating unquantifiability!

Only connect!

'And God said, Let us make man in our image, after our likeness: and let them have dominion over the fish of the sea, and over the fowl of the air, and over the cattle, and over all the Earth, and over every creeping thing that creepeth upon the Earth.' What a lot of problems that little passage from Genesis has caused! For 'dominion' has usually been interpreted as 'domination', which has in turn provided a licence for the wholesale exploitation of the Earth. Christianity has often participated in suppressing a sense of reverence for the Earth, despite the 'pagan' hangover of the Harvest Festival.

One of the most crucial tasks for Christians today is therefore to reinterpret the meaning of 'dominion' in terms of stewardship and ecological responsibility for life on Earth. But this is only the beginning, for it must be acknowledged that the established Churches have got themselves into a fearful pickle. Though it must be obvious to all Church leaders that today's spiritual vacuum derives from the ascendancy of scientific materialism, they have so tamely accepted that religion and politics are two separate things that they are all but incapable of making any useful contribution to resolving today's appalling problems. I speak here of the Church as an *institution*, and mean no offence to the many *individuals* within those Churches who are in the forefront of social and political change. To put it bluntly, is it any wonder that most people ignore the Church, when on the one hand it professes to follow the example of Christ, and on the other refuses to take a stand against weapons of mass destruction, against the redundant 'Protestant' work ethic, or against the assaults of materialism? As Erik Dammann says in *The Future in Our Hands*:

How can we go about our daily business as if the rest of the world did not exist? How can we sit in our churches and talk of love? How dare we teach our children about justice and humanity without doing anything at all for those 82,000 children who are starving to death *every day*? How can we, without cringing, without even thinking of cringing, set an increase of consumption as a goal for ourselves, when we know what this means for others?[8]

Tough questions, I admit. But I can't help but be astonished at the sheer lack of urgency among Church leaders today; ours is a world crying out for leadership, for some kind of spiritual guidance. And yet, as the winds of change whistle up their richly caparisoned copes, where on earth are they? Can't they see that thousands are already engaged in rediscovering the essence of Christian spirituality, without excessive concern for orthodoxy or dogma? Can't they see the green shoots creeping up between the flagstones of their deserted cloisters? (I ask these questions and make these criticisms as a hopelessly imperfect

Christian, who has great difficulty with many parts of the Creed, but one of whose greatest joys is growling his way through Evensong in remote country churches!)

It seems to me so obvious that without some huge groundswell of spiritual concern the transition to a more sustainable way of life remains utterly improbable. In an extraordinary dialogue between Arnold Toynbee and Daisaku Ikeda, Toynbee puts it this way:

It seems unquestionable that man's power over his environment has already reached a degree at which this power will lead to self-destruction if man continues to use it to serve his greed. People who have become addicts to greed tend to take a short-term view: 'After me, the deluge.' They may know that if they fail to restrain their greed, they will be condemning their children to destruction. They may love their children, yet this love may not move them to sacrifice part of their present affluence for the sake of safeguarding their children's future.

And he concludes this section by saying:

The present threat to mankind's survival can be removed only by a revolution-ary change of heart in individual human beings. This change of heart must be inspired by religion in order to generate the will power needed for putting arduous new ideals into practice.[9]

I think I would accept this analysis, and would argue therefore that some kind of spiritual commitment, or religion in its true meaning (namely, the reconnection between each of us and the source of all life), is a fundamental part of the transformation that ecologists are talking about.

Bang goes the atheist vote! But even atheists might admit that it would be no bad thing to have a few spiritually minded allies, if only to offset some of the horrors still perpetrated in the name of religion. I can't see where the god of Ayatollah Khomeini fits into the ecological pantheon, and I can't help wondering what the connection is between the words of Christ and the rantings of Ian Paisley or the ghastly bigotry of the so-called 'Moral Majority' in the USA. A green theology will have more in common with the 'liberation theology' of many poorer countries, so that the false split between politics and religion may be removed, so that voices may be raised from every pulpit exhorting us to become 'lifeists' rather than materialists, so that we may rediscover the oneness of humanity and all creation. Thomas Merton, the American Trappist monk, puts it like this: 'We are already one. But we imagine we are not. And what we have to recover is our original unity. What we have to be is what we are.'

Only connect!

Buddhist Ecology

E. F. SCHUMACHER
Small is Beautiful

E. F. Schumacher was an academic, economist and journalist. Economic adviser to the British National Coal Board from 1950 to 1970, he was also the originator of the concept of Intermediate Technology for developing countries and founded the Intermediate Technology Development Group. His seminal book *Small is Beautiful* was first published in 1973 and it sounded out a note that immediately caught public attention. His prime thesis was that industry and economic strategy had become so gargantuan that they had lost their humaneness. He therefore argued the need for technology and economy appropriate to the situation. His arguments became foundation stones for much green activism and ecological awareness, as well as for the field of developmental politics. His own foundations, however, were as much spiritual as they were economic and he openly advocated what he called Buddhist Economics.

What is it that we really require from the scientists and technologists? I should answer: We need methods and equipment which are

– cheap enough so that they are accessible to virtually everyone;
– suitable for small-scale application; and
– compatible with man's need for creativity.

Out of these three characteristics is born non-violence and a relationship of man to nature which guarantees permanence. If only one of these three is neglected, things are bound to go wrong. [...]

While the materialist is mainly interested in goods, the Buddhist is mainly interested in liberation. But Buddhism is 'The Middle Way' and therefore in no way antagonistic to physical well-being. It is not wealth that stands in the way of liberation but the attachment to wealth; not the enjoyment of pleasurable things but the craving for them. The keynote of Buddhist economics, therefore, is simplicity and non-violence. From an economist's point of view, the marvel of the Buddhist way of life is the utter rationality of its pattern – amazingly small means leading to extraordinarily satisfactory results.

For the modern economist this is very difficult to understand. He is used to measuring the 'standard of living' by the amount of annual consumption, assuming all the time that a man who consumes more is 'better off' than a man who consumes less. A Buddhist economist would consider this approach excessively irrational: since consumption is merely a means to human well-being, the aim should be to obtain the maximum of well-being with the minimum of consumption. Thus, if the purpose of clothing is a certain amount of temperature comfort and an attractive appearance, the task is to attain this purpose with the smallest possible effort, that is, with the smallest annual destruction of cloth and with the help of designs that involve the smallest possible input of toil. The less toil there is, the more time and strength is left for artistic creativity. It would be highly uneconomic, for instance, to go in for complicated tailoring, like the modern West, when a much more beautiful effect can be achieved by the skilful draping of uncut material. It would be the height of folly to make material so that it should wear out quickly and the height of barbarity to make anything ugly, shabby or mean. What has just been said about clothing applies equally to all other human requirements. The ownership and the consumption of goods is a means to an end, and Buddhist economics is the systematic study of how to attain given ends with the minimum means.

Modern economics, on the other hand, considers consumption to be the sole end and purpose of all economic activity, taking the factors of production – land, labour, and capital – as the means. The former, in short, tries to maximize human satisfactions by the optimal pattern of consumption, while the latter tries to maximize consumption by the optimal pattern of productive effort. It is easy to see that the effort needed to sustain a way of life which seeks to attain the optimal pattern of consumption is likely to be much smaller than the effort needed to sustain a drive for maximum consumption. We need not be surprised, therefore, that the pressure and strain of living is very much less in, say, Burma than it is in the United States, in spite of the fact that the amount of labour-saving machinery used in the former country is only a minute fraction of the amount used in the latter.

Simplicity and non-violence are obviously closely related. The optimal pattern of consumption, producing a high degree of human satisfaction by means of a relatively low rate of consumption, allows people to live without great pressure and strain and to fulfil the primary injunction of Buddhist teaching: 'Cease to do evil; try to do good.' As physical resources are everywhere limited, people satisfying their needs by means of a modest use of resources are obviously less likely to be at each other's throats than people depending upon a high rate of use. Equally, people who live in highly self-sufficient local communities are less likely to get involved in large-scale violence than people whose existence depends on world-wide systems of trade.

From the point of view of Buddhist economics, therefore, production from local resources for local needs is the most rational way of economic life, while dependence on imports from afar and the consequent need to produce for export to unknown and distant peoples is highly uneconomic and justifiable only in exceptional cases and on a small scale. Just as the modern economist would admit that a high rate of consumption of transport services between a man's home and his place of work signifies a misfortune and not a high standard of life, so the Buddhist economist would hold that to satisfy human wants from faraway sources rather than from sources nearby signifies failure rather than success. The former tends to take statistics showing an increase in the number of ton/miles per head of the population carried by a country's transport system as proof of economic progress, while to the latter – the Buddhist economist – the same statistics would indicate a highly undesirable deterioration in the *pattern* of consumption.

Another striking difference between modern economics and Buddhist economics arises over the use of natural resources. Bertrand de Jouvenel, the eminent French political philosopher, has characterized 'Western man' in words which may be taken as a fair description of the modern economist:

He tends to count nothing as an expenditure, other than human effort; he does not seem to mind how much mineral matter he wastes and, far worse, how much living matter he destroys. He does not seem to realize at all that human life is a dependent part of an ecosystem of many different forms of life. As the world is ruled from towns where men are cut off from any form of life other than human, the feeling of belonging to an ecosystem is not revived. This results in a harsh and improvident treatment of things upon which we ultimately depend, such as water and trees.[1]

The teaching of the Buddha, on the other hand, enjoins a reverent and non-violent attitude not only to all sentient beings but also, with great emphasis, to trees. Every follower of the Buddha ought to plant a tree every few years and look after it until it is safely established, and the Buddhist economist can demonstrate without difficulty that the universal observation of this rule would result in a high rate of genuine economic development independent of any foreign aid. Much of the economic decay of South-East Asia (as of many other parts of the world) is undoubtedly due to a heedless and shameful neglect of trees.

Modern economics does not distinguish between renewable and non-renewable materials, as its very method is to equalize and quantify everything by means of a money price. Thus, taking various alternative fuels, like coal, oil, wood, or water-power: the only difference between them recognized by modern economics is relative cost per equivalent unit. The cheapest is automatically the one to be preferred, as to do otherwise would be irrational and 'uneconomic'. From a Buddhist point of view, of course, this will not do; the essential difference between non-renewable fuels like coal and oil on the one hand and renewable fuels like wood and water-power on the other cannot be simply overlooked. Non-renewable goods must be used only if they are indispensable, and then only with the greatest care and the most meticulous concern for conservation. To use them heedlessly or extravagantly is an act of violence, and while complete non-violence may not be attainable on this earth, there is nonetheless an ineluctable duty on man to aim at the ideal of non-violence in all he does.

Just as a modern European economist would not consider it a great economic achievement if all European art treasures were sold to America at attractive prices, so the Buddhist economist would insist that a population basing its economic life on non-renewable fuels is living parasitically, on capital instead of income. Such a way of life could have no permanence and could therefore be justified only as a purely temporary expedient. As the world's resources of non-renewable fuels – coal, oil and natural gas – are exceedingly unevenly distributed over the globe and undoubtedly limited in quantity, it is clear that their exploitation at an ever-increasing rate is an act of violence against nature which must almost inevitably lead to violence between men.

This fact alone might give food for thought even to those people in Buddhist countries who care nothing for the religious and spiritual values of their heritage and ardently desire to embrace the materialism of modern economics at the fastest possible speed. Before they dismiss Buddhist economics as nothing better than a nostalgic dream, they might wish to consider whether the path of economic development outlined by modern economics is likely to lead them to places where they really want to be.

Holistic Commerce

BEN COHEN and JERRY GREENFIELD
Ben & Jerry's Double-Dip

In 1977 Ben Cohen and Jerry Greenfield started their ice cream company, Ben & Jerry's Homemade Inc. This corporation, alongside Anita Roddick's The Body Shop, has provided a major model of what a holistic business looks like and how it can run. Their way of working demonstrates how right livelihood can be achieved in an extremely successful corporation in the modern commercial world.

A values-led business is still a business. You can't always please everyone. You have to make rules, make tough decisions, prioritize the things you want to do. No matter what you do, some people are always going to feel you're not treating them fairly.

But if you're thrown into the chair you can choose to be the same person you always were. You don't need to put on a suit and tie if you'd rather wear a T-shirt. You don't need to hire an ad agency if you want to tell your own truth. You can choose not to believe the so-called conventional rules of business, to trust your own reasoning and beliefs instead of – or along with – soliciting advice from lawyers, accountants, and other businesspeople. You can still lead with your values, even when the experts tell you what they told us so many times: 'Nobody's ever done that before. You'd be crazy to do that. It won't work.' But just because something's never been done doesn't mean it never can be.

That's why we're writing this book: to show that you can run a profitable company by doing things in a way that's true to you and to your values, as long as you also do a good job of paying attention to the business basics of manufacturing, customer service, human resources, sales, marketing, and finance.

There's a spiritual aspect to business

Most people would agree that there's a spiritual part of our lives as individuals. Yet when a group of individuals gets together in the form of a business, all of a sudden they throw out that whole idea. We all know as individuals that spirituality – the exchange of love, energy, kindness, caring – exists. Just because the idea that the good you do comes back to you is written in the Bible and not in some business textbook doesn't make it any less valid. We're all interconnected. As we give we receive. As we help others we are helped in return. As your business supports the community, the community will support your business.

Most companies try to conduct their businesses in a spiritual vacuum. But it's absurd to think that just because spiritual connection isn't tangible or quantitatively measurable, it doesn't exist. When people are aware that there's a company that's trying to help their community, they want to support that company. They want to buy goods and services from that company. They want to be associated with that company. And that's what values-led business is all about.

But the reality is, we'll never actualize our spiritual concerns until we integrate them into business, which is where we spend most of our time, where our energy as human beings is organized in a synergistic way, and where the resources exist that allow us to be at our most powerful.

In a way, a values-led business is a self-marketing business. Just by the act of integrating a concern for the community into your day-to-day business activities – buying your brownies from a bakery run by a religious institution that puts economically disenfranchised people to work, and your coffee from a worker co-op that returns the proceeds to the farmers, for example – you're creating a spiritual connection between you and your customers. And that moves them to support you.

Some cynics ask, 'How can you claim you have a spiritual connection to your customers? How do you know whether they buy your ice cream because they like the flavours or because they have a spiritual connection with you?' Spiritual connection is impossible to quantify.

All we know is that when we meet people on the street, when people speak in focus groups, and when consumers write us letters about why they like Ben & Jerry's – and about fourteen thousand people a year do write us letters – they talk as much about what the business does as they do about the product we sell. They talk about a sense of meaning and interrelatedness and support for our efforts to help disenfranchised people.

This is a new role for business to play. A role it's not accustomed to and wasn't created for. That's why business has to re-create itself. Because if the most powerful force doesn't take responsibility for society as a whole, society – and eventually the business itself, which is dependent on that society – will be destroyed. Our country has now become the most unequal society in the industrialized world. Twenty years ago, the richest 1 per cent of people in America owned 19 per cent of the wealth. In 1992 (the most recent figures available) the richest 1 per cent of Americans owned 37 per cent – twice as much – of the nation's wealth. And the bottom 90 per cent of the population owned just 28 per cent of the nation's riches. If this trend continues we will not long endure.

There's so little in society these days that people can feel a part of or believe in. Politicians – forget it. Institutional religion isn't as relevant to most people as it used to be. School – not much. Families are in disarray. Business – it controls society and doesn't care about people. In the world in which we live, the spiritual has been taken out of our day-to-day life. So we go to work during the week and focus solely on earning our pay cheques and maximizing profit. Then on the weekends we go to church or temple and devote what's left of our energy to the spiritual part of our lives. But the reality is that we will never actualize those spiritual concerns until we integrate them into business.

In the midst of this desolate landscape, when people find a company that cares, they want to connect with it. Doing business with that company is something they can feel good about. [. . .]

Greyston brownies: an alternative supplier success story

In the early days our sourcing was pretty traditional. We were buying good quality products from conventional sources. Cones and paper from Sweetheart, Oreos from Nabisco, Heath Bars from Heath.

Our first experience with an alternative supplier came as a result of the new plant we built in 1987 in Springfield. The whole operation was dependent on the very thin, chewy, fudgy brownies we were buying from a fairly small baker. The bakery was doing a great job, but we realized that it was in the best interest of the company to develop a secondary supplier. That way, if something happened to our primary source, we could keep the plant running and our people working.

We looked and looked for someone else who could bake those brownies. Then Ben went to a Social Ventures Network meeting and met Bernie Glassman, a Jewish-Buddhist-former-nuclear-physicist-monk. Bernie had a bakery called Greyston in inner-city Yonkers, New York. It was owned by a non-profit religious institution; its purpose was to train and employ economically disenfranchised people as well as to fund low-income housing and other community-service activities.

Ben said, 'We're looking for someone who can bake these thin, chewy, fudgy brownies. If you could do that, we could give you some business, and you could give us the brownies we need, and that would be great for both of us.'

Bernie understood exactly how great that would be, and he put a tremendous amount of effort – and time and money he didn't have – into developing a brownie to meet our specifications. Bernie's people made some excellent brownies, but they weren't exact duplicates of what we were getting. So we kept going back and forth, back and forth; tweak this, tweak that. Eventually they got it right and Greyston was approved as a secondary supplier.

The first order we gave Greyston was for a couple of tons. For us, that was a small order. For Greyston, it was a huge order. It caused their system to break down. The brownies were coming off the line so fast that they ended up getting packed hot. Then they needed to be frozen. Pretty soon the bakery freezer was filled up with these steaming fifty-pound boxes of hot brownies. The freezer couldn't stay very cold, so it took days to freeze the brownies. By the time they were frozen they had turned into fifty-pound blocks of brownie. And that's what Greyston shipped to us.

Ben: When the production people received those blocks they said, 'We can't use this stuff. Pack it up. Send it back.'
Jerry: I think we can say, Ben, that they were beside themselves.
Ben: So we called up Bernie and we said, 'Those two tons you shipped us were all stuck together. We're shipping them back.' Bernie said, 'I can't afford that. I need the money to meet my payroll tomorrow. Can't you unstick them?' And we said, 'Bernie, this really gums up the works over here.'
Jerry: It was a real disaster. People were extremely upset that we were making them work harder, and we wouldn't just ship the brownies back. They said, 'This is great for the social mission. But what about the quality mission? The product didn't meet spec. Why don't we ship it back as we would if it were any other supplier?'

We kept going back and forth with Greyston, trying to get the brownies right. Eventually we created a new flavour, Chocolate Fudge Brownie, so we could use the brownie pieces we ended up with when we broke up the brownie blocks. But we still had problems getting what we needed from Greyston. So we kept making our line workers work harder, and trying to explain to them why we were making an exception for this supplier. That explanation didn't go across too well. Working with Greyston didn't seem so socially beneficial to our production workers.

Finally we started having people from Greyston come and speak to our employees. They'd tell our people their histories and how Greyston was helping them and how our business was helping Greyston.

Jerry: What really made a difference was when the people from Greyston came and observed the people working in our plants . . .
Ben: . . . trying to deal with those brownie blocks they were shipping us.
Jerry: And then our people going to Greyston and seeing what it was like for them working there.
Ben: Everyone started understanding what we were putting one another through in order to get this thing right.

Now Greyston is one of our solid suppliers. The quality of the brownies they sell us is consistently excellent. They deliver on time. They do what they say they're going to do. And the benefit is mutual.

It took a lot to make Greyston a good supplier for us. We had our quality people working with them, our production people, our finance people. We fronted them money; we paid in advance for product. When they had management problems we sent people to help them with that. When they had quality problems, we worked with them instead of cutting them off.

In retrospect, we made a mistake in the way we presented Greyston to our employees. We told them Greyston was going to be just another supplier, that we'd treat them like any other supplier. They were our first alternative supplier, and we ourselves didn't know then that we needed to plan on treating those vendors differently. We need to give them more support and guidance at the beginning. A lot of times they're not geared up to make as much product as we need as fast as we need it.

If the company isn't convinced of the benefits of using alternative suppliers, there's less tolerance for the inevitable problems that arise, and more pressure to switch to a mainstream supplier when they occur. When we first started buying brownies from Greyston, we didn't have our production workers on board. It was a decision that came down from on high. We didn't adequately explain to people within the company how our decision was going to affect them. If we'd arranged exchanges between the two companies before we started doing business with Greyston, people's responses might have been different.

Beyond the Information Age

HAZEL HENDERSON
Paradigms in Progress

Academic, futurist and international organizational consultant, Hazel Henderson is one of the most effective international propagandists for a holistic approach to economics and government. Whereas other activists may have been timid about asserting their holistic and futuristic leanings, Hazel Henderson has treated cynics and sceptics as if they were contemporary flat-earthers in need of shaking into reality. Her clarity and confidence have done much to bring holistic ideas into citadels such as multinational corporations, banks and non-governmental organizations.

The Age of Light lies beyond the Information Age. The Information Age is no longer an adequate image for the present, let alone a guide to the future. It still focuses on hardware technologies, mass production, narrow economic models of efficiency and competition, and is more an extension of industrial ideas and methods than a new stage in human development. Information is an abundant resource rather than a scarce commodity (as in economic theory) and demands new cooperative rules from local to global levels.

Information itself does not enlighten. We cannot clarify what is *mis*information, *dis*information, or propaganda in this media dominated, 'spin-doctored' environment. Focusing on mere information has led to an overload of ever-less meaningful billions of bits of fragmented raw data and sound bites rather than the search for meaningful new patterns of knowledge.

My view of the dawning Age of Light involves a repatterning of the exploding Information Age. This requires nothing less than a paradigm shift to a holistic view of the entire human family, now inextricably linked by our globe-girdling technologies. The Earth is re-perceived as a living Planet, and the most appropriate view is organic, based on the self-organizing models of the life sciences. Biological sciences become more useful spectacles, and it is no accident that biotechnologies are becoming our most morally-ambiguous tools. [. . .]

The Age of Light will follow on from the Solar Age as humans gradually learn that it is light and action that are fundamental in the universe. The technologies of the Age of Light are already appearing. Beyond electronics, these phototronic technologies are miracles of speed and miniaturization, such as the new 0.25 micron 'superchip' (400 times thinner than a human hair). These superchips now on the drawing board can pack hundreds of millions of transistors – ten times today's record. In the year 2000, 0.1 micron widths will be the cutting edge, small enough to cram billions of transistors on a single chip. Even today's advanced optical printing methods will have to give way to higher frequencies in the spectrum, using x-ray lithography. In 1991, San Jose, California's Cypress Semiconductor Corporation announced (*Business Week*, 3 June 1991) that it had purchased from Hampshire Instruments, Inc. of Rochester, New York, a new system that generates the x-rays, not with a room-size synchrotron (or atom smasher) that costs $30 million, but with a laser costing a modest $4 million.[1]

Another aspect of these new technologies of the Age of Light is the level of integration achieved with the biological sciences, as they shift from the 'inert' classical physics world-view to the organic living system perspectives of biology and ecology . . . However far out and 'high tech' they all claim to be, and indeed are, they, like most technologies before them, owe their inspiration to Nature. After all, Gaia, the great designer, has been optimizing these energy capture-utilization-storage systems for billions of years. Gaia is also the pre-eminent innovator and experimenter, who excels in sheer artistry as well. Further evidence that humans are still imitating Nature is the growing industrial research field of biomimetics (literally 'mimicking Nature') described in the *Business Week* cover story, 'The New Alchemy'. For example, new ceramic materials mimic the molecular structure of abalone shells to make impact resistant armour for military tanks and aircraft. As the article points out, 'Nature's materials have passed the test of time.' Eric K. Drexler's vision of 'nanotechnology' in his 1986 book, *Engines of Creation*,[2] predicted the shape of much of this new biomimetic research, such as Argonne National Laboratories work on improving structural materials by 'flirting with Creation', developing entirely new materials atom by atom using 'nanophase materials' such as crystals less than 100 nanometres across – smaller than most viruses. Japan's Ministry of International Trade and Industry (MITI) has launched a ten-year programme on 'nanotech initiatives' which it hopes industry will fund to the tune of $100 million or more.[3]

The Age of Light is an image that reminds us that it is the light from the sun that drives the earth's processes and powers its cycles of carbon, nitrogen, hydrogen, and water and the climate 'machine'. It is these light-driven processes – which are then mediated by the photosynthesis of plants – that maintain conditions for us to continue our evolution beyond the Information Age. Our present technologies are already maturing from their basis in electronics and are shifting to phototronics. These new lightwave technologies include fibre optics, lasers, optical scanning, optical computing, photovoltaics, and other photoconversion processes.

As we progress in these areas we will notice how each one leads us into a deeper appreciation of Nature's technological genius; we have modelled our earlier breakthroughs, such as flight, on that of birds. Nature's light-conversion technologies, the basic of which is photosynthesis, still serve as design criteria and marvels of miniaturization, such as the chloroplast cells all green plants use to convert photons into usable glycogen, hydrocarbons and cellulose. This is still the basic production process on which all humans rely and when our photovoltaic cells can match the performance of the chloroplast, we will be on the right track. Thus the Age of Light is more than the new lightwave technologies emerging from the computer, robotics and artificial intelligence labs. The Age of Light will be characterized by our growing abilities to cooperate with and learn from Nature. The Age of Light will build on today's biotechnology, still in its exploratory, often exploitative, moral infancy.

The Age of Light will bring a new awareness and reverence for living systems and the exquisite information technology of DNA, the wisdom and coding of all living experience on this Planet. The Age of Light will go far beyond industrial, manipulative modes towards deeper interconnecting, co-creative designing with and learning from Nature, as we become a species consciously co-evolving with all life forms on this unique water Planet. The Age of Light will also be one of a time compression, as we include our holistic, intuitive, right-brain hemisphere cognition with our more analytical, left-brain functioning, and as our computers catch up in their abilities for parallel processing with the simultaneity of our own brains' synapses. The peerless design of the human brain still presents the ultimate challenge to computer designers, despite the much-vaunted progress in so-called 'artificial intelligence' systems. For example, a leading designer of Cray Computer Company's efforts to create a supercomputer mimicking more closely the parallel processing ability of human brains, recently left to pursue other areas of endeavour. Most leading-edge technologies based on light, whether information, solar energy or biotechnologies and gene splicing also mimic Nature's design, such as monoclonal antibodies, interferon and other methods based on learning from the human immune system. The 'nanotechnologies' or protein-based assemblers that Eric Drexler (mentioned earlier) envisions, are designed by mimicking the functions of amino acids.

At the same time we are learning much more about our own bodies' responses to light, and how humans deprived of full-spectrum, natural light in indoor living and working conditions can suffer weakening of their endocrine and immune systems. Thus the wisest of us recognize that our Earth still has much to teach us – if we can humble ourselves and quiet our egos long enough to really listen and see, hear, smell and feel all her wonders. When we can feel this kind of attunement to the whole creation, we are transported with natural delight to the 'high' that psychologist Abraham Maslow called 'peak experiences'. As we reintegrate our awareness in this way, we no longer crave endless consumption of goods beyond those needed for a healthy life, but seek new challenges in our societies for order, peace and justice, and to develop our spirituality. It is in this way that humans can overcome the dismal Second Law of Thermodynamics in the continual striving for learning and wisdom. We no longer blind our imagination with the dismal deterministic view of a universe winding down like a closed system. Since Prigogine, we know that the universe is full of surprises, innovation and evolutionary potential.[4] In fact, Cartesian science's search for certainty, equilibrium, predictability and control is a good definition of death. We should happily embrace the new view that uncertainty is fundamental, since it also implies that everything can change – for the better – in a twinkling of an eye! As we move on to post-Cartesian science, we can acknowledge the earlier period of the Scientific Enlightenment of Descartes and Newton, Liebniz and Galileo. Its instrumental rationality and manipulation of Nature did lead to that greatest outpouring of technological hardware and managerial virtuosity which we call the Industrial Revolution.

As we have seen, the whole process of human development is teleological and evolutionary, and therefore cannot be explained or predicted by existing reductionistic scientific paradigms. This great purposeful unfolding of human potentialities towards goals – bettering human societies, perfecting the means of production and fostering conditions of people's lives so that they might fulfill themselves – is essentially a spiritual, as well as an instrumental and materialistic, endeavour.

Greening the Self – A Buddhist Approach

JOANNA MACY

World As Lover, World As Self

Joanna Macy explicitly provides what many people need, a clear approach which integrates spirituality, personal integrity and environmental awareness. Her point of departure is as a student of Buddhism who also understands environmental sciences and has a passionate empathy with both the beauty and suffering of nature and of people. In his introduction to her *World As Lover, World As Self*, the Vietnamese Buddhist monk and poet, Thich Nhat Hanh, wrote beautifully: 'Joanna Macy speaks the truth with the roar of a lioness, and all beings throughout the universe are patting her head and caressing her in gratitude and appreciation.'

Something important is happening in our world that you are not going to read about in the newspapers. I consider it the most fascinating and hopeful development of our time, and it is one of the reasons I am so glad to be alive today. It has to do with what is occurring to the notion of the *self*.

The self is the metaphoric construct of identity and agency, the hypothetical piece of turf on which we construct our strategies for survival, the notion around which we focus our instincts for self-preservation, our needs for self-approval, and the boundaries of our self-interest. Something is shifting here.

The conventional notion of the self with which we have been raised and to which we have been conditioned by mainstream culture is being undermined. What Alan Watts called 'the skin-encapsulated ego' and Gregory Bateson referred to as 'the epistemological error of Occidental civilization' is being unhinged, peeled off. It is being replaced by wider constructs of identity and self-interest – by what you might call the ecological self or the eco-self, co-extensive with other beings and the life of our planet. It is what I will call 'the greening of the self'.

At a recent lecture on a college campus, I gave the students examples of activities which are currently being undertaken in defence of life on Earth – actions in which people risk their comfort and even their lives to protect other species. In the Chipko, or tree-hugging, movement in north India, for example, villagers fight the deforestation of their remaining woodlands. On the open seas, Greenpeace activists are intervening to protect marine mammals from slaughter. After that talk, I received a letter from a student I'll call Michael. He wrote:

I think of the tree-huggers hugging my trunk, blocking the chainsaws with their bodies. I feel their fingers digging into my bark to stop the steel and let me breathe. I hear the bodhisattvas in their rubber boats as they put themselves between the harpoons and me, so I can escape to the depths of the sea. I give thanks for your life and mine, and for life itself. I give thanks for realizing that I too have the powers of the tree-huggers and the bodhisattvas.

What is striking about Michael's words is the shift in identification. Michael is able to extend his sense of self to encompass the self of the tree and of the whale. Tree and whale are no longer removed, separate, disposable objects pertaining to a world 'out there'; they are intrinsic to his own vitality. Through the power of his caring, his experience of self is expanded far beyond that skin-encapsulated ego. I quote Michael's words not because they are unusual but, to the contrary, because they express a desire and a capacity that is being released from the prison-cell of old constructs of self. This desire and capacity are arising in more and more people today as, out of deep concern for what is happening to our world, they begin to speak and act on its behalf.

Among those who are shedding these old constructs of self, like old skin or a confining shell, is John Seed, director of the Rainforest Information Centre in Australia. One day we were walking through the rainforest in New South Wales, where he has his office, and I asked him, 'You talk about the struggle against the lumbering interests and politicians to save the remaining rainforest in Australia. How do you deal with the despair?'

He replied, 'I try to remember that it's not me, John Seed, trying to protect the rainforest. Rather, I am part of the rainforest protecting itself. I am that part of the rainforest recently emerged into human thinking.' This is what I mean by the greening of the self. It involves a combining of the mystical with the practical and the pragmatic, transcending separateness, alienation, and fragmentation. It is a shift that Seed himself calls 'a spiritual change', generating a sense of profound interconnectedness with all life.

This is hardly new to our species. In the past poets and mystics have been speaking and writing about these ideas, but not people on the barricades agitating for social change. Now the sense of an encompassing self, that deep identity with the wider reaches of life, is a motivation for action. It is a source of courage that helps us stand up to the powers that are still, through force of inertia, working for the destruction of our world. This expanded sense of self serves to empower effective action.

When you look at what is happening to our world – and it is hard to look at what's happening to our water, our air, our trees, our fellow species – it becomes clear that unless you have some roots in a spiritual practice that holds life sacred and encourages joyful communion with all your fellow beings, facing the enormous challenges ahead becomes nearly impossible.

Robert Bellah's book *Habits of the Heart* is not a place where you are going to read about the greening of the self. But it is where you will read *why* there has to be a greening of the self, because it describes the cramp that our society has gotten itself into with its rampant, indeed pathological, individualism. Bellah points out that the individualism that sprang from the Romantic movement of the eighteenth and nineteenth centuries (the seeds of which were planted much earlier than that) is accelerating and causing great suffering, alienation and fragmentation in our century. Bellah calls for a moral ecology which he defines as a moral connectedness or interdependence. He says, 'We have to treat others as part of who we are, rather than as a "them" with whom we are in constant competition.'

To Robert Bellah, I respond, 'It is happening.' It is happening in the arising of the ecological self. And it is happening because of three converging developments. First, the conventional small self, or ego-self, is being impinged upon by the psychological and spiritual effects we are suffering from facing the dangers of mass annihilation. The second thing working to dismantle the ego-self is a way of seeing that has arisen out of science itself. It is called the systems view, stemming from general systems theory or cybernetics. From this perspective, life is seen as dynamically composed of self-organizing systems, patterns that are sustained in and by their relationships. The third force is the resurgence in our time of non-dualistic spiritualities. Here I am speaking from my own experience with Buddhism, but it is also happening in other faith-systems and religions, such as 'creation spirituality' in Christianity. These developments are impinging on the self in ways that are undermining it, or helping it to break out of its boundaries and old definitions. Instead of ego-self, we witness the emergence of an eco-self!

The move to a wider ecological sense of self is in large part a function of the dangers that are threatening to overwhelm us. Given nuclear proliferation and the progressive destruction of our biosphere, polls show that people today are aware that the world, as they know it, may come to an end. I am convinced that this loss of certainty that there will be a future is the pivotal psychological reality of our time. The fact that it is not talked about very much makes it all the more pivotal, because nothing is more preoccupying or energy-draining than that which we repress.

Why do I claim that this erodes the old sense of self? Because once we stop denying the crises of our time and let ourselves experience the depth of our own responses to the pain of our world – whether it is the burning of the Amazon rainforest, the famines of Africa, or the homeless in our own cities – the grief or anger or fear we experience cannot be reduced to concerns for our own individual skin.

When we mourn the destruction of our biosphere, it is categorically distinct from mourning over our own individual death. We suffer with our world – that is the literal meaning of compassion. It isn't some private craziness. Yet, when I was weeping over the napalming of villages in Vietnam twenty years ago, I was told that I was suffering from a hangover of Puritan guilt. When I expressed myself against President Reagan, they said I had unresolved problems regarding my own father. How often have you had your concerns for political and ecological realities subjected to reductionistic pop-therapy? How often have you heard, 'What are you running away from in your life that you are letting yourself get so concerned about those homeless people?

Perhaps you have some unresolved issues? Maybe you're sexually unfulfilled?' It can go on and on. But increasingly it is being recognized that a compassionate response is neither craziness nor a dodge. It is the opposite; it is a signal of our own evolution, a measure of our humanity.

We are capable of suffering with our world, and that is the true meaning of compassion. It enables us to recognize our profound inter-connectedness with all beings. Don't ever apologize for crying for the trees burning in the Amazon or over the waters polluted from mines in the Rockies. Don't apologize for the sorrow, grief, and rage you feel. It is a measure of your humanity and your maturity. It is a measure of your open heart, and as your heart breaks open there will be room for the world to heal. That is what is happening as we see people honestly confronting the sorrows of our time. And it is an adaptive response.

Earth Mysteries and Ley Lines

JOHN MICHELL
The New View Over Atlantis

John Michell is the most important British figure in the Earth Mysteries movement, the endeavour to experience the inner and mystical aspects of landscape. Drawing initially on the earlier work of authors such as Alfred Watkins and Guy Underwood, he describes how the landscape of the British Isles is covered with a patchwork of long straight lines which connect ancient monuments and significant features of the countryside. Michell explains, using accessible maths and geometry, how many of these monuments were built to sacred proportions. He also refers to many other examples in different parts of the globe including the classical civilizations of the Mediterranean, tribal cultures and the Chinese approach of Feng Shui.

At the same time as Mrs Maltwood in Somerset was tracing her vision of the zodiacal giants, the members of the Woolhope Club, a Hereford antiquarian society, were investigating an extraordinary discovery in the surrounding countryside by one of their number, Mr Alfred Watkins. His claim, that he had seen the whole country covered by a network of straight lines, linking the centres and sites of antiquity, seemed incredible, but such was the quality of the evidence he produced that it was impossible to dismiss without further inquiry.

Mr Watkins was a merchant well known and respected in his own county. His father was a farmer of a long established Herefordshire family, who moved to Hereford to start a number of enterprises, including a flour mill and a brewery. Early in life Alfred Watkins entered his father's business, travelling about the county as outrider or brewer's representative. In the course of his journeys he developed strong antiquarian interests. At that time the pattern of the countryside was little disturbed. Railways had only recently replaced the coach and the carrier's cart as the chief means of rural communication. Hereford, until 1853 linked commercially with the outer world only by a branch canal from Gloucester, was still a remote city. Country people lived where they were born and repeated the stories they had heard from their fathers. Alfred Watkins delighted in these legends, particularly when they related to the features of a landscape with which he had become intensely familiar. Riding about the country he came to know every remote corner of Herefordshire as well as almost every member of its population. His son, Allen Watkins, remembered how, when they travelled together, everyone they passed greeted his father as a friend. To him as a little boy it seemed quite natural that his father should be so well known.

One hot summer afternoon, 20 June 1921, Alfred Watkins was at Blackwardine in Herefordshire. On a high hilltop he stopped and looked at his map before meditating on the view below him. Suddenly, in a flash, he saw something which no one in England had seen for perhaps thousands of years.

Watkins saw straight through the surface of the landscape to a layer deposited in some remote prehistoric age. The barrier of time melted and, spread across the country, he saw a web of lines linking the holy places and sites of antiquity. Mounds, old stones, crosses and old crossroads, churches placed on pre-Christian sites, legendary trees, moats and holy wells stood in exact alignments that ran over beacon hills to cairns and mountain peaks. In one moment of transcendental perception Watkins entered a magic world of prehistoric Britain, a world whose very existence had been forgotten.

Describing the historic event of that summer afternoon, in the delightful little biography he wrote of his father, the late Allen Watkins pictured it as follows:

Then without warning it all happened suddenly. His mind was flooded with a rush of images forming one coherent plan. The scales fell from his eyes and he saw that over many long years of prehistory, all trackways were in straight lines marked out by experts on a sighting system. The whole plan of the Old Straight Track stood suddenly revealed.

His lightning comprehension bore all the marks of being an ancestral memory of the Old Straight Track, just as John Bunyan's ancestral memory of the same thing was at work when he wrote *The Pilgrim's Progress* and Hilaire Belloc's when he wrote *The Path to Rome*.

'The whole thing came to me in a flash,' he told me afterwards.

Just a year or two previously a similar flash of understanding had occurred to the seer and poet, A. E. (George Russell), during one of his rambles among the ancient hills and sanctuaries of Ireland. In his *Candle of Vision* he spoke of seeing 'the many coloured land', the essential landscape made luminous by the glowing springs and channels of its own vital energies, and realizing that it was but an eye-blink away from normal vision. At one moment, he wrote, 'I knew the Golden Age was all about me, and it was we who had been blind to it, but that it had never passed away from the world.'

Watkins marked out the churches and ancient sites on a one-inch Ordnance Survey map, and the truth of his vision was confirmed. Often he found eight and nine and even more sites aligned across quite short stretches of country. Extended on to neighbouring maps, the lines could sometimes be traced for many miles, often ending on a mountain peak or high hill. [. . .]

Some mystical concept, now lost, must have inspired the regular laying out of the country. In *The Old Straight Track* Watkins concludes: 'I feel that ley-man, astronomer-priest, druid, bard, wizard, witch, palmer, and hermit, were all more or less linked by one thread of ancient knowledge and power, however degenerate it became in the end.'

In the course of their researches Watkins and his friends grew more and more convinced that there was something more behind the ley system than a network of traders' tracks. It was as if some flow of current followed the course of these man-made alignments. Members of the Straight Track Club reported instances of birds and animals migrating along certain fixed lines, described the dead straight antelope paths of the Himalayas, and wrote papers on the regular systems of tracks and landmarks in Norway, Palestine, Africa and America. Watkins himself, an expert bee-keeper, noticed how bees, taken away and released at some distance from their hives, first describe hesitant circles in the air, and then, as if tuning in to some invisible current, make a 'bee-line' for home. His deep love of the countryside and knowledge of its ways, particularly since its hidden structure had been revealed in the discovery of leys, had given him a true understanding of the conformity of all aspects of life and growth, both large and small, to certain basic patterns. With the eye of a natural philosopher he perceived the correspondences throughout nature. Ant hills, he observed, fall into certain patterns and alignments. Like the sighting mounds upon leys, they are conical and flat topped, covered with turf. Moreover his measurements showed that the proportion in size between an ant and an ant heap is the same as that between a man and Silbury Hill. In all this Watkins raised the same kind of elusive questions as did the South African naturalist E. P. Marais, who in his book, *The Soul of the White Ant*, discovered that the man-sized white ant mounds of Africa contain a brain, heart, liver, digestive and circulation systems, and exercise all the same abilities as the human body save that of locomotion.

To the end of his life, despite much stern, even abusive criticism, Alfred Watkins continued to enlarge and confirm his discovery, without ever finding the ultimate clue to the meaning of the ley system. The evidence for its existence became overwhelming. Leys traced on one sheet of the map were found to continue exactly those started on another. Over and over again a search of the ground revealed stones, mounds and sections of old track unmarked on the map. Parish boundaries were found to align upon leys. More than once, at ley centres, places where several leys cross, investigation disclosed an ancient stone or cross which the Ordnance Survey had overlooked. All this Watkins recorded fairly and honestly. Though he never solved the riddle of leys, he came to recognize an unexpected aspect of their function. Anyone who has followed their paths across country will find that his life has been enriched by the experience. The knowledge that this gigantic ruin, the old fabric of alignments, can be traced in every corner of the country, while, like Avebury before 1648, remaining elusive to both reason and the eye, is a powerful inducement to wonder and humility, two qualities that particularly marked Alfred Watkins. In *The Old Straight Track* he expresses his vision in these words:

Imagine a fairy chain stretched from mountain peak to mountain peak, as far as the eye could reach, and paid out until it touched the 'high places' of the earth at a number of ridges, banks, and knolls. Then visualize a mound, circular earthwork, or clump of trees, planted on these high points, and in low points in the valley other mounds ringed round with water to be seen from a distance. Then great standing stones brought to mark the way at intervals, and on a bank leading up to a mountain ridge or down to a ford the track cut deep so as to form a guiding notch on the skyline as you come up. In a *bwlch* or mountain pass the road cut deeply at the highest place straight through the ridge to show as a notch afar off. Here and there and at two ends of the way, a beacon fire used to lay out the track. With ponds dug on the line, or streams banked up into 'flashes' to form reflecting points on the beacon track so that it might be checked when at least once a year the beacon was fired on the traditional day. All these works exactly on the sighting line. The wayfarer's instructions are still deeply rooted in the peasant mind today, when he tells you – quite wrongly now – 'You just keep straight on.'

Plant Spirits

DOROTHY MACLEAN
The Findhorn Garden

Dorothy Maclean, along with Eileen and Peter Caddy, is one of the founders of the Findhorn Foundation on the east coast of northern Scotland – a community recognized by many people as the most important centre of learning and experimentation in the New Age culture. At the heart of the Foundation is a profound respect for the innate spirituality in both people and nature. Dorothy Maclean is particularly interested in nature spirits and her work has been instrumental in bringing animism into the holistic framework.

My contact with the devas opened up in a natural way, rising organically from my life background. My two brothers and I were brought up by the most delightful and loving parents in a beautiful old house next to a wood in Canada. We had gardens of vegetables and flowers, but I was not especially attracted to cultivated plants. I loved wandering in the wild places.

I went to university with a lot of questions, but despite all the talk about the profundities of life, I found no satisfactory answers. Eventually I started paying attention to that voice within that had long been asking me to listen, and I began to write down the daily guidance I was receiving. During a period of spiritual training which was teaching me to place the will of this indwelling God first in my life, I met Peter and Eileen Caddy. Before moving to Findhorn, we worked together on the staff of the hotel where Peter was manager, putting this principle into action.

When I speak of God's will, I am aware that this might call up a stereotyped picture of an old gentleman somewhere out in the sky, making automatons of us by imposing an external will. This is not my meaning, but I do not know of another way in which to convey it. To me, God is an indwelling presence, the core of what I am and what everything is. God is life itself, speaking through all life. And God's will is the path we tread which develops the best for us and for all we encounter. *Let My will be a mystery for you to find in each moment,* my guidance told me. *Seek it within the little and the big. It includes all people and all things, all questions and all answers.*

Our first winter at Findhorn had been an especially harsh one for the area, with frequent gale-force winds adding to the snow and rain. But by early May, 1963, the first radishes and lettuce Peter had sown in the patio garden were coming up, and he was busy preparing another area for peas and beans and a few other vegetables. The spring weather was growing warm enough for us to sit outside on the patio during our daily time of quiet together. This was a delightful opportunity to experience God's presence in everything around me.

During that period of time, my guidance had been telling me to be open for new ideas and inspiration: *Be prepared, My child, and on the lookout for My promptings. Expect new ideas to come into your head. This is a further period of training for you and it entails many new things.* The guidance I received on the morning of 8 May was indeed the beginning of something new: *One of the jobs for you as My free child is to feel into the nature forces, such as the wind. Feel its essence and purpose for Me, and be positive and harmonize with that essence. It will not be as difficult as you immediately imagine because the beings of these forces will be glad to feel a friendly power. All forces are to be felt into, even the sun, the moon, the sea, the trees, the very grass. All are part of My life. All is one life. Play your part in making life one again, with My help.*

Well, I thought that was very nice, because as far as I was concerned, there was nothing I would like better than to sit in the sun and commune with nature. But when Peter saw this guidance, that's not how he understood it. 'You can use that to help with the garden!' he said, feeling that direct contact with the nature forces might give him the answers he needed to his questions about the garden. Sure enough, the next day I was told in guidance, *Yes, you are to cooperate in the garden. Begin this by thinking about the nature spirits, the higher over lighting nature spirits, and tune into them. That will be so unusual as to draw their interest here. They will be overjoyed to find some members of the human race eager for their help. That is the first step.*

By the higher nature spirits, I mean those such as the spirits of clouds, of rain, and of vegetables. The smaller individual nature spirits are under their jurisdiction. In the new world these realms will be quite open to humans – or I should say, humans will be open to them. Seek into the glorious realms of nature with sympathy and understanding, knowing that these beings are of the Light, willing to help, but suspicious of humans and on the lookout for the false, the snags. Keep with Me and they will find none, and you will all build towards the new.

I thought such instructions rather a tall order, taxing my credulity and certainly beyond my talents. I knew only a little about nature spirits and, although I was aware of the angelic hierarchy, I had not known that there were devas overlighting vegetables. I told Peter I couldn't do it and stalled for several weeks, despite his encouragement. However, instructions from the inner divinity – and Peter's promptings – are not lightly disregarded!

One evening in meditation I reached a powerful state of heightened consciousness, and I thought, now I'll contact one of those higher nature spirits. Since vegetables had been mentioned, I thought I might contact the spirit of some plant we were growing at Findhorn. I had always been fond of the garden pea which we had grown at home in Canada, and I could feel in sympathy in all ways with that plant. So I tried to focus on the essence of what the pea was to me and the love I felt for it. I got an immediate response in thought and feeling which I put into the following words: *I can speak to you, human. I am entirely directed by my work which is set out and moulded and which I merely bring to fruition, yet you have come straight to my awareness. My work is clear before me – to bring the force fields into manifestation regardless of obstacles, and there are many in this man-infested world. While the vegetable kingdom holds no grudge against those it feeds, man takes what he can as a matter of course, giving no thanks. This makes us strangely hostile.*

What I would tell you is that as we forge ahead, never deviating from our course for one moment's thought, feeling or action, so could you. Humans generally seem not to know where they are going or why. If they did, what a powerhouse they would be. If they were on the straight course of what is to be done, we could cooperate with them! I have put across my meaning and bid you farewell.

When I showed this to Peter, he said, 'Fine, now you can find out what to do about these tomatoes and what it is these lettuces might need.' And I would take his questions to the deva of the species concerned and get straightforward practical advice.

At this point I might say that the term 'deva' is a Sanskrit word meaning shining one. On the whole, I have chosen to use this word rather than the English equivalent, 'angel', which calls up stereotyped images that are more of a barrier than a help in understanding the true nature of these beings.

Baking bread

Mix some flour with enough water to form a dough, a touch of salt perhaps; shape it, bake it, the result is bread in its simplest, most fundamental form:

coarse, crusty
with rich true-spirited flavour
that one soon learns to love and crave.

Everything else is extra: yeast, milk, oil, sweetening, eggs. Extra to make bread more palatable, more 'civilized', more chewable and sliceable; yet in a way the extras only detract from the primitive simplicity of grain-tasting unyeasted bread.

The range of breads and other bakery goods is extraordinary, from the simplest flour-salt-water to the fanciest butter-eggs-milk-yeasted pastry (see a good gourmet cookbook). Yet basically it's just you and the dough – ripening, maturing, baking, blossoming together.

The Tassajara Bread Book, Edward Espe Brown,
Shambhala Publications, Boulder, 1970

Holistic Health and Healing

Introduction

It is in the field of healthcare that the holistic approach has probably had its greatest impact over the last thirty years. Originally the medical and scientific establishment was deeply distrustful of all holistic and complementary approaches, regarding these alternative strategies as at best naive and at worst fatally dangerous. This attitude is understandable, for Western medicine has its rigorous foundation in the certainties of empirical science and because medical doctors daily face life and death crises. Indeed the success of Western medicine can be witnessed in infant survival rates, the extension of life and the general relief of pain – all undreamt of a century or more ago.

In the face of such a successful track record, based in a scientific approach, the complementary therapies can easily be seen as irrelevant and dangerous. But public demand for a holistic approach and the pragmatic reality of its effectiveness have forced mainstream medicine to widen its boundaries to include the complementary strategies.

The fundamental tenet of the holistic approach is that the human body is not an isolated physical organism, but is part of a complex system which includes the emotions, mind, attitudes and spirit of a total human being – a complex organism of many dynamic energies. The sources of physical health then are not just physical. Sooner or later psychological and spiritual distress will manifest itself in actual physical symptoms. Physical symptoms are therefore often a wake-up call to pay attention to an inner dysfunction.

The holistic approach also draws on the classical healing systems from non-Western sources – the ayurvedic tradition of India, the acupuncture and energy medicine of China, and the herbal remedies, physical touch and spiritual healing which have been part of all pre-scientific traditions.

A central idea in all these approaches is that real health depends on the ability to express and be who we really are. Definitions of this 'core self' vary, but in general there is a sense of the human soul or spirit. If we are unable to express our spirit authentically, then psychological and emotional energy coagulates – which anchors down into the physical body as illness and disease.

In holistic approaches to healthcare, the major object is to understand and help the patient's whole system come back into a healthy flow. This necessarily requires the active cooperation of the patient and is one of the reasons why holistic healthcare has been so successful. Unlike much Western scientific medicine it empowers individuals to be involved in their own recovery and healing.

In this section, the extracts do not illustrate particular therapeutic schools, but give a general taste of the way of thinking that permeates the subject.

Childbirth

INA MAY GASKIN
Spiritual Midwifery

The movement to a less clinical and more natural form of childbirth is a fundamental aspect of holism.

In 1971 a group of San Franciscans led by Stephen Gaskin formed an idealistic and free-thinking organic farming community called the Farm in Tennessee. If they had a central set of beliefs, Ina May Gaskin suggested it was: 'Clean air, sane people and healthy babies'. The women soon realized that they needed to bring childbirth under their control and trained as midwives. They offered childbirth facilities to any woman provided she arrived six weeks before her term ended, and embraced women with unwanted pregnancies. Whenever possible, the birth was natural. But as well as acknowledging and working sensitively with the physical body, they were also aware of the energies that surround childbirth and relationship. Ina May's book *Spiritual Midwifery* became a bible for mothers seeking a more natural birthing.

We are a group of midwives who deliver babies and provide primary health care for our spiritual community of eleven hundred long-haired vegetarians. We have been a self-sufficient farming community since 1971, when the first three hundred of us settled on our land near Summertown, Tennessee. We originally came together in San Francisco, attending open meetings held by Stephen in the late 1960s.

We are not just a community. We are a church. We hold our land in common, and share fortunes (as in the Book of Acts in the Bible, 2:44–45: 'And all who believed were together and had all things in common: and they sold their possessions and goods and distributed them to all, as any had need'). No money is exchanged for goods or services among the people of our community.

It was even before we settled in Tennessee that we knew we were going to have to learn how to deliver our own babies. The first group of three hundred settlers spent several months following Stephen on a national lecture tour, then travelling on to Tennessee in a caravan of remodelled schoolbuses and vans, which were both our homes and our transportation. There were several pregnant ladies among us, including me (Ina May). No one on the Caravan had ever delivered a baby before. Our funds were limited to what savings we had among us and what we could earn on the way, so having each lady delivered in a hospital was out of the question. Besides this, several of us had given birth in hospitals previous to the Caravan and had been unsatisfied with the way we and our babies were treated. We wanted our men to be with us during the whole process of childbirth, and we didn't want to be anaesthetized against our will, and we didn't want to be separated from our babies after their births. We were already looking for a better way. [. . .]

In some relationships, one partner will be in the habit of shortchanging the other in energy transactions.

At one birthing, the mother's first, the husband was a big help to her. During a rush he would squeeze her back, trying to rub in exactly the right place for her and keeping his full attention on her to the very end of the rush. After a rush, he would smooch her, give her a lot of love and encouragement, and she wouldn't acknowledge that he had said anything to her. It was uncomfortable because the way she was being with him left the energy unbalanced. He had been giving her his best, and she hadn't acted like it was good enough to be noticed. He was so obviously feeling her labour with her and trying to share her load in any way that he could that she needed to give some energy back to make it feel right. I thought at the time that it must look to him like maybe she regretted having got familiar enough with him to have gotten pregnant. When I mentioned this (I tried to do it humorously), she laughed and then she let him know that I hadn't been far off in my guess, and then she let him know that she loved him and that it was okay. From then on, they did fine. He helped her a lot, she accepted his help, and they had a nice baby girl not long afterward.

At another birthing, just before the birth of the baby, the lady would tell her husband that she loved him, feeling the energy of the baby very strong and wanting some graceful way to channel it, and he would just nod – wouldn't tell her that he loved her too and give her back as much as she had just given him. The midwives told him that it wasn't fair to be stingy about the energy that way, that this was the same energy that was trying to get his child born. They told him that he was really lucky to have such a nice lady, and encouraged him to have a good time at this birthing since it was one of the highest experiences that he would ever have. He loosened up and their baby was soon born.

Inhibition can block birthing energy.

If I suspect that inhibition is slowing down the progress of labour, I pay attention to the situation for a while, and observe the couple go through a few rushes. I look to see if this couple really loves each other. At the same time I am watching them, I am trying not to impose my own presence on them so much that they don't have any room to be together. Sometimes I will see that the husband is afraid to touch his wife's tits because of the midwives' presence, so I touch them, get in there and squeeze them, talk about how nice they are, and make him welcome. That way he can be uninhibited and loving at the same time. One of the strongest things a man can do to help his lady during their birthing is to let her know he loves her in all the ways that he can. *A marriage should be reliable, fun, and uninhibited.*

Stephen taught us in the beginning that stimulation of the ladies' breasts had a powerful connection with bringing about contractions of the uterus. Our group of midwives had known this and used it as a tool for two or three years before we heard that the medical community, in doing experiments, had discovered that there is a powerful endocrine hormone called oxytocin that is produced by the pituitary gland, which can be prompted to do this by stimulation of the breasts. We had been using this in starting labour in the woman, or, where labour had begun, in speeding it up. We prefer to do this by pleasanter means than an IV drip.

One time I was delivering a single lady whose cervix was fully dilated, but she wasn't able to move the baby. Her pelvic measurements were ample, but she couldn't get herself gathered together so that all her energy was working the same way. Usually it is possible to teach a mother how to push if she is pretty free of subconscious. She can usually learn in a few tries how to get all that energy focused into pushing. But sometimes, no matter how many times you go through it with a lady and demonstrate and do it with her, she always seems to move her leg or something at just the time when the energy is building. She moves that way, or forgets and lets out her breath or does something that you know she could be doing better. When I have a case like this, I usually begin to suspect there is some kind of subconscious that is tying up the energy. I have noticed that it is often sexual subconscious if the energy is blocked once the cervix is already dilated.

So in this case I started talking about it and since she was a single lady, I asked her about what the baby's father was like and what her relationship with him had been. It turned out that she didn't like him too much – she thought he was good-looking, but she didn't really like him too much. As she talked about it, and everybody in the room heard what she had to say about him, it seemed to free up a lot of energy that she had tied up in hostile feelings about him, and she could feel better about her baby being half that guy's genetic make-up. He wasn't going to have anything to do with the raising of the child, but she needed to feel okay about the part of the baby that was him.

I remember a similar situation with a married lady who had already had one baby with her husband. All through their relationship they questioned whether they ought to be together. Then they got pregnant again. They split up and got back together several times during the pregnancy and finally they just agreed not to do it together. During her labour, she had to come to peace about having his baby. The baby didn't want to come out until she felt okay about the regrets over what had gone on so far.

When someone says, 'I love you' and means it, it opens up his throat – it literally does it. And when the throat opens up so does the cervix. I've been checking a lady's dilation at the same time she'd say that, and I could feel a distinct difference in her tissue, in how stretchy she was, that was exactly synchronous with her saying, *'I love you.'* It made me really understand that words are vibrations and that some combinations of words have greater power than others. 'I love you' is very strong.

One thing to remember is not to babble away all your energy by talking about insignificant or irrelevant things while the birthing is happening.

Sometimes labouring mothers get amazingly beautiful during a rush; you can see the prettiest one of that lady that you ever saw. These are very important moments to look for. Just to appreciate the way somebody is being tends to manifest it: nothing needs to be said.

'The flow of energy through a system tends to organize that system.'
– Harold Morowitz

One of our single mothers who came to the Farm to have her baby was very unsatisfied with how she looked. At the time she came to us, she had a large patch of pimples on each cheek, and she would spend quite a bit of time looking critically at herself in the mirror, which didn't tend to help her complexion any. (What you pay attention to, you get more of.) I was present during part of her labour, when she was approaching transition. She was being very brave, and as I looked into her eyes during a rush, I would see that her pimples tended to fade whenever she could stay on top of the energy during a rush. If she would start to lose control a little bit and tighten up her face, the redness would come on again and the pimples would look exaggerated. By the time her son was born, she had managed the energy well enough that her pimples were about half as red as they had been at the onset of labour, and when I saw her again a few days later, her face was completely healed. Instead of looking in a mirror and not liking what she saw, she had been looking in her son's eyes. He wasn't critical a bit. He had that pure vision that newborns have, and he just loved her.

Childcare

JEAN LIEDLOFF
The Continuum Concept

Let me declare an interest and say that if I had to recommend only one book in this anthology, it would be this one. Having spent two and a half years living in the South American jungle with a 'Stone Age' tribe, Jean Liedloff observed the 'natural' way of caring for babies and infants, a continuum of body warmth, affectionate acceptance and ongoing nurture. If, as babies and infants, we do not receive this, we become psychologically awkward, deficient and wounded. Healthy cultures have passed this warm parenting style down from generation to generation and there is no break in the continuum.

How can we learn about continuum and non-continuum infant life? We can make a start by observing people like the Yequana and look again more carefully at members of our own cultures. The worlds of infants in arms in Stone Age and in civilized cultures are as different as day and night.

From birth, continuum infants are taken everywhere. Before the umbilicus comes off, the infant's life is already full of action. He is asleep most of the time, but even as he sleeps he is becoming accustomed to the voices of his people, to the sounds of their activities, to the bumpings, jostlings and moves without warning, to stops without warning, to lifts and pressures on various parts of his body as his caretaker shifts him about to accommodate her work or her comfort, and to the rhythms of day and night, the changes of texture and temperature on his skin and the safe, right feel of being held to a living body. His urgent need to be there would be noticeable to him only if he were removed from his place. His unequivocal expectation of these circumstances, and the fact that these and no other are his experience, simply carry on the continuum of his species. He is feeling right, therefore he seldom has any need to signal by crying or to do anything but suckle when the impulse arises and enjoy satisfying the stimulus to do so, and equally to enjoy the stimulus and satisfaction of defecating. Otherwise he is engaged in learning what it is like to be.

During the in-arms phase, the time between birth and the voluntary commencement of crawling, a baby is receiving experience and with it fulfilling his innate expectations, graduating to new expectations or desires and then fulfilling them in their turn. He moves very little when he is awake and is generally in a relaxed and passive state. His muscles have tone: he is not in the rag-doll condition in which he sleeps, but he uses only the economical minimum of muscular activity needed to pay attention to the events that concern him at each stage, to eat and to defecate. He also has the task, which falls to him fairly early, though not immediately after birth, of balancing his head and body (for paying attention, eating and defecating) in an infinite variety of postures depending upon the actions and positions of the person holding him.

He may be lying on a lap in only occasional contact with arms and hands that are working at something above him, like paddling a canoe, sewing or preparing food. Then he might suddenly feel the lap tilting him outward and a hand gripping his wrist. The lap drops away and the hand tightens its grip and lifts him through the air to a new contact with the trunk of the body, whereupon the hand lets go and an elbow takes up a supporting position by pinning him against a hip and rib cage before bending to pick something up with the free hand, upending him momentarily then proceeding to walk, run, then walk again, bobbing him up and down in several rhythms and giving him a variety of jolts. He may then be passed to someone else and feel himself losing contact with one person and coming into the new temperature, texture, smell and sound of another, a bonier one perhaps, or one with the reedy voice of a child or the resonance of a man's. Or he may be lifted again by one arm and dunked into cool water, splashed and stroked, then scraped with the side of a hand until the water stops trickling down his body. He may then be replaced, damp on damp, in his place on the hip until the contact area generates great heat while the areas exposed to air grow colder. He may then feel the sun's warmth come through, or the extra chill of a breeze. He may feel both, as he is taken through sunshine to the shade of a forest path. He may be almost dry, then drenched by pelting rain, and later refind comfort in a radical change from cold and wet to shelter and a fire at his outer side, which warms him faster than his other side is being warmed by his companion's body.

If there is a party while he is asleep, he will be bounced about quite violently while his mother hops and stamps in time to the music. Through daytime sleep, similar adventures befall him. At night his mother sleeps beside him, her skin next to his, as always, while she breathes and moves and sometimes snores a little. She wakens often during the night to tend the fire, holding him close as she rolls out of her hammock and slips to the floor, where he is sandwiched between her thigh and ribs as she rearranges the logs. If he awakens hungry in the night he signals with a soft grunt if he cannot find her breast; she will then give it to him, and again his well-being will be re-established, without ever having come near to straining the limits of his continuum. His life, full of action, is consistent with the lives lived by millions of his predecessors and meets the expectations of his nature.

He does very little, then, at this stage, but a great quantity and variety of experience come to him through his adventures in the arms of a busy person. As his requirements change, when the preceding ones have been satisfactorily met and he is psychologically developed and ready for the next ones, he signals, according to his innate impulses, and the signals are correctly interpreted by the corresponding innate mechanisms in his beholders. When he smiles and gurgles, it excites pleasure in them and an impulse to elicit the delightful sounds as long and often as possible. The right stimuli are quickly identified and, encouraged by the rewarding response of the baby, repeated. Later, as the level of pleasure and excitement diminishes with repetition, his cues and responses push the behaviour pattern to alter in the direction that will sustain the high pleasure quotient.

Games of approach and retreat are examples of this. They may begin with an affectionate kiss on the infant's face or body. He smiles and gurgles. Another kiss follows. More signs of pleasure and encouragement come from the baby. The tone of his happy voice and the sparkle in his eyes do not signal for peace and quiet, nor for comforting, nor for feeding or repositioning, but for excitement. Instinctively, his accomplice rubs her nose on his chest and when this meets with success, she very soon creates even more gleeful signals with a vibrating b-b-b-b-b-b from lips brushing the surface of his body.

The infant, anticipating his own reaction, now starts gurgling and squealing with excitement as the pleasure-giving mouth approaches. The man, woman or child who owns the mouth finds that the rewarding sounds from the baby can be increased by teasing, that is, delaying the approach to the point where maximum effect is maintained: not too long for the baby to remain attentive, nor too short a time to obtain all the anticipatory response possible.

The next step in the game is to hold the baby at arm's length and then pull him into the close contact, or safe, position. The contrast between the fringe zone and safety zone, the relationship between moving outward and coming back unharmed, the triumph of having tested one's own separability from the safety zone and returning successful, is the beginning of the progression of events and psychobiological maturing that will lead to graduation from the in-arms phase with maximum competence and eagerness for the next adventures on the age-old agenda.

As the arm's-length position is tried and mastered, a toss with a loosening of the grip at the zenith follows. When the infant shows that he is ready for something more daring, he is thrown and caught. He is allowed to fly higher and drop further as his confidence increases, as the borderline at which he exhibits fear is pushed back and his radius of confidence expands.

Games that test the same qualities in the context of the separate senses are also learned from infants by their companions. The reassuring sight of a mother or familiar is cut off and restored in the same progressive way in games of peek-a-boo. Increasingly sudden or loud sounds are sprung upon the infant's ear – as, for example, 'Boo!' – followed by the reassuring news that it is only Mummy or whoever, and there is no cause for alarm. Toys of the jack-in-the-box kind remove the startling stimulus to the world outside and test greater degrees of resilience. There can be games that follow the pattern but are initiated by the adult. The Yequana take advantage of the baby's predisposition to this sort of performance and, keeping his rules and respecting his go-ahead signals, dip him into more and more challenging waters. A daily bath is routine from birth, but every infant is also dipped into fast rivers, first only his feet, then his legs, then his entire body. The water goes from swift to swifter and on to plunging rapids and falls, and the time of exposure lengthens too, as the baby's response reveals growing confidence. Before he can walk or even think, a Yequana baby is well on the way towards expertise in judging the force, direction and depth of water by sight. His people are among the finest white-water canoeists in the world.

The senses are given an enormous quantity and variety of events and objects upon which to practise, refine their functions and coordinate their messages to the brain.

The first experiences are predominantly of the body of a busy mother. The movings about are bases for taking up the pace of an active life. The pace becomes a characteristic of the world of living and it is associated always with the cosy rightness of the self, for it is learned in arms.

If a baby is held much of the time by someone who is only sitting quietly, it will not serve him in learning the quality of life and action, though it will keep away negative feelings of abandonment, separateness, and much of the worst torment of longing. The fact that babies actively encourage people to treat them to excitement is indication that they expect and require action upon which to develop. A mother sitting still will condition a baby to think of life as dull and slow, and there will be a restlessness in him and frequent promptings from him to encourage more stimulation. He will bounce up and down to show what he wants, or wave his arms to initiate a faster pace in her actions. Similarly, if she insists upon treating him as though he were fragile, she will suggest to him that he is. But if she handles him in a rough and off-hand way, he will think of himself as strong, adaptable and at home in a vast variety of circumstances. Feeling fragile not only is unpleasant but also interferes with the efficiency of the developing child and, later, of the adult.

The sights, sounds, smells, textures and tastes are first dominated by the sheltering body and later, with the development of greater faculties, include a broadening range of events and objects. Associations are made. The darkness of the hut is always present when there is a smell of cooking and almost always when there is the smell of wood smoke. The light is bright at baths and during most of the joggling of walking trips. The temperature in the dark is more comfortable, generally, than in the bright outdoors, which is often blazingly hot or chilly with wind and rain; but any and all of the changes are acceptable and the variations expected, for there was always variety in babies' experience. The basic condition of being in arms has been met, so the infant is free to be stimulated and enriched by whatever he senses. Happenings that would frighten an unprepared adult are barely noticed by an infant in arms. Figures suddenly loom close above his eyes, treetops spin high overhead. Things go dark or light without warning. Thunder and lightning, barking dogs, deafening roars of waterfalls, splitting trees, flaring fires, surprise dousings in rain or river water do not perturb him. Given the conditions in which his species evolved, silence or a prolonged *lack* of change in sensory stimuli is alarming.

When he does cry for some reason during a moment when a group of adults is in conversation, his mother hisses softly in his ear to distract him. If this fails, she takes him away until he is quiet. She does not set her will against the infant's, she exiles herself with him without showing any sign of judgement of his behaviour or displeasure at being inconvenienced. When he drools on her, she seldom notices. If she wipes his mouth with the back of her hand, it is in the half-attentive manner with which she grooms her own person. When he wets or defecates, she may laugh, and, as she is seldom alone, so do her companions, and she holds the infant away from her as quickly as she can until he finishes. It is a sort of game to see how fast she can hold him away, but the laughter is louder when she gets the worst of it. Water sinks into the dirt floor in moments, and excrement is cleared away immediately with leaves. Vomiting, or 'spitting up', an everyday event in our infants' lives, is so rare that I can remember seeing it happen only once in my years with the Indians, and that baby had a high fever.

The notion that nature has evolved one species to suffer from indigestion every time it drinks its mother's milk has, amazingly, not been questioned by civilized experts. 'Burping', patting the baby firmly on the back while he is held against one's shoulder, is advocated to help him 'bring up the air he has swallowed'. The baby often vomits on the shoulder in the process. Stressed as our babies are, it is little wonder that they are chronically ill. The tension, kicking, arching, flexing and squealing are symptoms of the same constant, deep discomfiture.

Yequana babies never require special treatment after nourishing themselves – any more than do the young of other animals. Perhaps part of the explanation lies in the fact that they nurse much more often during the day and night than our civilized babes are permitted to do. It seems more likely, though, that the whole answer rests in our permanently stressed condition, for even when Yequana babies were cared for by children most of the day, and therefore unable to resort to their mothers at will, they showed no sign of colic.

If a child lives with criticism
 it learns to condemn.
If a child lives with hostility
 it learns to fight.
If a child lives with ridicule
 it learns to be shy.
If a child lives with shame
 it learns to be guilty.
If a child lives with tolerance
 it learns to be patient.
If a child lives with encouragement
 it learns confidence.
If a child lives with praise
 it learns to appreciate.
If a child lives with fairness
 it learns justice.
If a child lives with security
 it learns to have faith.
If a child lives with approval
 it learns to like itself.
If a child lives with acceptance and friendship
 it learns to find love both in itself and in the world.

Anonymous

Esoteric Healing – The Basic Rules

ALICE BAILEY
Esoteric Healing

Alice Bailey was the telepathic secretary of the Tibetan teacher, Djwahl Kuhl. She wrote some twenty books, many of which have been reprinted over twenty times and which have reached millions of people. One of her most influential books is *Esoteric Healing*, which presents a coherent and detailed explanation of how illness is caused by inner dynamics and how it can be healed. Most teachers and writers in the field of spiritual healing are directly or indirectly indebted to this work.

Law I

All disease is the result of inhibited soul life. This is true of all forms in all kingdoms. The art of the healer consists in releasing the soul so that its life can flow through the aggregate of organisms which constitute any particular form.

Law II

Disease is the product of and subject to three influences: first, a man's past, wherein he pays the price of ancient error; second, his inheritance, wherein he shares with all mankind those tainted streams of energy which are of group origin; third, he shares with all the natural forms that which the Lord of Life imposes on His body. These three influences are called the 'Ancient Law of Evil Sharing'. This must give place some day to that new 'Law of Ancient Dominating Good' which lies behind all that God has made. This law must be brought into activity by the spiritual will of man.

Rule one

Let the healer train himself to know the inner stage of thought or of desire of the one who seeks his help. He can thereby know the source from whence the trouble comes. Let him relate the cause and the effect and know the point exact through which relief must come.

Law III

Disease is an effect of the basic centralization of a man's life energy. From the plane whereon those energies are focussed proceed those determining conditions which produce ill health. These therefore work out as disease or as freedom from disease.

Law IV

Disease, both physical and psychological, has its roots in the good, the beautiful and the true. It is but a distorted reflection of divine possibilities. The thwarted soul, seeking full expression of some divine characteristic or inner spiritual reality, produces, within the substance of its sheaths, a point of friction. Upon this point the eyes of the personality are focussed and this leads to disease. The art of the healer is concerned with the lifting of the downward focussed eyes unto the soul, the true Healer within the form. The spiritual or third eye then directs the healing force and all is well.

Rule two

The healer must achieve magnetic purity, through purity of life. He must attain that dispelling radiance which shows itself in every man when he has linked the centres in the head. When this magnetic field is established, the radiation then goes forth.

Law V

There is naught but energy, for God is Life. Two energies meet in man, but another five are present. For each is to be found a central point of contact. The conflict of these energies with forces and of forces twixt themselves produce the bodily ills of man. The conflict of the first and second persists for ages until the mountain top is reached – the first great mountain top. The fight between the forces produces all disease, all ills and bodily pain which seek release in death. The two, the five and thus the seven, plus that which they produce, possess the secret. This is the fifth Law of Healing within the world of form.

Rule three

Let the healer concentrate the needed energy within the needed centre. Let that centre correspond to the centre which has need. Let the two synchronize and together augment force. Thus shall the waiting form be balanced in its work. Thus shall the two and the one, under right direction, heal.

Law VI

When the building energies of the soul are active in the body, then there is health, clean interplay and right activity. When the builders are the lunar lords and those who work under the control of the moon and at the behest of the lower personal self, then you have disease, ill health and death.

Law VII

When life or energy flows unimpeded and through right direction to its precipitation (the related gland), then the form responds and ill health disappears.

Rule four

A careful diagnosis of disease, based on the ascertained outer symptoms, will be simplified to this extent – that once the organ involved is known and thus isolated, the centre in the etheric body which is in closest relation to it will be subjected to methods of occult healing, though the ordinary, ameliorative, medical or surgical methods will not be withheld.

Law VIII

Disease and death are the results of two active forces. One is the will of the soul, which says to its instrument: I draw the essence back. The other is the magnetic power of the planetary life, which says to the life within the atomic structure: The hour of reabsorption has arrived. Return to me. Thus, under cyclic law, do all forms act.

Rule five

The healer must seek to link his soul, his heart, his brain and his hands. Thus can he pour the vital healing force upon the patient. *This is magnetic work*. It cures disease or increases the evil state, according to the knowledge of the healer.

The healer must seek to link his soul, his brain, his heart and auric emanation. Thus can his presence feed the soul life of the patient. *This is the work of radiation*. The hands are needed not. The soul displays its power. The patient's soul responds through the response of his aura to the radiation of the healer's aura, flooded with soul energy.

Law IX

Perfection calls imperfection to the surface. Good drives evil from the form of man in time and space. The method used by the Perfect One and that employed by Good is harmlessness. This is not negativity but perfect poise, a completed point of view and divine understanding.

Rule six

The healer or the healing group must keep the will in leash. It is not will that must be used, but love.

Law X

Hearken, O Disciple, to the call which comes from the Son to the Mother, and then obey. The Word goes forth that form has served its purpose. The principle of mind then organizes itself and then repeats that Word. The waiting form responds and drops away. The soul stands free.

Respond, O Rising One, to the call which comes within the sphere of obligation; recognize the call emerging from the Ashram or from the Council Chamber where waits the Lord of Life Himself. The Sound goes forth. Both soul and form together must renounce the principle of life and thus permit the Monad to stand free. The soul responds. The form then shatters the connection. Life is now liberated, owning the quality of conscious knowledge and the fruit of all experience. These are the gifts of soul and form combined.

Note: This last law is the enunciation of a new law which is substituted for the Law of Death, and which has reference only to those upon the later stages of the Path of Discipleship and the stages upon the Path of Initiation.

Application of the Laws and Rules

In the last few pages I greatly clarified the issue by indicating – even at the risk of somewhat discouraging you – certain of the essential requirements of the healer in the New Age, and also certain of the contacts which he will have to make with facility and promptness when attempting to heal. I likewise defined for you the nature of Law. This was preliminary to a consideration of the Laws to which the healer must conform and the Rules which he will automatically and intuitively obey. We might consider these Laws and Rules in relation to the healer and also in relation to each other, for several of the Rules are closely related to a Law which controls the healer.

From the definition of law, as given above, it will be apparent to you that in the last analysis disease, death, untruth, falsity and despair are inherent in the planet itself, because our planetary Logos is an 'imperfect God'. After the present great world crisis, incident to our planetary Logos having moved forward upon the cosmic Path, and therefore having taken a cosmic initiation, His imperfections are demonstrably lessened; there will be less distress and disease on earth once the necessary planetary adjustments have been made. This you yourselves will not see take place, for adjustments on such a large scale take centuries to effect. What I have, therefore, to say upon the future healing of disease will not be of practical value for a long time to come, but the theory and the indications of possibility must be considered and discussed. Also, for a long time, medical practice and surgical knowledge will play their useful parts in preventive medicine, alleviative practices and curative processes. To these increasingly will be added many psychological methods of healing, and these will go hand in hand with the two above; to these again the services of the spiritual healers will be added. In this way, a rounded-out approach to the whole man will be steadily developed, and the need for this is today recognized by forward thinking physicians everywhere. Thus, and also through the method of trial and error, much will be learned.

The healing processes I outline and indicate through these Laws and Rules are basically new. They are not based on affirmations, as in Christian Science and other mental healing cults; they are not posited on affirmed origins and on claiming results which will only be possible when the race has reached a far higher standard of perfection than is at present seen or that is immediately capable of development. As I have several times said in this treatise, there is nothing fundamentally wrong in the claims made by these groups and organizations anent the man who has arrived at soul expression and at realization of the Christ consciousness. What is wrong is the claim that the ordinary man (obviously not at this advanced point in evolution) can perform these miracles of healing either in himself or for others. Very few people have as yet reached this point, and the healer in these cults and organizations who has done so is a rarity indeed. The healer in the New Age will recognize limitation and conditioning circumstances, plus destiny.

Psychoneuroimmunology

CANDACE PERT
Molecules of Emotion

Candace Pert began her career as a neuroscientist with the discovery of the opiate receptor. In many ways it is her research, published in scientific journals, which provides much of the background for what is called emotional literacy or emotional intelligence. In *Molecules of Emotion* she describes the history of her pioneering research into how the chemicals in our bodies form an information network which links mind and body in a way previously considered impossible and unthinkable. The rigour and scientific evidence of her argument provide an irrefutable basis for a holistic understanding of the human personality and of the body-mind continuum.

Let me summarize the basic idea I have been developing. The three classically separated areas of neuroscience, endocrinology, and immunology, with their various organs – the brain; the glands; and the spleen, bone marrow, and lymph nodes – are actually joined to each other in a multidirectional network of communication, linked by information carriers known as neuropeptides. There are many well-studied physiological substrates showing that communication exists in both directions for every single one of these areas and their organs. Some of the research is old, some of it is new. For example, we've known for over a century that the pituitary gland spews out peptides throughout the body. But it's only been a few years that we've known that peptide-producing cells like those in the brain also inhabit the bone marrow, the place where immune cells are 'born'.

The word I want to emphasize in regard to this integrated system is *network*, which comes from the relatively new field of information theory. In a network, there is a constant exchange and processing and storage of information, which is exactly what happens, as we have seen, as neuropeptides and their receptors bind across systems. The informational nature of these biochemicals led Francis Schmitt of MIT to introduce, in 1984, the term *information substances*, a wonderfully descriptive way of referring to all of the messenger molecules and their receptors as they go about their job of linking brain, body, and behaviour. Schmitt did us a great favour by giving us a metaphor to explain the purpose of the complex overlapping of these multiple-functioning substances as they move from one system to another, one job to another. He included in his new generic category both long-familiar substances such as the classical neurotransmitters and the steroid hormones, and newly discovered ones such as peptide hormones, neuropeptides, and growth factors – all ligands that trigger receptors and initiate a cascade of cellular processes and changes.

So what we have been talking about all along is information. In thinking about these matters, then, it might make more sense to emphasize the perspective of psychology rather than of neuroscience, for the term *psycho* clearly conveys the study of mind, which encompasses but also goes beyond the study of the brain. I like to speculate that what the mind is is the flow of information as it moves among the cells, organs, and systems of the body. And since one of the qualities of information flow is that it can be unconscious, occurring below the level of awareness, we see it in operation at the autonomic, or involuntary, level of our physiology. The mind as we experience it is immaterial, yet it has a physical substrate, which is both the body and the brain. It may also be said to have a non-material, non-physical substrate that has to do with the flow of that information. The mind, then, is that which holds the network together, often acting below our consciousness, linking and coordinating the major systems and their organs and cells in an intelligently orchestrated symphony of life. Thus, we might refer to the whole system as a psychosomatic information network, linking *psyche*, which comprises all that is of an ostensibly non-material nature, such as mind, emotion, and soul, to *soma*, which is the material world of molecules, cells, and organs. Mind and body, psyche and soma.

This view of the organism as an information network departs radically from the old Newtonian, mechanistic view. In the old paradigm, we saw the body in terms of energy and matter. Hardwired reflexes, caused by electrical stimulation across the synapse, ran the body in a more or less mechanical, reactive fashion, with little room for flexibility, change, or intelligence. With information added to the process, we see that there is an intelligence running things. It's not a matter of energy acting on matter to create behaviour, but of intelligence in the form of information running all the systems and creating behaviour. Walter B. Cannon, William James's debater, was on to this when he referred to the 'wisdom of the body'; and today certain manipulative healers such as chiropractors refer to it as the body's 'innate intelligence'. But, classically, there is no such thing as an intelligent organism, and to say so is heresy to the old guard who cling to a concept of the body as unintelligent, a bundle of mass and matter stimulated by electrical impulses in a predictable way. Theirs is the ultimate godless, mechanical universe, peopled by clock-like organisms, as conceived by Cartesian and Newtonian models.

While much of the activity of the body, according to the new information model, does take place at the autonomic, unconscious level, what makes this model so different is that it can explain how it is also possible for our conscious mind to enter the network and play a deliberate part. Let's look, for example, at the role of opiate receptors and endorphins in modulating pain. Pain researchers all agree that the area called the periaqueductal grey, located around the aqueduct between the third and fourth ventricles of the midbrain, is filled with opiate receptors, making it a control area for pain. (It is also loaded with receptors for virtually all the neuropeptides that have been studied.)

Now, we've all heard of the yogis of the East and practitioners of certain mystical disciplines who have been able, through breath training, to alter their perceptions of physical pain. (Other people, known as mothers, demonstrate mastery equal to that of the yogis, when, with proper training such as Lamaze, they use breathing techniques to control pain in childbirth.) What seems to be going on here is that these people are able to plug into their PAG (their periaqueductal grey), gaining access to it with their conscious intention, and then, I believe, are able to reset their pain thresholds. Reframed by conscious expectations and beliefs, the pain is abolished, reinterpreted as either a neutral experience or even pleasure. The question is: how can the mind mediate and modulate an experience of pain? What role does consciousness play in such matters?

To answer, I must return to the idea of a network. A network is different from a hierarchical structure that has a ruling 'station' at the top and a descending series of positions that play increasingly subsidiary roles. In a network, theoretically, you can enter at any nodal point and quickly get to any other point; all locations are equal as far as the potential to 'rule' or direct the flow of information. Let's see how a concept like this explains the process by which a conscious intention can reach the PAG and use it to control pain.

Conscious breathing, the technique employed by both the yogi and the woman in labour, is extremely powerful. There is a wealth of data showing that changes in the rate and depth of breathing produce changes in the quantity and kind of peptides that are released from the brain stem. And vice versa! By bringing this process into consciousness and doing something to alter it – either holding your breath or breathing extra fast – you cause the peptides to diffuse rapidly throughout the cerebrospinal fluid, in an attempt to restore homeostasis, the body's feedback mechanism for restoring and maintaining balance. And since many of these peptides are endorphins, the body's natural opiates, as well as other kinds of pain-relieving substances, you soon achieve a diminution of your pain. So it's no wonder that so many modalities, both ancient and New Age, have discovered the power of controlled breathing. The peptide-respiratory link is well documented: virtually any peptide found anywhere else can be found in the respiratory centre. This peptide substrate may provide the scientific rationale for the powerful healing effects of consciously controlled breath patterns.

We are all aware of the bias built into the Western idea that the mind is totally in the head, a function of the brain. But your body is not there just to carry around your head. I believe the research findings I have described indicate that we need to start thinking about how the mind manifests itself in various parts of the body and, beyond that, how we can bring that process into consciousness.

Mind in body

The concept of a network, stressing the interconnectedness of all systems of the organism, has a variety of paradigm-breaking implications. In the popular lexicon, these kinds of connections between body and brain have long been referred to as 'the power of the mind over the body'. But in light of my research, that phrase does not describe accurately what is happening. Mind doesn't dominate body, it *becomes* body – body and mind are one. I see the process of communication we have demonstrated, the flow of information throughout the whole organism, as evidence that the body is the actual outward manifestation, in physical space, of the mind. *Bodymind*, a term first proposed by Dianne Connelly, reflects the understanding, derived from Chinese medicine, that the body is inseparable from the mind. And when we explore the role that emotions play in the body, as expressed through the neuropeptide molecules, it will become clear how emotions can be seen as a key to the understanding of disease.

We know that the immune system, like the central nervous system, has memory and the capacity to learn. Thus, it could be said that intelligence is located not only in the brain but in cells that are distributed throughout the body, and that the traditional separation of mental processes, including emotions, from the body is no longer valid.

If the mind is defined by brain-cell communication, as it has been in contemporary science, then this model of the mind can now be seen as extending naturally to the entire body. Since neuropeptides and their receptors are in the body as well, we may conclude that the *mind* is in the body, in the same sense that the mind is in the brain, with all that that implies.

To see what this means in practice, let's return for a moment to the example of the gut. The entire lining of the intestines, from the oesophagus through the large intestine, and including each of the seven sphincters, is lined with cells – nerve cells and other kinds of cells – that contain neuropeptides and receptors. It seems entirely possible to me that the density of receptors in the intestines may be why we feel our emotions in that part of the anatomy, often referring to them as 'gut feelings'. Studies have shown that excitement and anger increase gut motility, while contentment decreases it. And then, because this is a two-way network, it's also the case that the movement of the gut as it digests food and excretes impurities can alter your emotional state. 'Dyspeptic' means grouchy and irritable, but originally it referred to having poor digestion. Or let's look again at the autonomic nervous system, which runs all the unconscious aspects of your body, such as breathing, digestion, and elimination. You would think that if any part of the body functioned independently of the mind, it would most surely be the autonomic nervous system. There, the ability to make your heart beat, your intestines digest, and your cells replicate is carried on below conscious awareness. And yet, surprisingly, as we discussed in the example of yogis and women in labour, consciousness *can* intervene at this level. This is the radical lesson of biofeedback, which many doctors now teach their patients so that they can control pain, heart rate, blood circulation, tension and relaxation, etc. – all processes previously thought to be unconscious. Up until the early sixties, we thought that the autonomic nervous system was run by two neurotransmitters, acetylcholine and norepinephrine. But it turns out that in addition to the classical neurotransmitters, all of the known peptides, the information molecules, can be found abundantly in the autonomic nervous system, distributed in subtly different intricate patterns all the way down both sides of your spine. It is these peptides and their receptors that make the dialogue between conscious and unconscious processes possible.

In summary, the point I am making is that your brain is extremely well integrated with the rest of your body at a molecular level, so much so that the term *mobile brain* is an apt description of the psychosomatic network through which intelligent information travels from one system to another. Every one of the zones, or systems, of the network – the neural, the hormonal, the gastrointestinal, and the immune – is set up to communicate with one another, via peptides and messenger-specific peptide receptors. Every second, a massive information exchange is occurring in your body. Imagine each of these messenger systems possessing a specific tone, humming a signature tune, rising and falling, waxing and waning, binding and unbinding, and if we could hear this body music with our ears, then the sum of these sounds would be the music that we call the emotions.

Emotions. The neuropeptides and receptors, the biochemicals of emotion, are, as I have said, the messengers carrying information to link the major systems of the body into one unit that we can call the body-mind. We can no longer think of the emotions as having less validity than physical, material substance, but instead must see them as cellular signals that are involved in the process of translating information into physical reality, literally transforming mind into matter. Emotions are at the nexus between matter and mind, going back and forth between the two and influencing both.

Crystal Healing

RICHARD GERBER
Vibrational Medicine

It would be a terrible omission in this anthology if it did not have a passage on crystals. If there is one area of holistic culture that evokes sardonic comment it is its interest in crystals. Yet in the following passage a medical doctor describes very precisely the relevance of crystals. Richard Gerber graduated in Medicine in Detroit and his research and practice have been rigorously dedicated to a holistic approach. His *Vibrational Medicine* is one of the very best and most thorough overviews of holistic medicine.

Quartz crystals have found their way into many of the electronic devices common to our present-day culture. As mentioned earlier, they are the central components of many of today's timepieces. The reason that quartz crystals are useful in telling time is that when they are stimulated with electricity, their oscillations are so regular and precise that they form a handy reference by which bits of time may be measured and displayed. This property of quartz crystals is a reflection of what is known as the 'piezoelectric effect'. When quartz crystals are subjected to mechanical pressure, they produce a measurable electrical voltage. Conversely, when an electrical current is applied to a crystal, it will induce mechanical movement. Most electronic devices utilize a slice or plate of quartz. Each plate of quartz has a particular natural resonant frequency which is dependent upon its thickness and size. If an alternating current is passed through the crystal plate, the charges oscillate back and forth at the resonant frequency of the crystal.

This phenomenon is the basis for crystal oscillator components used in many electronic systems to generate and maintain very precise energy frequencies. Another demonstration of the piezoelectric effect is seen when the crystal at the tip of the phonograph needle transduces mechanical vibration from patterns in the record grooves into electrical oscillation. This electrical oscillation is then translated by the electronics of the record player into music and words.

Quartz crystals are actually composed of silicon dioxide (SiO_2). While quartz crystals form the components of many electronic systems, it is the crystals of elemental silicon which have been used as primary components of computer and solar technologies. [. . .]

Of particular interest to our discussion is the application of these functions of quartz crystals towards subtle energetic healing of human illness. According to crystal researcher Marcel Vogel, a senior scientist with IBM for 27 years:

The crystal is a neutral object whose inner structure exhibits a state of perfection and balance. When it's cut to the proper form and when the human mind enters into relationship with its structural perfection, the crystal emits a vibration which extends and amplifies the powers of the user's mind. Like a laser, it radiates energy in a coherent, highly concentrated form, and this energy may be transmitted into objects or people at will.

Although the crystal may be used for 'mind to mind' communication, its higher purpose . . . is in the service of humanity for the removal of pain and suffering. With proper training, a healer can release negative thoughtforms which have taken shape as disease patterns in a patient's physical body.

As psychics have often pointed out, when a person becomes emotionally distressed, a weakness forms in his subtle energy body and disease may soon follow. With a properly cut crystal, however, a healer can, like a surgeon cutting away a tumour, release negative patterns in the energy body, allowing the physical body to return to a state of wholeness.

The key concept which Dr Vogel has presented is that the quartz crystal is capable of amplifying and directing the natural energies of the healer. The subtle energies of the healer's field become focused and coherent in a manner similar to a laser. Ordinarily, light is incoherent, with rays of energy moving randomly in many directions at once. In the ruby laser, the crystal creates an amplification effect by organizing rays of light into a coherent, orderly beam that has a tremendously powerful energetic effect. The quartz crystal works similarly with the subtle energies of the healer. [. . .]

A number of healers have adapted the use of the quartz crystal to amplify their natural healing abilities. Dr Dolores Krieger, the creator of Therapeutic Touch, has also worked with augmenting healing energies by utilizing quartz crystals. She was shown this technique by Oh Shinnah, who is a trained psychologist, a crystal healer, and a Native American Indian. It is interesting to note that many Native American healers, and especially the tribal shamans of cultures throughout the world, have quartz crystals among their collections of power objects. In such widely separated peoples as the Jivaro in South America and the tribes of Australia, the quartz crystal is considered the strongest power object of all.

The quartz crystal can have other energetic abilities besides merely focusing the subtle energies of the healer. When healing energy is focused through the quartz crystal, it is sent into the body of the patient and distributed to the areas most in need of an energy balancing. There is an almost innate intelligence to this focused energy as it is always directed to the body regions where it is needed. The quartz crystal may be held in the hand while touching the patient, and the healing energies sent through the palm chakra. As the energies pass through the crystal, they are both amplified and directed to the part of the subtle anatomy which requires energetic reorganization and healing. Although there is a natural tendency for the crystal to distribute the energies properly, it is still wise to place the crystal over the part of the body which is painful or most affected by illness.

Quartz crystals may be useful for rebalancing and cleansing abnormally functioning or 'blocked' chakras. When cleansing a chakra, the crystal is placed over the particular chakra body region and energy is sent through the crystal. The cleansing action may be induced by either the energies of the healer or the individual in need of chakra rebalancing. If the healer is the active energy source, subtle energy is transmitted from the healer's palm chakra, through the crystal, and into the individual's unbalanced chakra, while the healer focuses his/her mind on the task at hand. Conversely, an individual can use the crystal to cleanse his/her own chakras by placing a single terminated crystal over the chakra with the point facing away from the body. In this technique, the individual directs energy from inside the body out through the chakra and the overlying crystal.

A number of visualization techniques can be used in conjunction with this method. With the crystal over the chakra, the individual can imagine breathing in energy of a particular colour (although white light is usually the most effective) and then visualize directing this light through the chakra on the exhaling breath. This method can be further augmented with the use of sound and chanting. For instance, while the individual is exhaling energy through the chakra, he or she can chant the 'om'. The sound energy can be visualized as projected or sung through a window meant to represent the chakra, in addition to directing light energy through the chakra window. [. . .]

As a rule, the healing energies transmitted by crystals seem to work at the level of our subtle energetic bodies. They assist the energies of the healer to correct dysfunction at a very primary level. Illness at the physical level is usually preceded by changes which have already occurred at the level of the etheric body. As we have discussed previously, energies from the astral and mental levels also have input into the etheric body. Therefore, dysfunctional emotional patterns may create changes in the astral form which are gradually transformed into energetic pattern changes at the level of the etheric and finally the physical body.

When correction occurs at the level of the astral and etheric bodies via healing energies transmitted through the crystal, the subtle energetic template is repatterned in such a way that normal tissue growth can occur, pain can be relieved, and coordination between the various energetic levels can take place more easily. One of the problems that can occur when healing with crystals, and with subtle energies in general, relates to the problem of disease recurrence. Many times a particular pain or illness stems from a negative thoughtform carried within the subtle energetic field of the individual. This thoughtform is the energy manifestation of some type of weighty or abnormal thought or emotion which has been held by the individual for a long period of time. Sometimes thoughtforms originate at unconscious levels and may relate to problematic issues that the sick individual has never actively addressed nor tried to resolve. Frequently, thoughtforms are charged with a particular emotion. The stronger the associated emotion that created the thoughtform, the more persistent the thoughtform will be in the auric field of the individual. Although one may use the crystal-amplified healing energies to disintegrate a negative thoughtform in an individual's subtle energetic field, the patient may recreate a thoughtform.

Affirmations

LOUISE HAY
Heal Your Body – The Mental Causes for Physical Illness and the Metaphysical Way to Overcome Them

Louise Hay has done more than any other writer to popularize the notion that physical illness is frequently the result of an inner attitude and that healing happens if you can transform this underlying attitude. This transformation can be helped by changing certain unconscious assumptions using affirmations; an affirmation is a statement or belief which you say mentally to yourself over and over again until finally it feels authentically true and resonates through your whole being; it is a method of changing unconscious thought patterns.

Louise Hay comes from a family of Christian Scientists, a faith which precisely believes that thought creates illness, but its reality struck home when she was diagnosed as having vaginal cancer. She linked this cancer to the fact that she was raped as a five-year-old and that deep psychological patterns needed healing before the cancer would go; and this proved to be the case as she underwent her own self-healing.

Mental equivalents: the mental thought patterns that form our experience

Both the good in our lives and the disease are the results of mental thought patterns which form our experiences. We all have many thought patterns that produce good, positive experiences, and these we enjoy. It is the negative thought patterns that produce uncomfortable, unrewarding experiences with which we are concerned. It is our desire to change our disease in life into perfect health.

We have learned that for every effect in our lives, there is a thought pattern that precedes and maintains it. Our consistent thinking patterns create our experiences. Therefore, by changing our thinking patterns, we can change our experiences.

What a joy it was when I first discovered the words *metaphysical causations*. This describes the power in the words and thoughts that create experiences. This new awareness brought me understanding of the connection between thoughts and the different parts of the body and physical problems. I learned how I had unknowingly created disease in myself and this made a great difference in my life. Now I could stop blaming life and other people for what was wrong in my life and my body. I could now take full responsibility for my own health. Without either reproaching myself or feeling guilty, I began to see how to avoid creating thought patterns of disease in the future.

For example, I could not understand why I repeatedly had problems with a stiff neck. Then I discovered that the neck represented being flexible on issues, being willing to see different sides of a question. I had been a very inflexible person, often refusing to listen to another side of a question out of fear. But, as I became more flexible in my thinking and able, with a loving understanding, to see another's viewpoint, my neck ceased to bother me. Now, if my neck becomes a bit stiff, I look to see where my thinking is stiff and rigid.

Replacing old patterns

In order to permanently eliminate a condition, we must first work to dissolve the mental cause. But most often, since we do not know what the cause is, we find it difficult to know where to begin. So, if you are saying, 'If I only knew what is causing this pain', I hope that this booklet will provide both a clue to find the causes and a helpful guide for building new thought patterns which will produce health in mind and body.

I have learned that for every condition in our lives, there is a NEED FOR IT. Otherwise, we would not have it. The symptom is only an outer effect. We must go within to dissolve the mental cause. This is why Willpower and Discipline do not work. They are only battling the outer effect. It is like cutting down the weed instead of getting the root out. So before you begin the New Thought Pattern affirmations, work on the WILLINGNESS TO RELEASE THE NEED for the cigarettes, or the headache, or the excess weight, or whatever. When the need is gone, the outer effect must die. No plant can live if the root is cut away.

The mental thought patterns that cause the most disease in the body are CRITICISM, ANGER, RESENTMENT and GUILT. For instance, criticism indulged in long enough will often lead to diseases such as arthritis. Anger turns into things that boil and burn and infect the body. Resentment long held festers and eats away at the self and ultimately can lead to tumours and cancer. Guilt always seeks punishment and leads to pain. It is so much easier to release these negative thinking patterns from our minds when we are healthy than to try to dig them out when we are in a state of panic and under the threat of the surgeon's knife.

The following list of mental equivalents has been compiled from many years of study, my own work with clients, and my lectures and work-shops. It is helpful as a quick-reference guide to the probable mental patterns behind the disease in your body. I offer these with love and a desire to share this simple method of helping to *Heal Your Body*.

Healing affirmations

Problem	Probable cause	New thought pattern
Abdominal Cramps	Fear. Stopping the process.	*I trust the process of life. I am safe.*
Abscess	Fermenting thoughts over hurts, slights and revenge.	*I allow my thoughts to be free. The past is over. I am at peace.*
Accidents	Inability to speak up for the self. Rebellion against authority. Belief in violence.	*I release the pattern in me that created this. I am at peace. I am worthwhile.*
Aches	Longing for love. Longing to be held.	*I love and approve of myself. I am loving and lovable.*
Acne	Not accepting the self. Dislike of the self.	*I am a Divine expression of life. I love and accept myself where I am right now.*

Addictions	Running from the self. Fear. Not knowing how to love the self.	*I now discover how wonderful I am. I choose to love and enjoy myself.*
Addison's Disease See: Adrenal Problems	Severe emotional malnutrition. Anger at the self.	*I lovingly take care of my body, my mind and my emotions.*
Adenoids	Family friction, arguments. Child feeling unwelcome, in the way.	*This child is wanted and welcomed and deeply loved.*
Adrenal Problems See: Addison's Disease	Defeatism. No longer caring for the self. Anxiety.	*I love and approve of myself. It is safe for me to care for myself.*
Aging Problems	Social beliefs. Old thinking. Fear of being one's self. Rejection of the now.	*I love and accept myself at every age. Each moment in life is perfect.*
AIDS	Feeling defenceless and hopeless. Nobody cares. A strong belief in not being good enough. Denial of the self. Sexual guilt.	*I am part of the Universal design. I am important and I am loved by Life itself. I am powerful and capable. I love and appreciate all of myself.*
Alcoholism	'What's the use?' Feeling of futility, guilt, inadequacy. Self-rejection.	*I live in the now. Each moment is new. I choose to see my self-worth. I love and approve of myself.*

Edgar Cayce – The Sleeping Prophet

THOMAS SUGRUE
There is a River

The important figure here is Edgar Cayce whose biography was written by Thomas Sugrue. Cayce is one of the most crucial figures in the American holistic and New Age movement. He had the ability, while in a sleeping trance, to give absolutely accurate medical diagnoses and to prescribe totally appropriate treatments which used all available therapies. He successfully treated many thousands of patients and, despite many attempts to expose him, his reputation maintained complete integrity. His 'miracles' helped both the public and many in the medical profession open up to new and more holistic approaches.

It was a quiet Sunday night in Montgomery, Alabama, late in October, 1910. A photographer of the H. P. Tressler staff, returning from a week's trip into the country, entered the studio building and trudged upstairs, lugging his equipment. He was a slim, tired-looking young man, with long legs and arms and a round, boyish face that made him seem younger than his thirty-three years.

A light was burning in the reception room of the studio. A man was curled up in one of the easy chairs, dozing. He leaped to his feet when the photographer walked in.

'Are you Edgar Cayce?' he asked.

The photographer nodded. 'Yes,' he said.

'We've been looking all over for you,' the man said. 'You're famous.'

He pulled a fistful of clippings from his pocket.

'*New York Times*, St Louis *Post-Dispatch*, Denver *Post*, Kansas City *Star* . . .'

He handed the clippings to Edgar. The first one was a page from the *New York Times* of Sunday, 9 October. From it stared two pictures that were familiar – they hung on the walls of the Cayce living room in Hopkinsville. One was of Edgar, the other of the squire. Between them on the newspaper page was a picture of Ketchum. A streamer headline said: ILLITERATE MAN BECOMES A DOCTOR WHEN HYPNOTIZED – STRANGE POWER SHOWN BY EDGAR CAYCE PUZZLES PHYSICIANS.

Edgar sank into a chair and began to read:

The medical fraternity of the country is taking a lively interest in the strange power said to be possessed by Edgar Cayce of Hopkinsville, Ky., to diagnose difficult diseases while in a semi-conscious state, though he has not the slightest knowledge of medicine when not in that condition. [. . .]

The first patient was admitted next day. He was an old friend of Edgar's, an engineer engaged in the construction of coke furnaces. In trying to finish a job within the allotted time he had overworked himself, caught cold, and neglected it. He had a chronic sinus irritation and his blood showed diabetic tendencies. His reading suggested baths, packs, osteopathy, medicine, and diet. The treatments were carried out; in two weeks a check reading discharged him as sufficiently well to go back to work, providing he continued some of the treatment at home.

To Edgar there was a peculiar joy in seeing all the treatments suggested by a reading carried out, with co-operation between the people administering them and an attempt to harmonize their effects on the patient.

Over the years certain ideas about health, the causes of disease, and cures, had been repeated over and over again in readings. There was a compound that was given for every person suffering from pyorrhoea; there was an inhalant suggested for one of the three types of hay fever; there was a salve for haemorrhoids; there were castor oil packs for appendicitis and intestinal complications; there were grape poultices for intestinal fevers; there was the suggestion to some people that they eat a few almonds a day to thwart a tendency towards cancer; there was the suggestion to others that they massage peanut oil into their skin to head off arthritis; there was a dose which time and again had proved efficacious in breaking up a common cold.

At the hospital these and other remedies could be checked and rechecked until their value was beyond doubt. Then they could be turned over to the medical profession and the public. There were skin lotions, intestinal antiseptics, treatments for stimulating the growth of hair, diets helpful to certain conditions, and mechanical appliances.

Two general types of appliance had for many years been prescribed in readings. One, the radioactive, was connected so that the electrical current of the body passed through the appliance, which acted as a transformer, sending the current back at a regular rate of impulse. In cases where the circulation was impaired, this meant a speeding up; where the circulation was too rapid, it meant a slowing down. This device was often specified in circulatory conditions, and for nervous disorders.

The other type, the wet cell, operated on the theory that a very low electrical charge set up in an ordinary wet solution of acid, metal, and copper sulphate can be discharged through solutions of gold chloride, camphor, iodine, etc., and the vibratory impulse can be carried to the body, causing it to extract more of the particular property in the solution from its digested foods. In commenting on the theory behind this, a reading said:

'The human body is made up of electronic vibrations, with each atom and element of the body, each organ and organism, having its electronic unit of vibration necessary for the sustenance of, and equilibrium in, that particular organism. Each unit, then, being a cell or a unit of life in itself has its capacity of reproducing itself by the first law as is known of reproduction-division. When a force in any organ, or element of the body, becomes deficient in its ability to reproduce that equilibrium necessary for the sustenance of the physical existence and its reproduction, that portion becomes deficient in electronic energy. This may come by injury or by disease, received from external forces. It may come from internal forces through lack of eliminations produced in the system, or by the lack of other agencies to meet its requirements in the body.'

These appliances, now properly built and maintained, were in the hospital, along with cabinets where sweat baths could be had while the fumes of needed elements enveloped the body, entering it through the opened pores.

There was all the regular equipment of a hospital, of course, and the orthodox physiotherapy laboratory: sinusoidal machines, ultraviolet and infra-red lamps, baths, cabinets, rubbing tables. Dr House, being both a medical doctor and an osteopath, supervised the allopathic treatments and administered the mechanical adjustments. Mrs House saw to it that each patient's diet was kept; she had charge of the kitchen and dining room. The nurses, in addition to their ordinary duties, learned to give the rubs prescribed for certain patients and took others to the beach – weather permitting – for sand packs. Hot sand was packed around a body wet with sea water. The readings said the sand at Virginia Beach had a large gold content and was highly radio-active.

When summer came the boys were put to work. Hugh Lynn and Tommy took over the job of acquainting newcomers and visitors with the history and theory of the readings. Gray, who liked to build things, took over the manufacture of radioactive appliances and the maintenance of the electrical machines.

'I don't see any use in going to college, Edgar,' he said; 'I can learn more here about the things that interest me than any school can teach me.'

'Good,' Edgar said. 'You can build yourself a workshop out back.'

Work was begun on several medicines which, though the procedure was clearly outlined in readings, were difficult to produce. Two of these were carbon ash and animated ash. In each case the ash had to be that of the wood of a bamboo tree, burned with the flame of a carbon lamp, and treated in a vacuum. These were to be taken internally, for such things as tuberculosis.

The readings had always been democratic in the selection of medi-cines as they were in the selection of treatments. No drug manufacturer was shown the slightest favour. Smith's preparation for one ailment might be preferred, while his product for another trouble was snubbed in favour of that of his rival, Jones. Often the readings suggested uses for the drugs which were not listed by the manufacturer. In one instance they helped the chemist perfect his formula, and then put it to a use which had not entered the inventor's head.

The chemist was a distinguished and learned Hindu, Dr Sunker A. Bisey, who had won his doctorate in chemistry at Oxford University in England. He had been concerned for years with the problem of producing iodine in a form that could be taken internally in doses large enough to have an appreciable effect on diseases caused by its lack in the body.

He had himself been psychic since birth, and was in the habit of taking his problems to bed with him, and sleeping on them. When he heard of Edgar and came to him with the problem of 'atomic iodine', the formula was almost perfected. The readings offered suggestions, and whether it was these or Dr Bisey's dreams, or his continued laboratory experiments, the product was eventually marketed successfully as Atomidine. Promptly the readings began to prescribe it for infantile paralysis, particularly as a preventive for this disease in times of epidemic. Dr Bisey hadn't thought of such a use: the readings gave the cause of infantile paralysis as a filterable virus which can enter the body through the mucous membranes (being carried in the air), or even by way of the sensitive skin under the arms, or in drinking water.

The explanation of infantile paralysis was only one of the things which Edgar felt hopeless about, so far as the world was concerned. Even with a hospital, how could such a thing be proved? How could anyone prove the statement that the appendix and tonsils should not be removed, because they act as focal points for poisons, gathering and sending them out through the proper channels? Only when overloaded to the point of breaking down should they be removed, the readings said, and such a breaking down meant that some part of the body was overproducing waste material.

What about the implication of a cycle in the metabolism of each body? The readings gave medicines in cycles: ten days, then a three-day rest, for example. Or, 'For this body it is best to take the prescription on Tuesdays and Thursdays.'

'Maybe science will discover those things someday,' Mrs House would say as they sat on the hospital porch after dinner.

'Keep the records,' Dr House would say. 'Keep everything. Someday they'll catch up with us.'

'If they do, and the records are here, that will at least prove that psychic phenomena aren't frauds,' Edgar would say.

Healing Herbs

DAVID HOFFMANN
The Holistic Herbal

Originally an academic in the field of ecology, David Hoffmann realized that he needed to be more directly involved in his work and became a student then practitioner of medical herbalism. Although many herbals have been published, *The Holistic Herbal* was instrumental in placing the ancient art of herbalism into a contemporary context.

'He causeth the grass to grow for the cattle, and herbs for the service of man.'
Psalm 104:14

Herbs, which comprise much of the realm of plants, are an interface within the body of Gaia. They are an interface between two realms of nature. Where humanity and plants meet, a synergistic energy can be created and exchanged. At such a point inner and outer ecology may resonate and become attuned. We have then an ecologically-integrated process that heals and harmonizes the inner environment (the human body) while being produced by an outer harmonized environment (nature).

Flowering plants first appeared in geological history during the Cretaceous period, about 135 million years ago. It took them only a very short period of time to diversify into the main flowering plant families we know today. This baffled botanists for a long time until they recognized that the plants evolved within the context of an ecological whole and not as isolated individuals. They evolved within the ecosystem they lived in. The rapid diversification took place through the interaction of plants and insects. The interface between plant and animal realms provided the evolutionary drive.

With the concept of Gaia in mind, we can see that evolution is an exercise in cooperation as well as one of competition, both processes forming a web of interactions and producing the complex tapestry of today's ecology, an interwoven dynamic system. The ecosystem can only be understood as a whole – as one integrated and self-maintaining unit. All that is needed for the maintenance of any part of the whole is supplied by it; in fact *has* to be supplied by the system, since there is nothing outside it. If the system did not take care of itself, it would not be viable and could not survive.

A specific example is the phenomenon of secondary plant products. A number of plants produce a range of complex chemicals that play no identifiable role within the metabolism of that plant; we call them secondary plant products. The only way to explain their function within the individual plant scientifically is to assume that it is a very complex way of isolating waste matter accumulated from the metabolic process of the plant, and this would be totally out of keeping with the genius of the realm of plants for efficiency and design.

Secondary plant products such as the alkaloids, the glycosides and many other groups have a strong and marked influence on human and animal physiology. They are the agents that distinguish herbs from other plants, as pharmaceutical chemists are finding out. This is not merely a fortuitous accident. It is in fact the hallmark of Gaia. By eating plants we are linked to a circulatory system within the biosphere and to the energy source of the sun, since plants synthesize their own nutrition via sunlight. The secondary plant products are taking part in this circulation to reach us and to facilitate homeostasis. In a profound and ingenious way, our food can be our healing.

The realm of plants provides everything our body needs for a balanced and integrated existence. However, we are more than just a body: we also have consciousness, which brings other factors on to the stage. We not only have to take our animal body into consideration, but also our emotions, our mind and our spiritual nature. Harmony is no longer simply a matter of right diet or even right herbs, but also a matter of right feelings, right thoughts, lifestyle, attunement, actions – harmony of right relationship to our world and ourselves. Choice comes into the healing process when we see which of these areas we need to work with most.

It is impossible to generalize about the relative value of techniques that work with the physical body, with the emotions or spiritual energies. All have their role and can work together for healing to take place. It can be said that health lies in correct diet, or right use of allopathic drugs, or a free flow of soul energy. All these statements are correct and all of them are relative.

Where does herbal medicine fit into this picture? By the nature of the plant form, herbs work on the physical body. They are acting to integrate and balance its physiological function and to augment its innate vitality. When the body is balanced, the process of integrating the other aspects of our being is helped and catalysed. While herbs will not replace relevant techniques like counselling or meditation, they will help the chalice of the body to be strong, receptive and supportive of the subtler aspects of human life.

Ecosystems and the biosphere

Every culture throughout the world – until very recently – used healing plants as the basis for their medicine. The therapeutic philosophy and rationale for plant use varies, but for thousands of years plants have demonstrated their efficiency and significance.

Each culture had a basic healing flora from which remedies were selected. This range of plants would vary from area to area depending on the local ecosystem. It is remarkable, however, to look at Wales, southern India, the North American plains or any other area and find herbs with equivalent actions. The plant species, or even the botanical types might be totally different, but the range of human problems that can be dealt with botanically is the same. While this supports the idea of Gaia providing a context for healing with the aid of herbs, it raises the question of whether today we should always stick to the flora provided by the local ecosystem within which we live.

The ecosystem available to us is no longer a local one, just as our human culture and consciousness is no longer a local one. We have become planetary beings, though not necessarily yet out of our own choice. Our food may come from anywhere in the world and modern information technology brings the world into our homes, opening our thoughts and emotional lives to a wide range of influences. We are already in many ways planetary citizens. As planetary beings within the body of Gaia, the whole of the world's flora is available to us and rightly so.

We also have to consider human impact on local ecosystems. In

Wales, for example, it used to be possible to obtain a large range of plants in natural habitats. Nowadays, due to intensive agriculture, to deforestation and reafforestation with foreign conifers, and the expansion and industrialization of towns, there are few truly natural and wild habitats left: the range of plants available to us locally is therefore greatly reduced. This has been part of the ecological impact of humanity, unaware as it has been of whole systems and the value of their interrelationships.

Herbs in healing

The potent healing qualities of herbs have been used in different therapeutic philosophies throughout history. We find plants used within the Indian ayurvedic system, in Chinese medicine alongside acupuncture and other techniques. They play a very important role in the spiritual healing ecology of the North American Indians. We see them being used as a source of drugs in the highly scientific and technological approach of modern pharmacy and allopathic medicine.

In fact allopathic medicine, now often called 'orthodox' medicine, has its roots in the use of herbs. Until about fifty years ago, nearly all the entries in pharmacopoeia describing the manufacture of drugs indicate a herbal origin. Only since the refinement of chemical technology and developments in chemotherapy has the use of herbs apparently diminished. Nonetheless it should be recognized that a majority of drugs still have their origin in plant material. Some very simple examples will illustrate this.

The amphetamines, which are based on the alkaloid ephedrine, supply stimulants and anti-asthmatic drugs and play an important role in medicine. Their exploitation followed the discovery of the active ingredient ephedrine in the Chinese herb Ma Huang, *Ephedra sinica*. The steroid drugs, the wonder drugs of the sixties now known to have unfortunate side effects, are still synthesized from a chemical extracted from the West African Wild Yam, *Dioscorea sp*. Aspirin, too, was discovered in the last century from a number of plants like Meadowsweet and Black Willow. In fact its name comes from the old botanical name of Meadowsweet, *Spirea*.

So we see that allopathic medicine still uses herbs, if in a limited way. Plants are approached as a source of active ingredients, specific bio-active chemicals that can be analysed, synthesized and used in the form of potent drugs. The body is seen as being essentially biochemical in nature, so when something goes wrong, it does so on the level of chemical processes and molecules. To get it to work correctly we thus have to use chemicals. If such an attitude is correct, why not use isolated constituents from plants? After all, nature provides powerful agents like morphine, still one of the best painkillers known, so why not approach plants this way? In the context of the scientific approach, to view the human being as a biochemical laboratory where specific chemicals have specific effects seems justified and valid.

But can we really reduce a human being to the level of molecules? The human being surpasses description in its beauty and dynamic complexity of form and function, in potential expression and creativity. Of course on the level of physical form our body is *also* biochemical, but its organization transcends by far the realms of biochemistry textbooks. Even if we were to comprehend fully the molecular complexities, we would not find what makes us human. There is a powerful and synergistic force at work within us – call it life, life force, vital force or other names – that *is* us and is involved with the whole of us on all levels, not just the biochemical. At death the same chemicals are present, but this energy of life and synthesis has gone. It is impossible to define this force, but the holistic approach is based on and works with a vision of humanity as animated by it.

Herbal medicine in its holistic sense recognizes humanity as an expression of life, enlivened with life force, and herbs can work with this whole being, not just specific symptoms. They do function through biochemical interactions and specific applications, but they do so in a way that augments the vital processes of the body. On the biochemical level, the numerous ingredients in a herb work in a synergistic way, with elements involved in the process that chemotherapy would not even consider as being active.

If we just looked at herbs as a source of valuable chemicals we would limit their healing power, for beyond the physical level they can also work on the level of the life force. As they heal our bodies, they may also heal our hearts and minds, for they open the body to a clear flow of integrating and synergistic vital energy.

Love

M. SCOTT PECK
The Road Less Traveled

The Road Less Traveled is one of the biggest selling self-help books in the holistic movement. Scott Peck is a dedicated Christian and was a psychiatrist in the US army. To his surprise he has become the most well-known and successful guru of the holistic culture. He gives both psychological and spiritual counsel without pandering to a search for quick-fixes or comfortable narcissism.

Love defined

Discipline, it has been suggested, is the means of human spiritual evolution. This section will examine what lies in back of discipline – what provides the motive, the energy for discipline. This force I believe to be love. I am very conscious of the fact that in attempting to examine love we will be beginning to toy with mystery. In a very real sense we will be attempting to examine the unexaminable and to know the unknowable. Love is too large, too deep ever to be truly understood or measured or limited within the framework of words. I would not write this if I did not believe the attempt to have value, but no matter how valuable, I begin with the certain knowledge that the attempt will be in some ways inadequate.

One result of the mysterious nature of love is that no one has ever, to my knowledge, arrived at a truly satisfactory definition of love. In an effort to explain it, therefore, love has been divided into various categories: eros, philia, agape; perfect love and imperfect love, and so on. I am presuming, however, to give a single definition of love, again with the awareness that it is likely to be in some way or ways inadequate. I define love thus: the will to extend one's self for the purpose of nurturing one's own or another's spiritual growth.

At the outset I would like to comment briefly on this definition before proceeding to a more thorough elaboration. First, it may be noticed that it is a teleological definition; the behaviour is defined in terms of the goal or purpose it seems to serve – in this case, spiritual growth. Scientists tend to hold teleological definitions suspect, and perhaps they will this one. I did not arrive at it, however, through a clearly teleological process of thinking. Instead I arrived at it through observation in my clinical practice of psychiatry (which includes self-observation), in which the definition of love is a matter of considerable import. This is because patients are generally very confused as to the nature of love. For instance, a timid young man reported to me: 'My mother loved me so much she wouldn't let me take the school bus to school until my senior year in high school. Even then I had to beg her to let me go. I guess she was afraid that I would get hurt, so she drove me to and from school every day, which was very hard on her. She really loved me.' In the treatment of this individual's timidity it was necessary, as it is in many other cases, to teach him that his mother might have been motivated by something other than love, and that what seems to be love is often not love at all. It has been out of such experience that I accumulated a body of examples of what seemed to be acts of love and what seemed not to be love. One of the major distinguishing features between the two seemed to be the conscious or unconscious purpose in the mind of the lover or nonlover.

Second, it may be noticed that, as defined, love is a strangely circular process. For the process of extending one's self is an evolutionary process. When one has successfully extended one's limits, one has then grown into a larger state of being. Thus the act of loving is an act of self-evolution even when the purpose of the act is someone else's growth. It is through reaching towards evolution that we evolve.

Third, this unitary definition of love includes self-love with love for the other. Since I am human and you are human, to love humans means to love myself as well as you. To be dedicated to human spiritual development is to be dedicated to the race of which we are a part, and this therefore means dedication to our own development as well as 'theirs'. Indeed, as has been pointed out, we are incapable of loving another unless we love ourselves, just as we are incapable of teaching our children self-discipline unless we ourselves are self-disciplined. It is actually impossible to forsake our own spiritual development in favour of someone else's. We cannot forsake self-discipline and at the same time be disciplined in our care for another. We cannot be a source of strength unless we nurture our own strength. As we proceed in our exploration of the nature of love, I believe it will become clear that not only do self-love and love of others go hand in hand but that ultimately they are indistinguishable.

Fourth, the act of extending one's limits implies effort. One extends one's limits only by exceeding them, and exceeding limits requires effort. When we love someone our love becomes demonstrable or real only through our exertion – through the fact that for that someone (or for ourself) we take an extra step or walk an extra mile. Love is not effortless. To the contrary, love is effortful.

Finally, by use of the word 'will' I have attempted to transcend the distinction between desire and action. Desire is not necessarily translated into action. Will is desire of sufficient intensity that it *is* translated into action. The difference between the two is equal to the difference between saying 'I would like to go swimming tonight' and 'I will go swimming tonight.' Everyone in our culture desires to some extent to be loving, yet many are not in fact loving. I therefore conclude that the desire to love is not itself love. Love is as love does. Love is an act of will – namely, both an intention and an action. Will also implies choice. We do not have to love. We choose to love. No matter how much we may think we are loving, if we are in fact not loving, it is because we have chosen not to love and therefore do not love despite our good intentions. On the other hand, whenever we do actually exert ourselves in the cause of spiritual growth, it is because we have chosen to do so. The choice to love has been made. [...]

In some respects (but certainly not in all) the act of falling in love is an act of regression. The experience of merging with the loved one has in it echoes from the time when we were merged with our mothers in infancy. Along with the merging we also re-experience the sense of omnipotence which we had to give up in our journey out of childhood. All things seem possible! United with our beloved we feel we can conquer all obstacles. We believe that the strength of our love will cause the forces of opposition to bow down in submission and melt away into the darkness. All problems will be overcome. The future will be all light. The unreality of these feelings when we have fallen in love is essentially the same as the unreality of the two-year-old who feels itself to be king of the family and the world with power unlimited.

Just as reality intrudes upon the two-year-old's fantasy of omnipotence so does reality intrude upon the fantastic unity of the couple who have fallen in love. Sooner or later, in response to the problems of daily living, individual will reassert itself. He wants to have sex; she doesn't. She wants to go to the movies; he doesn't. He wants to put money in the bank; she wants a dishwasher. She wants to talk about her job; he wants to talk about his. She doesn't like his friends; he doesn't like hers. So both of them, in the privacy of their hearts, begin to come to the sickening realization that they are not one with the beloved, that the beloved has and will continue to have his or her own desires, tastes, prejudices and timing different from the other's. One by one, gradually or suddenly, the ego boundaries snap back into place; gradually or suddenly, they fall out of love. Once again they are two separate individuals. At this point they begin either to dissolve the ties of their relationship or to initiate the work of real loving.

By my use of the word 'real' I am implying that the perception that we are loving when we fall in love is a false perception – that our subjective sense of lovingness is an illusion. Full elaboration of real love will be deferred until later in this section. However, by stating that it is when a couple falls out of love they may begin to really love I am also implying that real love does not have its roots in a feeling of love. To the contrary, real love often occurs in a context in which the feeling of love is lacking, when we act lovingly despite the fact that we don't feel loving. Assuming the reality of the definition of love with which we started, the experience of 'falling in love' is not real love for the several reasons that follow.

Falling in love is not an act of will. It is not a conscious choice. No matter how open to or eager for it we may be, the experience may still elude us. Contrarily, the experience may capture us at times when we are definitely not seeking it, when it is inconvenient and undesirable. We are as likely to fall in love with someone with whom we are obviously ill matched as with someone more suitable. Indeed, we may not even like or admire the object of our passion, yet, try as we might, we may not be able to fall in love with a person whom we deeply respect and with whom a deep relationship would be in all ways desirable. This is not to say that the experience of falling in love is immune to discipline. Psychiatrists, for instance, frequently fall in love with their patients, just as their patients fall in love with them, yet out of duty to the patient and their role they are usually able to abort the collapse of their ego boundaries and give up the patient as a romantic object. The struggle and suffering of the discipline involved may be enormous. But discipline and will can only control the experience; they cannot create it. We can choose how to respond to the experience of falling in love, but we cannot choose the experience itself.

Falling in love is not an extension of one's limits or boundaries; it is a partial and temporary collapse of them. The extension of one's limits requires effort; falling in love is effortless. Lazy and undisciplined individuals are as likely to fall in love as energetic and dedicated ones. Once the precious moment of falling in love has passed and the boundaries have snapped back into place, the individual may be disillusioned, but is usually none the larger for the experience. When limits are extended or stretched, however, they tend to stay stretched. Real love is a permanently self-enlarging experience. Falling in love is not.

Falling in love has little to do with purposively nurturing one's spiritual development. If we have any purpose in mind when we fall in love it is to terminate our own loneliness and perhaps ensure this result through marriage. Certainly we are not thinking of spiritual development. Indeed, after we have fallen in love and before we have fallen out of love again we feel that we have arrived, that the heights have been attained, that there is both no need and no possibility of going higher. We do not feel ourselves to be in any need of development; we are totally content to be where we are. Our spirit is at peace. Nor do we perceive our beloved as being in need of spiritual development. To the contrary, we perceive him or her as perfect, as having been perfected. If we see any faults in our beloved, we perceive them as insignificant – little quirks or darling eccentricities that only add colour and charm.

Aging

DEEPAK CHOPRA
Ageless Body, Timeless Mind

Deepak Chopra is a medical doctor with a specialist background in endocrinology and the Ayurvedic tradition of Asian Indian medicine. His background also includes a close involvement with the Transcendental Meditation schools. Through his bestselling books, lectures and workshops, he was the most visible and influential proponent of the holistic approach to healthcare in the 1980s and 1990s.

1. There is no objective world independent of the observer

The world you accept as real seems to have definite qualities. Some things are large, others small; some things are hard, others soft. Yet none of these qualities means anything outside of your perception. Take any object, such as a folding chair. To you the chair isn't very large, but to an ant it is immense. To you the chair feels hard, but a neutrino would whiz through it without slowing down, because to a subatomic particle the chair's atoms are miles apart. The chair seems stationary to you, but if you observed it from outer space, you would see it revolving past you, along with everything else on Earth, at a thousand miles per hour. Likewise, anything else you can describe about the chair can be completely altered simply by changing your perception. If the chair is red, you can make it appear black by looking at it through green glasses. If the chair weighs five pounds, you can make it weigh two pounds by putting it on the moon or a hundred thousand pounds by putting it in the gravitational field of a dense star.

Because there are no absolute qualities in the material world, it is false to say that there even is an independent world 'out there'. The world is a reflection of the sensory apparatus that registers it. The human nervous system takes in only the most minute fraction, less than one part per billion, of the total energy vibrating in the environment. Other nervous systems, such as that of a bat or a snake, reflect a different world, coexisting with ours. The bat senses a world of ultrasound, the snake a world of infra-red light, both of which are hidden from us.

All that is really 'out there' is raw, unformed data waiting to be interpreted by you, the perceiver. You take 'a radically ambiguous, flowing quantum soup', as physicists call it, and use your senses to congeal the soup into the solid three-dimensional world. The eminent British neurologist, Sir John Eccles, pierces the sensory illusion with one startling but irrefutable assertion: 'I want you to realize that there is no colour in the natural world and no sound – nothing of this kind; no textures, no patterns, no beauty, no scent . . .' In short, none of the objective facts upon which we usually base our reality is fundamentally valid.

As disturbing as this may sound, there is incredible liberation in realizing that you can change your world – including your body – *simply by changing your perception*. How you perceive yourself is causing immense changes in your body right now. To give an example: in America and England, mandatory retirement at age sixty-five sets an arbitrary cut-off date for social usefulness. The day before a worker turns sixty-five, he contributes labour and value to society; the day after, he becomes one of society's dependants. Medically, the results of this perceptual shift can be disastrous. In the first few years after retirement, heart attack and cancer rates soar, and early death overtakes men who were otherwise healthy before they retired. 'Early retirement death', as the syndrome is called, depends on the perception that one's useful days are over; this is only a perception, but for someone who holds it firmly, it is enough to create disease and death. By comparison, in societies where old age is accepted as part of the social fabric, elders remain extremely vigorous – lifting, climbing, and bending in ways that we do not accept as normal in our elderly.

If you examine old cells, such as ones that form liver spots on the skin, through a high-powered microscope, the scene is as devastated as a war zone. Fibrous streaks run here and there; deposits of fat and undiscarded metabolic wastes form unsightly clumps; dark, yellowish pigments called lipofuscin have accumulated to the point where they litter ten to thirty per cent of the cell's interior.

This scene of devastation was created by subcellular processes that went wrong, but if you look through less materialistic lenses, you will see that old cells are like maps of a person's experience. Things that made you suffer are imprinted there, along with things that brought you joy. Stresses you long ago forgot on the conscious level are still sending out signals, like buried microchips, making you anxious, tense, fatigued, apprehensive, resentful, doubtful, disappointed – these reactions cross the mind-body barrier to become part of you. The clogged, toxic deposits in old cells don't appear uniformly; some people acquire much more than others, even when there is little genetic difference between them. By the time you reach age seventy, your cells will look unique, mirroring the unique experiences you processed and metabolized into your tissues and organs.

Being able to process the raw, chaotic vibrations of the 'quantum soup' and turn them into meaningful, orderly bits of reality opens up enormous creative possibilities. However, these possibilities exist only when you are aware of them. While you are reading this book, a huge portion of your consciousness is engaged in creating your body without your participation. The so-called involuntary or autonomic nervous system was designed to control functions that have slipped out of your awareness. If you began walking down the street in a daze, the involuntary centres in your brain would still be coping with the world, keeping on the lookout for danger, poised to activate the stress response at a moment's notice.

A hundred things you pay no attention to – breathing, digesting, growing new cells, repairing damaged old ones, purifying toxins, preserving hormonal balance, converting stored energy from fat to blood sugar, dilating the pupils of the eyes, raising and lowering blood pressure, maintaining steady body temperature, balancing as you walk, shunting blood to and from the muscle groups that are doing the most work, and sensing movements and sounds in the surrounding environment – continue ceaselessly.

These automatic processes play a huge part in aging, for as we age, our ability to coordinate these functions declines. A lifetime of unconscious living leads to numerous deteriorations, while a lifetime of conscious participation prevents them. The very act of paying conscious attention to bodily functions instead of leaving them on automatic pilot will change how you age. Every so-called involuntary function, from heartbeat and breathing to digestion and hormone regulation, can be consciously controlled. The era of biofeedback and meditation has taught us that – heart patients have been trained in mind-body laboratories to lower their blood pressure at will or to reduce the acid secretions that create ulcers, among dozens of other things. Why not put this ability to use in the aging process? Why not exchange old patterns of perception for new ones? There are abundant techniques, as we will see, for influencing the involuntary nervous system to our advantage.

2. Our bodies are composed of energy and information

To transform the patterns of the past you must know what they are made of. Your body appears to be composed of solid matter that can be broken down into molecules and atoms, but quantum physics tells us that every atom is more than 99.9999 per cent empty space, and the subatomic particles moving at lightning speed through this space are actually bundles of vibrating energy. These vibrations aren't random and meaningless, however; they carry information. Thus, one bundle of vibrations is coded as a hydrogen atom, another as oxygen; each element is in fact its own unique code.

Codes are abstract, and so ultimately is our cosmos and everything in it. Chasing the physical structure of the body down to its ultimate source dead-ends as molecules give way to atoms, atoms to subatomic particles, and these particles to ghosts of energy dissolving into an empty void. This void is mysteriously imprinted with information even before any information is expressed. Just as thousands of words exist silently in your memory without being spoken, the quantum field holds the entire universe in unexpressed form; it has been that way since the Big Bang, when billions of galaxies were compressed into a space millions of times smaller than the period at the end of this sentence. Yet even before that infinitesimal dot, the structure of the universe existed in unmanifest form.

The essential stuff of the universe, including your body, is non-stuff, but it isn't ordinary non-stuff. It is thinking non-stuff. The void inside every atom is pulsating with unseen intelligence. Geneticists locate this intelligence primarily inside DNA, but that is only for the sake of convenience. Life unfolds as DNA imparts its coded intelligence to its active twin, RNA, which in turn goes out into the cell and imparts bits of intelligence to thousands of enzymes, which then use their specific bit of intelligence to make proteins. At every point in this sequence, energy and information have to be exchanged or there could be no building life from lifeless matter.

The human body derives its primary energy by burning sugar, which is transported to the cells in the form of glucose, or blood sugar. The chemical structure of glucose is closely related to common table sugar, sucrose. But if you burn table sugar, you don't get the exquisite, complex structures of a living cell; you just get a charred lump of ash and traces of water and carbon dioxide in the air.

Metabolism is more than a burning process; it is an intelligent act. The same sugar that remains inert in a sugar cube supports life with its energy because the body's cells infuse it with new information. The sugar may contribute its energy to a kidney, heart, or brain cell, for example. All of these cells contain completely unique forms of intelligence – the rhythmic twitching of a heart cell is completely different from the electrical discharges of a brain cell or the sodium exchanges of a kidney cell.

As marvellous as this wealth of diverse intelligence is, at bottom there is one single intelligence shared by the whole body. The flow of this intelligence keeps you alive, and when it ceases to flow, at the moment of death, all the knowledge stored in your DNA is rendered useless. As we age, this flow of intelligence becomes compromised in various ways. The specific intelligence of the immune system, the nervous system, and the endocrine system all start falling off; these three systems are now known by physiologists to function as the master controls of the body. Your immune cells and endocrine glands are outfitted with the same receptors for brain signals as your neurons are; therefore, they are like an extended brain. Senility cannot be looked upon, then, simply as a disease confined to our grey matter; when intelligence is lost in the immune or the endocrine system, senility of the whole body is creeping in.

Since all this happens at an unseen, unmanifest level, the losses go unnoticed until they have progressed to a very late stage and are expressed as a physical symptom. The five senses cannot go deep enough to experience the billions of quantum exchanges that create aging. The rate of change is at once too fast and too slow: too fast because individual chemical reactions take less than 1/10,000th of a second, too slow because their cumulative effect will not show up for years. These reactions involve information and energy on a scale millions of times smaller than a single atom.

Age deterioration would be unavoidable if the body was simply material, because all material things are prey to entropy, the tendency of orderly systems to become disorderly. The classic example of entropy is a car rusting in a junkyard; entropy breaks down the orderly machinery into crumbling rust. There is no chance that the process will work the other way – that a rusty scrap heap will reassemble itself into a new car. But entropy doesn't apply to intelligence – an invisible part of us is immune to the ravages of time. Modern science is just discovering the implications of all this, but it has been imparted for centuries through spiritual traditions in which masters have preserved the youthfulness of their bodies far into old age.

India, China, Japan, and to a lesser extent the Christian West have given birth to sages who realized their essential nature as a flow of intelligence. By preserving that flow and nurturing it year after year, they overcame entropy from a deeper level of Nature. In India, the flow of intelligence is called *Prana* (usually translated as 'life force'), which can be increased and decreased at will, moved here and there, and manipulated to keep the physical body orderly and young. As we will see, the ability to contact and use Prana is within all of us. A yogi moves Prana using nothing more than attention, for at a deep level, attention and Prana are the same – life is awareness, awareness is life.

3. Mind and body are inseparably one

Intelligence is much more flexible than the mask of matter that hides it. Intelligence can express itself either as thoughts or as molecules. A basic emotion such as fear can be described as an abstract feeling or as a tangible molecule of the hormone adrenalin. Without the feeling there is no hormone; without the hormone there is no feeling. In the same way, there is no pain without nerve signals that transmit pain; there is no relief from pain without endorphins that fit into the pain receptors to block those signals. The revolution we call mind-body medicine was based on this simple discovery: wherever thought goes, a chemical goes with it. This insight has turned into a powerful tool that allows us to understand, for example, why recent widows are twice as likely to develop breast cancer, and why the chronically depressed are four times more likely to get sick. In both cases, distressed mental states get converted into the biochemicals that create disease.

In my medical practice, I can see two heart patients afflicted with angina pectoris, the typical squeezing, breathless pain that is typical of heart disease. One patient will be able to run, swim, and perhaps even mountain-climb, totally ignoring his pain or not even having any, while the other nearly faints with pain when he gets up out of his armchair.

My first instinct will be to look for a physical difference between them, but I might or might not find anything. Cardiologists expect anginal pain to appear when at least one of the three coronary arteries is fifty per cent blocked. This blockage is almost always in the form of an atheroma, a lesion on the inside of the arterial wall built up by dead cells, blood clots, and fatty plaque. The fifty per cent blockage is only a rule of thumb, however. Some angina patients are disabled by pain when they have only a single small lesion barely obstructing blood flow in one artery, while other patients suffering from massive, multiple blockages of up to eighty-five per cent have been known to run marathons. (Angina is not always caused by physical blockage, I should add. Arteries are lined with a layer of muscle cells that can go into spasm and squeeze the vessel closed, but this is a highly individual reaction.)

In mind-body terms, my two patients are expressing their different interpretations of pain. Every patient stamps his condition with a unique perspective, and pain (or any other symptom) emerges into awareness only after it interacts with all the past influences at work in the mind-body system. There is no single response for all people or even for the same person at two different times. Pain signals are raw data that can be turned to many purposes. High-exertion athletics, such as long-distance running, subject an athlete to pain that he interprets as a sign of accomplishment ('no pain, no gain'); but the same pain, inflicted under other circumstances, would be completely unwelcome. Track runners admire a coach who pushes them to their limits; they might hate the same treatment in boot camp.

Medicine is just beginning to use the mind-body connection for healing – defeating pain is a good example. By giving a placebo, or dummy, drug, thirty per cent of patients will experience the same pain relief as if a real painkiller had been administered. But the mind-body effect is much more holistic. The same dummy pill can be used to kill pain, to stop excessive gastric secretions in ulcer patients, to lower blood pressure, or to fight tumours. (All the side effects of chemotherapy, including hair loss and nausea, can be induced by giving cancer patients a sugar pill while assuring them that it is a powerful anti-cancer drug, and there have been instances where injections of sterile saline solution have actually led to remissions of advanced malignancy.)

Since the same inert pill can lead to such totally different responses, we must conclude that the body is capable of producing *any* biochemical response once the mind has been given the appropriate suggestion. The pill itself is meaningless; the power that activates the placebo effect is the power of suggestion alone. This suggestion is then converted into the body's intention to cure itself. Therefore, why not bypass the deception of the sugar pill and go directly to the intention? If we could effectively trigger the intention not to age, the body would carry it out automatically.

We have extremely exciting evidence to prove that such a possibility exists. One of the most dreaded diseases of old age is Parkinson's, a neurological disorder that produces uncontrollable muscle movements and a drastic slowing down of bodily motions such as walking, eventually resulting in a body so stiff that the patient cannot move at all. Parkinson's has been traced to an unexplained depletion of a critical brain chemical called dopamine, but there is also a simulated Parkinson's caused when the dopamine-producing cells of the brain have been destroyed chemically by certain drugs. Imagine a patient afflicted with this type of Parkinson's in an advanced stage of frozen motion. Trying to walk, he can only take a step or two before halting in place, as stiff as a statue.

However, if you draw a line on the floor and say, 'Step over that', the person will miraculously be able to walk right over it. Despite the fact that the production of dopamine is completely involuntary and its stores are seemingly exhausted (as shown by the fact that his brain cannot signal his leg muscles to take another step), merely by having the intention to walk, the brain is awakened. The person may freeze again after only a few seconds, but again you can ask him to step over an imaginary line, and his brain will respond. By extension, the infirmity and inactivity exhibited by many old people is often just dormancy. By renewing their intention to live active, purposeful lives, many elderly people can dramatically improve their motor abilities, strength, agility, and mental responses.

Intention is the active partner of attention; it is the way we convert automatic processes into conscious ones. Using simple mind-body exercises, almost any patient can learn in a few sessions to convert a racing heartbeat, asthmatic wheezing, or free-floating anxiety into a more normal response. What seems out of control can be brought back into control with the proper technique. The implications for aging are enormous. By inserting an intention into your thought processes, such as, 'I want to improve in energy and vigour every day', you can begin to assert control over those brain centres that determine how much energy will be expressed in activity. The decline of vigour in old age is largely the result of people *expecting* to decline; they have unwittingly implanted a self-defeating intention in the form of a strong belief, and the mind-body connection automatically carries out this intention.

Our past intentions create obsolete programming that seems to have control over us. In truth, the power of intention can be reawakened at any time. Long before you get old, you can prevent such losses by consciously programming your mind to remain youthful, using the power of your intention.

Death and Healing

STEPHEN LEVINE

Who Dies?

Along with Elisabeth Kübler-Ross, Stephen Levine has been one of the most influential pioneers in opening up contemporary culture to a deeper and more compassionate understanding of death. He is a poet and teacher of meditation, a colleague of Ram Dass and Director of the Hanuman Foundation Dying Project. His work has helped to make clear the deep healings that can happen during people's approach to death.

The balance of the mind and heart is reflected in the body. When the heart and mind are not in harmony there sometimes occurs what we call disease (dis-ease). But I suspect this is not the only cause of illness. Many saintly beings have died of cancer (Ramana Maharshi, Suzuki Roshi, Ramakrishna). Some seem to take on illness as a means of purification, or as a friend put it, 'Cancer is the gift for the person who has everything.' It may be that for some beings illness does not arise out of disharmony but is a 'cleaning of the slate', a finishing of old business.

Healing is the title we give to the phenomenon of the mind and heart coming back into balance. When this harmony is restored we say that someone is healed. But often we have a preconception about what healing is. Our attachment to ideas of healthiness obstructs a deeper perspective on what illness and healing may be all about. The deepest healing seems to take us beyond identification with that which causes and experiences sickness.

A woman we know had worked very hard to overcome her cancer. After several months of meditation and deep psychological nit-picking it seemed as though the cancer was no longer present. For some months she felt strong and healthy and clear. Then one day in meditation she sensed the cancer once again in her body. Tests confirmed her intuition. A healing circle was called. Some of the most respected holistic and

Native American healing persons on the West Coast came to her home and formed a silent circle about her. For more than an hour they channelled their energy into her. Some in the room later related that the power was nearly palpable. A week later thirty new metastases, secondary tumours, appeared in different parts of her body. She said the healing had worked. She felt the next perfect step in her evolution had occurred. She prepared for death by continuing to open to life.

It appears that the balancing of the heart and mind can either displace illness from the body or in some cases draw that being into harmony outside the body. In either case, healing occurs. When the attachment to preconceived results is let go of, there is little to maintain imbalance. As our friend wryly noted one day, 'Survival is highly overrated.'

When the healer's priority becomes that each individual directly experiences their original nature, healing becomes a lens that focuses the potentialities of the moment. But if the priority is to change people, to 'heal them', to take something away from them, then perhaps the most that can be expected is that the body may become somewhat stronger, but the weakness in the mind, the clinging that has always obscured the heart, is not affected or encouraged to dissolve.

As long as we are thinking of healing as opposed to dying, there will be confusion. As long as we separate life from death, we separate the mind from the heart and we will always have something to protect, something more to be, another cause for inharmony and illness. When the attitude towards healing is in balance, the attitude towards death is as well.

As my friend said after she discovered the thirty new tumours, 'The healing worked. Now I see that for me the perfect healing is to open to whatever happens next with love and awareness. There is nothing for me to do but listen, open, and be.'

Sharing with various healers – nurses, doctors, herbalists, acupuncturists, psychics, polarity therapists, body workers, aura balancers, etc. – I have sensed at times a tendency, slight or grandiose, that they believed they were doing the healing. It is perhaps that state of pride and separateness that most obstructs the conduit for the healing powers always available in the universe. But the greater the sense of separateness, of 'someone doing something', the more attachment to results. They are not allowing healing, they are clamouring for it. But the heart closes in the presence of such personal force, and harmony becomes less likely. It is by surrendering into the underlying suchness that one seems to be able to make available the essential harmony of being to another. Anything that reinforces the feeling of the 'healed' as a separate entity removed from the universe intensifies the separation of heart and mind while it magnifies the fear of death and the disharmony that amplifies disease.

The true healer is invisible. He or she only allows the potential of the moment to come to fruition. Ramana Maharshi, the Indian saint and teacher, was known as a great healer. Thousands had come to him and gone away in balance. There is a story that one day a doctor from the northern part of India came to visit him and asked, 'I understand you are a great healer; I would like to know more about how you do it.' But Ramana replied with an honesty and pureness, 'No, I am not a healer, I don't heal anyone.' The visitor said, 'I've heard you have healed thousands.' Ramana seemed sort of bewildered and said, 'No, I don't heal.' At that point one of Ramana's devotees turned to him and said, 'Bhagwan, what I think the doctor means is that the healing comes through you.' 'Oh, yes! The healing comes through.' He wasn't playing a confrontation Zen game, he was just being who he was. He wasn't doing anything but allowing those energies which flourish in the universe to compassionately focus on any being who came near.

It is not unlike the story of the Tibetan lama Kalu Rinpoche, a much revered meditation master and teacher of incredible tenderness and fierce wisdom, who was visiting the home of a friend one day. He was approached by a number of people who were interested in the occult and various yogic powers that were rumoured possible by those who had undergone the initiations of his particular lineage. They asked him, 'Can you fly?' 'No,' he said. 'I don't fly.' 'Can you read the future and the past?' 'No, I don't read the future and the past.' The group was becoming perturbed and one of them turned to him and said, 'Well, just what is it that you do do?' And he said softly, 'I simply practise compassion for all sentient beings.'

When you are in just that kind of space you are not forcing anything. You are not pushing away life or death. You are in reality not even attacking disease. You are just allowing balance to occur by being in balance yourself. Many healers have said to me, 'I know God is doing the healing, I am just His stand-in.' That is the space out of which healing can manifest.

Love is the optimum condition for healing. The healer uses whatever he intuits will be of the greatest aid, but his energy cannot come from the mind. His power comes from the openness of his heart. He senses something greater than the body's predicament. He goes to the source out of which all healing occurs, not attempting to disturb or obstruct that which may allow the next perfect step. He does not second guess the universe.

Indeed, in many healers, it is the attachment to someone getting well, the attachment to results that limits the depth and potential of the healing. In the Tibetan healing tradition those who have made a commitment to use their energies for the benefit of others, in the beginning course of their training as healers, are first taught to open deeply to death. For the first two or three years of their training they work with the dying so there is a comfort and familiarity with every possibility. They are taught to exclude nothing from their perception of the perfection of things. Life and death are seen as the perfect expression of being, each in its own moment, in its appropriate time. The healer addresses the process of being rather than its separate manifestation. The true healer goes to the root of being and allows it to flower as it will in perfect symmetry to the tendencies that have brought that individual to the teaching known as disease.

This quality of unconditional love and availability to others can be seen in some of those who survived the Nazi death camps. Victor Frankl speaks about a few of those beings who escaped the gas chambers and survived the typhus, dysentery, pneumonia, and despair – the rabbis, nurses, doctors, laymen, and priests who wished to help others, surviving year after year while most others just disintegrated. Reflecting on those times he said, 'It did not really matter what we expected of life but rather we had to ask ourselves what life expected of us.' It was their selfless love that allowed them to maintain balance when many about them wilted and fell.

Often when we speak of healing the question is asked, 'How do you know when to stop healing and begin to prepare for death?' The question once again comes from a partial understanding. In reality the opening to healing and the preparation for death are the same.

When we are differentiating between healing and preparing for death we are forgetting that each are aspects of a single whole. It is all within the attitude with which one comes to life. If we don't use our symptoms as a message of our holding, then any attempt at healing which seeks to suppress that teaching slays a much deeper aspect of being. Is the healing that affects only the body in our best interest? On the other hand, if one welcomes death as an escape, that is a rejection of life, and the same imaginary differences between life and death will occur. In either case we never touch the deathless. We never encourage the exploration of undifferentiated being out of which all healing and wisdom arise.

I have known a few who fought their disease tooth and nail, and only when they prepared to die did their heart and mind come into balance and manifest healing in the body.

Because I do not think I need stress the obvious value of healing, of having a body in which to learn and serve, I do not believe it is necessary to underscore the benefit of physical healing, but I might here attempt to balance some of the misconceptions about the natural form of healing inherent in death. Death is not the enemy. The 'enemy' is ignorance and lovelessness. Identifying with the contents of the mind we seldom trust the spaciousness of the heart. Indeed, it may be that much illness is a result of our distrust of our greater nature: the disharmony that results when we pull back from the truth.

For many it may be illness that for the first time causes them to look within. For some it might be the only experience that would get them to pay attention, to begin exploring the mind/body, to develop a sense of wholeness. For many it could be said that sickness is grace, for it brings them into contact with themselves in a way that none of the stumblings of a lifetime's attempt to maintain self-image have accomplished. It causes an examination of that which attempts to protect us from life.

Feminism and the Goddess

Introduction

From the perspective of the holistic movement, men in robes pontificating on what people are supposed to believe is neither attractive nor creative. Often it is oppressive and cruel.

The general gender imbalance in the world today – men predominately making the decisions about what we do and what we believe – has been manifest for millennia and usually at its worst in the world's religious movements. Whatever the culture or the continent, religions have been led by men and have actively excluded women from the priesthood. Where are the women priests and religious leaders when we look at Judaism, Christianity, Islam, Buddhism or Hinduism?

The exclusion of women has been not only an outrageous affront to half the population of the planet, it has also created an imbalance in the way that culture and religion and society are formed. Half the people have been missing! This is a profound fragmentation. It is also part of the whole dynamic which creates environmental and social crisis.

It is in the very nature of the holistic movement, therefore, totally to support and accept the central role of women. In fact, I would suggest that it is precisely in the holistic movement that feminism thus far has had its major triumph. In holistic culture – in the literature, the teachers, the organizations and the communities – there is little argument about the place of women, for women are solidly there both at the centre and in leadership. Many of the major figures (teachers, therapists and writers) are women. Many holistic gatherings and workshops have more women attending and leading the proceedings than men.

This pushing aside of male dominance has allowed women's spirituality to surface without the fear of inquisition and execution. The last decades have a seen a huge shift in society's attitude to witchcraft and Wicca. Women's experiences of spirit and transformation, and the renaissance of the Goddess, are essential foundations of holistic awareness.

It is also in the holistic context that women have not sought the basic rights of equality through endeavouring to be like men. In a holistic context, there is a deep appreciation that female *is* different from male and, perhaps in these times, is better.

The feminist approach is not just a different way of thinking about reality and identity, it is a different way of feeling and intuiting it. It means, in contradistinction to the masculine approach, a new appreciation of creativity, power, nurture, cycles and healing. It means an understanding of spirituality that is not so much transcendent and external, but a fecund life force emerging out of the Cosmic Mother, out of the Earth, out of the womb and out of all of us.

Feminism and Witchcraft

STARHAWK
The Spiral Dance

Without a doubt Starhawk has been the most influential, well-known and radical spiritual feminist. She has been prepared to state with great clarity that witchcraft is in fact the survivor of the religion of the Goddess and to make equally clear that there is no dividing line between Goddess spirituality and feminist politics. Although she fully understands and stands against patriarchal religion and culture, her writing is fully inclusive of, and affectionate towards, men. Her explicit motive is the healing of the whole community and the creation of balance. She successfully manages to bring together the threads of environmentalism, social justice, urban politics, feminism and Goddess spirituality.

The importance of the Goddess symbol for women cannot be overstressed. The image of the Goddess inspires women to see ourselves as divine, our bodies as sacred, the changing phases of our lives as holy, our aggression as healthy, our anger as purifying, and our power to nurture and create, but also to limit and destroy when necessary, as the very force that sustains all life. Through the Goddess, we can discover our strength, enlighten our minds, own our bodies, and celebrate our emotions. We can move beyond narrow, constricting roles and become whole.

The Goddess is also important for men. The oppression of men in Father God-ruled patriarchy is perhaps less obvious but no less tragic than that of women. Men are encouraged to identify with a model no human being can successfully emulate: to be mini-rulers of narrow universes. They are internally split, into a 'spiritual' self that is supposed to conquer their baser animal and emotional natures. They are at war with themselves: in the West, to 'conquer' sin; in the East, to 'conquer' desire or ego. Few escape from these wars undamaged. Men lose touch with their feelings and their bodies, becoming the 'successful male zombies' described by Herb Goldberg in *The Hazards of Being Male*: 'Oppressed by the cultural pressures that have denied him his feelings, by the mythology of the woman and the distorted and self-destructive way he sees and relates to her, by the urgency for him to "act like a man", which blocks his ability to respond to his inner promptings both emotionally and physiologically, and by a generalized self-hate that causes him to feel comfortable only when he is functioning well in harness, not when he lives for joy and personal growth.'[1]

Because women give birth to males, nurture them at the breast, and in our culture are primarily responsible for their care as children, 'every male brought up in a traditional home develops an intense early identification with his mother and therefore carries within him a strong feminine imprint.'[2] The symbol of the Goddess allows men to experience and integrate the feminine side of their nature, which is often felt to be the deepest and most sensitive aspect of self. The Goddess does not exclude the male; she contains him, as a pregnant woman contains a male child. Her own male aspect embodies both the solar light of the intellect and wild, untamed animal energy.

Our relationship to the earth and the other species that share it has also been conditioned by our religious models. The image of God as outside of nature has given us a rationale for our own destruction of the natural order, and justified our plunder of the earth's resources. We have attempted to 'conquer' nature as we have tried to conquer sin. Only as the results of pollution and ecological destruction become severe enough to threaten even urban humanity's adaptability have we come to recognize the importance of ecological balance and the interdependence of all life. The model of the Goddess, who is immanent in nature, fosters respect for the sacredness of all living things. Witchcraft can be seen as a religion of ecology. Its goal is harmony with nature, so that life may not just survive, but thrive.

The rise of Goddess religion makes some politically oriented feminists uneasy. They fear it will sidetrack energy away from action to bring about social change. But in areas as deeply rooted as the relations between the sexes, true social change can only come about when the myths and symbols of our culture are themselves changed. The symbol of the Goddess conveys the spiritual power both to challenge systems of oppression and to create new, life-oriented cultures. [. . .]

The feminist movement is a magicospiritual movement as well as a political movement. It is spiritual because it is addressed to the liberation of the human spirit, to healing our fragmentation, to becoming whole. It is magical because it changes consciousness, it expands our awareness and gives us a new vision. It is also magic by another definition: 'the art of causing change in accordance with will'.

If we are to reclaim our culture, we cannot afford narrow definitions.

And when we have won clear, 'we must return to the circle'. The circle is the ecological circle, the circle of the interdependence of all living organisms. Civilization must return to harmony with nature.

The circle is also the circle of community. The old family structures, the networks of support and caring are breaking down. Religion has always been a prime source of community, and a vital function of feminist spirituality is to create new networks of involvement. Community also implies broader issues of how equitably power, wealth, and opportunities are shared among different groups, and the issues of who cares for children, the aged, the sick, and the disabled. When the Divine becomes immanent in the world, these are all areas of spiritual concern.

The circle is also the circle of Self. Our view of the Self – what it is, how it perceives, in what modes it functions – has changed greatly. Feminist spirituality is also an inner journey, a personal vision quest, a process of self-healing and self-exploration.

To return to the circle does not necessarily mean to embrace Witchcraft specifically. I hope the religion of the future will be multifaceted, growing out of many traditions. Perhaps we will see a new cult of the Virgin Mary and a revival of the ancient Hebrew Goddess. Native American traditions and Afro-American traditions may flourish in an atmosphere in which they are given the respect they deserve. Eastern religions will inevitably change as they grow in the West – and part of that change may be in the roles they assign women.

But there are valuable underlying concepts in Witchcraft, on which other feminist traditions can draw. The most important is the understanding of the Goddess, the divine, as immanent in the world, manifest in nature, in human beings, in human community. The All-That-Is-One is not now and never has been separate from this existing physical world. She is here, now, *is* each of us in the eternal changing present;

219

is no one but you, is nowhere but where you are – and yet is everyone. To worship Her is to assert, even in the face of suffering and often against all reason, that life is good, a great gift, a constant opportunity for ecstasy. If we see it become a burden of misery for others, we have the responsibility to change it.

Because the Goddess is manifest in human beings, we do not try to escape our humanness, but seek to become fully human. The task of feminist religion is to help us learn those things that seem so simple, yet are far more demanding than the most extreme patriarchal disciplines. It is easier to be celibate than to be fully alive sexually. It is easier to withdraw from the world than to live in it; easier to be a hermit than to raise a child; easier to repress emotions than to feel them and express them; easier to meditate in solitude than to communicate in a group; easier to submit to another's authority than place trust in oneself. It is not easy to be a Witch, a bender, a shaper, one of the Wise; nor is it safe, comfortable, 'laid back', mellow, uplifting, or a guarantee of peace of mind. It requires openness, vulnerability, courage, and work. It gives no answers: only tasks to be done, and questions to consider. In order to truly transform our culture, we need that orientation towards life, towards the body, towards sexuality, ego, will, towards all the muckiness and adventure of being human.

Witchcraft offers the model of a religion of poetry, not theology. It presents metaphors, not doctrines, and leaves open the possibility of reconciliation of science and religion, of many ways of knowing. It functions in those deeper ways of knowing which our culture has denied and for which we hunger.

The world-view of Witchcraft is cyclical, spiral. It dissolves dualities and sees opposites as complements. Diversity is valued; both poles of any duality are always valued because between them flows the on-off pulse of polar energy that sustains life. That cycle is the rhythm of the dance, to which the Hunter, the seeker, is always drawn back.

Finally, the Craft provides a structural model: the coven, the circle of friends, in which there is leadership, but no hierarchy, small enough to create community without loss of individuality. The form of ritual is circular: we face each other, not an altar or a podium or a sacred shrine, because it is in each other that the Goddess is found. Every Witch is Priestess or Priest: there are no hierophants, no messiahs, no avatars, no gurus. The Goddess says, 'If that which you seek, you find not within yourself, you will never find it without. For I have been with you from the beginning.'

The Paradise Papers

MERLIN STONE
The Paradise Papers – The Suppression of Women's Rites

Merlin Stone was first introduced to images of the Goddess through her work as a sculptress. She immediately began to question why and how it was that the Goddess had disappeared almost completely from Western culture. In *The Paradise Papers* she describes how widespread the Goddess had been and how She was overthrown by male-dominated religions.

Forty-nine years before the birth of Christ, a man from Roman Sicily wrote of his travels in northern Africa and some of the Near Eastern countries, recording his observations of people along the way. He was keenly interested in cultural patterns and was certainly one of the forerunners of the fields of anthropology and sociology. This man was known as Diodorus Siculus, Diodorus of Sicily. Many statements reporting the high or even dominant status of women were included in his writings. We may question why he, more than any other classical writer, recorded so much information about women warriors and matriarchy in the nations all about him. He does not belittle the men who lived in such social systems; that does not appear to be his aim. Indeed, he seemed to be rather admiring and respectful of the women who wielded such power.

It was Diodorus who reported that the women of Ethiopia carried arms, practised communal marriage and raised their children so communally that they often confused even themselves as to who the natural mother had been. In parts of Libya, where the Goddess Neith was highly esteemed, accounts of Amazon women still lingered even in Roman times. Diodorus described a nation in Libya as follows:

All authority was vested in the woman, who discharged every kind of public duty. The men looked after domestic affairs just as the women do among ourselves and did as they were told by their wives. They were not allowed to undertake war service or to exercise any functions of government, or to fill any public office, such as might have given them more spirit to set themselves up against the women. The children were handed over immediately after birth to the men, who reared them on milk and other foods suitable to their age.

Diodorus wrote of warrior women existing in Libya, reporting that these women had formed into armies which had invaded other lands. According to him, they revered the Goddess as their major deity and set up sanctuaries for Her worship. Though he gives no specific name, the accounts probably refer to the Libyan warrior Goddess known as Neith, who was also revered under that name in Egypt.

In prehistoric Egypt, the Goddess held supremacy in Upper Egypt (the south) as Nekhebt, symbolized as a vulture. The people of Lower Egypt, which includes the northern delta region, worshipped their supreme Goddess as a cobra, using the name Ua Zit (Great Serpent). From about 3000 BC onwards the Goddess, known as Nut, Net or Nit, probably derived from Nekhebt, was said to have existed when nothing else had yet been created. She then created all that had come into being. According to Egyptian mythology, it was She who first placed Ra, the sun god, in the sky. Other texts of Egypt tell of the Goddess as Hathor in this role of creator of existence, explaining that She took the form of a serpent at that time.

In Egypt the concept of the Goddess always remained vital. The introduction of male deities, just as the dynastic periods begin (about 3000 BC) will be more thoroughly discussed in chapter four. This probably lessened Her original supremacy as it was known in Neolithic societies. But Goddess worship continued and in conjunction with this, the women of Egypt appear to have benefited in many ways.

Diodorus wrote at great length of the worship of the Goddess Isis (the Greek translation for Au Set), who had incorporated the aspects of both Ua Zit and Hathor. Isis was also closely associated with the Goddess as Nut, who was mythologically recorded as Her mother; in paintings Isis wore the wings of Nekhebt. Diodorus explained that, according to Egyptian religion, Isis was revered as the inventor of agriculture, as a great healer and physician and as the one who first established the laws of justice in the land.

He then recorded what we today may find a most startling description of the laws of Egypt, explaining that they were the result of the reverence paid to this mighty Goddess. He wrote, 'It is for these reasons, in fact, that it was ordained that the queen should have greater power and honour than the king and that among private persons the wife should enjoy authority over the husband, husbands agreeing in the marriage contract that they will be obedient in all things to their wives.'

Frazer commented on the relationship between the veneration of Isis and the customs of female kinship and stated that 'In Egypt, the archaic system of mother-kin, with its preference for women over men in matters of property and inheritance, lasted down to Roman times . . .'

There is further evidence that Egypt was a land where women had great freedom and control of their own lives, and perhaps of their husbands' as well. Herodotus of Greece, several centuries before Diodorus, wrote that in Egypt, 'Women go in the marketplace, transact affairs and occupy themselves with business, while the husbands stay home and weave.' His contemporary, Sophocles, stated that 'Their thoughts and actions all are modelled on Egyptian ways, for there the men sit at the loom indoors while the wives work abroad for their daily bread.'

Professor Cyrus Gordon wrote in 1953 of life in ancient Egypt. He tells us that 'In family life, women had a peculiarly important position for inheritance passed through the mother rather than through the father . . . This system may well hark back to prehistoric times when only the obvious relationship between mother and child was recognized, but not the less apparent relationship between father and child.'

Dr Murray suggested that 'Women's condition was high, due perhaps to their economic independence.' S. W. Baron writes that in Egyptian papyri, 'many women appear as parties in civil litigations and independent business transactions even with their own husbands and fathers'. One of the earliest archaeologists of the pyramids of Egypt, Sir William Flinders Petrie, wrote in 1925 that 'In Egypt all property went in the female line, the woman was the mistress of the house; and in early tales she is represented as having entire control of herself and the place.'

Discussing the position of women in ancient Egypt, theologian and archaeologist Roland de Vaux wrote in 1965 that 'In Egypt the wife was often the head of the family, with all the rights such a position entailed.' Obedience was urged upon husbands in the maxims of Ptah-Hotep. Marriage contracts of all periods attest the extremely independent social and economic position of women. According to Mayer, who is quoted in the Vaertings' study, 'Among the Egyptians the women were remarkably free . . . as late as the fourth century BC there existed side by side with patriarchal marriage, a form of marriage in which the wife chose the husband and could divorce him on payment of compensation.'

Love poems, discovered in Egyptian tombs, strongly hint that it was the Egyptian women who did the courting, oft-times wooing the male by plying him with intoxicants to weaken his protestations. Robert Briffault wrote of an Egyptian woman clerk who later became a governor and eventually the commander and chief of an army.

A most enlightening and significant study on the social structure and position of women in Egypt was done in 1949 by Dr Margaret Murray. Painstakingly tracing the lineage of royal families in Egypt, she eventually proved that, at the level of royalty, the Egyptian culture at most periods was matrilineal. Royalty was studied because records for these people were most available. According to Murray it was the daughters, not the sons, who were the actual inheritors of the royal throne. She suggests that the custom of brother/sister marriage then developed, allowing a son to gain access to the royal privilege in this way. She writes that matrilineal rights to the throne were the reason that Egyptian princesses for so many centuries were married within the family and were not available for international marriage alliances. This may clarify why the Goddess Isis, whom Frazer stated was a more important deity than Her brother/husband Osiris, and whom Diodorus cited as the origins of the generally high position of women in Egypt, was known as The Throne.

But even in Egypt women were slowly losing their prestigious position. Sir Flinders Petrie, incidentally a deeply respected colleague of Dr Murray's at the University of London, discussed the role of priestesses in ancient Egypt. He pointed out how their position had changed between the time of the earliest dynasties (3000 BC onwards) to the Eighteenth Dynasty (1570–1300 BC). According to the available records, the Goddess known as Hathor, much the same deity as Isis, was in earliest times served by sixty-one priestesses and eighteen priests, while the Goddess as Neith was attended solely by priestesses. By the time of the Eighteenth Dynasty women were no longer even part of the religious clergy, but served only as temple musicians. It was in the Eighteenth Dynasty that Egypt was made to feel the greatest influence of the Indo-Europeans, a factor again discussed at greater length in chapters four and five. Incidentally, the use of the word 'pharaoh', generally summoning up images even more powerful than the word 'king', actually comes from the term *par-o*, which literally means 'great house'. It was only from the time of the Eighteenth Dynasty that the word was used to signify the royal male of that household.

Professor Saggs wrote in 1962 of the societies of Mesopotamia, which includes both Sumer and Babylon. Mesopotamia generally refers to the areas of Iraq along and between the Tigris and Euphrates Rivers, starting at the Persian Gulf and reaching up to Anatolia. He examined the relationship of the reverence for Goddesses to the status of women in Sumer (about 3000 BC–1800 BC, in southern Iraq), concluding that in the earliest periods women were much better off than in the later periods, and that they gradually lost ground over the years. [. . .]

Even today Hebrew males are taught to offer the daily prayer, 'Blessed Art Thou O Lord our God, King of the Universe, who has not made me a woman.'

Mohammed stated, 'When Eve was created, Satan rejoiced.'

As the Hebrew myth of the creation was later adopted into the sacred literature of Christianity, with all the other writings of the Old Testament, the writers and religious leaders who followed Christ assumed the same pose of contempt for the female, continuing to use religion to lock women further into the role of passive and inferior beings, and thus the more easily controlled property of men. As the years went on and the position and status of women continued to lose ground, the Church held fast to its goals of creating and maintaining a male-dominated society. For hadn't it been one of the first decrees of the god who made the world and all life? Women were to be regarded as mindless, carnal creatures, both attitudes justified and 'proved' by the Paradise myth.

In Paul's letter to the Ephesians we read, 'Wives, submit yourselves unto your own husbands as unto the Lord. For the husband is the head of the wife even as Christ is the head of the Church and he is the saviour of the body. Therefore as the Church is subject unto Christ, so let the wives be to their own husbands in everything' (Eph. 5:22–24).

This brings to mind the quote from Hosea in which the husband so totally identified himself with the male deity that his words became the words of Yahweh. In the new religion not only the priests, but all men, were to be considered as direct messengers of the Lord, not merely in Church but in the privacy of a woman's kitchen or even in her bed.

Using the now familiar Eden myth, Paul asserted that this was the reason that women must be obedient, denying themselves even the faculty of their vocal chords, not to mention their minds. We read in I Timothy 2:11–14, 'Let the woman learn in silence with all subjection. But I suffer not a woman to teach, nor to usurp authority over the man, but to be in silence. For Adam was first formed and then Eve and Adam was not deceived, but the woman being deceived was in the transgression.'

And in Corinthians the word of the creation legend was brought home once again. 'The head of every man is Christ; and the head of the woman is the man; and the head of Christ is God. For a man indeed ought not to cover his head for as much as he is the image and glory of God, but the woman is the glory of the man. For the man is not of the woman but the woman of the man. Neither was man created for the woman but the woman for the man' (1 Cor. 11:3,7,9).

Statements carefully designed to suppress the earlier social structure continually presented the myth of Adam and Eve as divine proof that man must hold the ultimate authority. The status of the male deity was the status of the male mortal, and it was surely no accident that the Levite priests of Yahweh had fought so bitterly for his position. So intent was Paul on declaring maleness to be first, that he was willing to blind himself to the biological truth of birth – 'For the man is not of the woman but the woman of the man.' Woman bears the pain but man takes the credit.

When the apostle Peter was in Anatolia, where the Goddess was still revered, he condemned the 'pagans' for the 'lust of defiling passion', much like the prophets of the Old Testament, angrily deriding those who 'revelled in the daytime'. He complained that these heathens still followed Baalim. Peter solemnly lectured, 'Likewise ye wives, be in subjection to your own husbands, for after this manner in the old time, the holy women also, who trusted in God, adorned themselves, being in subjection to their own husbands' (I Pet. 3:1).

St Clement, father of the Roman Church, denied women – in the name of the Lord – the pleasure and health and strength-building effects of such physical sports as wrestling and running, claiming that it was in greater accord with the Bible that women's activities be confined to spinning, weaving and cooking.

St John Chrysostom, a Christian teacher of the fifth century, warned, 'The woman taught once and ruined everything. On this account . . . let her not teach.'

St Augustine of the same period claimed that man, but not woman, was made in God's image and woman therefore is not complete without man, while he is complete alone.

Taking his cue from these same biblical ideas, Martin Luther asserted in his writings that it was quite natural for women to be secondary to men. In his 'Vindication of Married Life' he wrote that men must continue to maintain their power over women, since man is higher and better than she, 'for the regiment and dominion belong to the man as the head and master of the house'.

Sixteenth-century Swiss reformer John Calvin also spoke out against political equality for women, stating that it would be a 'deviation from the original and proper order of nature'. He spoke favourably of polygamy, suggesting that it would help to keep women from being unwed and childless.

Goddess Versus Puritanism

ROBERT GRAVES
The White Goddess

Essentially a poet, Robert Graves made his living from articles and books, including the famous novel *I, Claudius* and his autobiographical classic of World War I, *Good-Bye to All That*. In 1946 he published his seminal *The White Goddess* which influenced the whole course of English poetry and provided a mythic context for feminism and the revival of the Goddess. In the book he painstakingly argued that the true source of poetry, the White Goddess, had been abandoned, not only by poets but also by mystics and spiritual leaders. She had been replaced by a patriarchal deity which, in concert with commercial, industrial and social structures, created a culture devoid of its true spiritual roots and disastrously imbalanced.

The extract starts with a prayer quoted by Graves, which comes from a twelfth-century English herbal (*Brit. Mus. MS. Harley, 1585, ff. 12v–13r*).

Earth, divine goddess, Mother Nature, who dost generate all things and bringest forth ever anew the sun which thou hast given to the nations; Guardian of sky and sea and of all Gods and powers; through thy influence all nature is hushed and sinks to sleep . . . Again, when it pleases thee, thou sendest forth the glad daylight and nurturest life with thine eternal surety; and when the spirit of man passes, to thee it returns. Thou indeed art rightly named Great Mother of the Gods; Victory is in thy divine name. Thou art the source of the strength of peoples and gods; without thee nothing can either be born or made perfect; thou art mighty, Queen of the Gods, Goddess, I adore thee as divine, I invoke thy name; vouchsafe to grant that which I ask of thee, so shall I return thanks to thy godhead, with the faith that is thy due . . .

Now also I make intercession to you, all ye powers and herbs, and to your majesty: I beseech you, whom Earth the universal parent hath borne and given as a medicine of health to all peoples and hath put majesty upon, be now of the most benefit to humankind. This I pray and beseech you: be present here with your virtues, for she who created you hath herself undertaken that I may call you with the good will of him on whom the art of medicine was bestowed; therefore grant for health's sake good medicine by grace of these powers aforesaid . . .

The early Gentile Christian borrowed from the Hebrew prophets the two religious concepts, hitherto unknown in the West, which have become the prime causes of our unrest: that of a patriarchal God, who refuses to have any truck with Goddesses and claims to be self-sufficient and all-wise; and that of a theocratic society, disdainful of the pomps and glories of the world, in which everyone who rightly performs his civic duties is a 'son of God' and entitled to salvation, whatever his rank or fortune, by virtue of direct communion with the Father.

Both these concepts have since been vigorously contested within the Church itself. However deeply Westerners may admire Jesus's single-minded devotion to the remote, all-holy, universal God of the Hebrew prophets, few of them have ever accepted whole-heartedly the antagonism between flesh and spirit implied in his cult. And though the new Godhead seemed philosophically incontrovertible, once the warlike and petulant Zeus-Jupiter, with his indiscreet amours and quarrelsome Olympian family, had ceased to command the respect of intelligent people, the early Church Fathers soon found that man was not yet ready for ideal anarchy: the All-Father, a purely meditative patriarch who did not intervene personally in mundane affairs, had to resume his thunderbolt in order to command respect. Even the communistic principle, for a breach of which Ananias and Sapphira had been struck dead, was abandoned as unpractical. As soon as the Papal power was acknowledged superior to that of kings, the Popes assumed magnificent temporal pomp, took part in power-politics, waged wars, rewarded the rich and well-born with indulgences for sin in this world and promises of preferential treatment in the next, and anathematized the equalitarian principles of their simple predecessors. And not only has Hebrew monotheism been modified at Rome by the gradual introduction of Virgin-worship, but the ordinary Catholic layman has long been cut off from direct communication with God: he must confess his sins and acquaint himself with the meaning of God's word, only through the mediation of a priest.

Protestantism was a vigorous reassertion of the two rejected concepts, which the Jews themselves had never abandoned, and to which the Mohammedans had been almost equally faithful. The Civil Wars in England were won by the fighting qualities of the Virgin-hating Puritan Independents, who envisaged an ideal theocratic society in which all priestly and episcopal pomp should be abolished, and every man should be entitled to read and interpret the Scriptures as he pleased, with direct access to God the Father. Puritanism took root and flourished in America, and the doctrine of religious equalitarianism, which carried with it the right to independent thinking, turned into social equalitarianism, or democracy, a theory which has since dominated Western civilization. We are now at the stage where the common people of Christendom, spurred on by their demagogues, have grown so proud that they are no longer content to be the hands and feet and trunk of the body politic, but demand to be the intellect as well – or, as much intellect as is needed to satisfy their simple appetites. As a result, all but a very few have discarded their religious idealism, Roman Catholics as well as Protestants, and come to the private conclusion that money, though the root of all evil, is the sole practical means of expressing value or of determining social precedence; that science is the only accurate means of describing phenomena; and that a morality of common honesty is not relevant either to love, war, business or politics. Yet they feel guilty about their backsliding, send their children to Sunday School, maintain the Churches, and look with alarm towards the East, where a younger and more fanatic faith threatens.

What ails Christianity today is that it is not a religion squarely based on a single myth; it is a complex of juridical decisions made under political pressure in an ancient law-suit about religious rights between adherents of the Mother-goddess who was once supreme in the West, and those of the usurping Father-god. Different ecclesiastical courts have given different decisions, and there is no longer a supreme judicature. Now that even the Jews have been seduced into evading the Mosaic Law and whoring after false gods, the Christians have drifted farther away than ever from the ascetic holiness to which Ezekiel, his Essene successors, and Jesus, the last of the Hebrew prophets, hoped to draw the world. Though the West is still nominally Christian, we have come to be governed, in practice, by the unholy triumdivate of Pluto god of wealth, Apollo god of science, and Mercury god of thieves. To make matters worse, dissension and jealousy rage openly between these three, with Mercury and Pluto blackguarding each other, while Apollo wields the atomic bomb as if it were a thunderbolt; for since the Age of Reason was heralded by his eighteenth-century philosophers, he has seated himself on the vacant throne of Zeus (temporarily indisposed) as Triumdival Regent.

Women's Psychology

MARION WOODMAN
The Pregnant Virgin

Marion Woodman, a Jungian psychoanalyst, has been a key figure in bringing together the female aspect of mythology with analytic psychology. Compassionate and empathetic to the suffering of psychological distress, she brings acute insights into the particular patterns that may work out in women's psychology. Her awareness as a therapist is therefore informed by Goddess mythology and the roles and actions of female figures in legends and fairy tales, as well as by an understanding of feminist politics. Her book *The Pregnant Virgin* is also representative of a whole genre of Jungian literature in which mythology is used as a way of understanding both psychological and social challenges. A male counterpoint would be Robert Bly's *Iron John*.

For many women born and reared in a patriarchal culture, initiation into mature womanhood occurs through abandonment, actual or psychological. It is the identity-conferring experience that frees them from the father.

Some women can accept their destiny in a traditional, patriarchal relationship, finding within its obvious limitations – social, intellectual, spiritual – compensations that are important to them. Others who accept that destiny but nevertheless resist its limitations are forced for financial, political or social reasons to stay within its framework.

However, an increasing number of women whose psychic centre has always radiated around the father, real or imagined, are determined to go through the initiation. These women are by inner necessity creators in the Keatsian sense of 'soul-makers',[1] that is, their quest for meaning drives them to find their own inner story. They reject collective masculine values as an intrusive imposition, but their search for a personal identity from within almost inevitably brings them into collision with the very forces they are struggling to integrate. In the effort to liberate themselves from the very real restrictions of a patriarchal culture, they ironically, even at a highly conscious level, tend to become its victims. The internal father, who in the soul-making process they sought to please, turns on them – or appears to – as soon as that father-image is projected on to a man, or they seek recognition and reward in those creative fields still largely dominated by men.

While this situation is now changing, there is still a long way to go. The psychic dynamics involved in the change are still far from understood. Men and women caught up in those dynamics, and even consciously committed to so-called enlightened relationships, are still not getting through to each other despite their heroic efforts to do so, efforts that refuse to admit failure even when failure is all they experience. This can become vividly clear in the analytic relationship, often a microcosm of what is happening on the cultural level.

The word abandonment comes from the Old English verb *bannan*, meaning 'to summon' (OED). To be among those summoned was to relinquish oneself to service. Abandonment means literally 'to be uncalled', symbolically 'to be without a destiny'. If one's destiny has been dictated by the father, however, then to be uncalled may be a blessing rather than a curse. Free of the father, the daughter may then truly *abandon herself* to the process of her own soul-making. This rite of passage contains within itself the double meaning of abandonment. Emily Dickinson sums this up in her usual elliptical style:

I'm ceded – I've stopped being Theirs –
The name They dropped upon my face
With water, in the country church
Is finished using, now.
And They can put it with my Dolls,
My childhood, and the string of spools,
I've finished threading too –

Baptized, before, without the choice,
But this time, consciously, of Grace
Unto supremest name
Called to my Full – The Crescent dropped
Existence's whole Arc, filled up,
With one small Diadem.

My second Rank – too small the first –
Crowned – Crowing – on my Father's breast
A half unconscious Queen
But this time Adequate Erect,
With Will to choose, or to reject,
And I choose, just a Crown.[2]

The 'half unconscious Queen', as I see her, is bonded, for better or for worse, to her creative imagination, a situation that originated in the psychological bonding to her father. Even in childhood such a woman is outside the ban (i.e. calling) that contains other children. In adolescence, while her sisters are conspiring about bangles, babies and bans of marriage, she is banished by her own decree. Her creativity is of a different nature: plays, canvasses, sonatas or chemical experiments. On some level she always feels banned from life and yearns for what other people take for granted. Yet while part of her feels abandoned, part of her knows that were she to forsake her own creativity she would be abandoning her own soul.

Many variables are involved in defining the creative woman. Some women are creative in their homemaking, creating a loving, spontaneous environment for their husbands and children – a place to go out from, a place to go back to. Others are creating in an extraverted professional situation. Some are successfully doing both. In this discussion, however, I am thinking of the creative woman as one who is compelled from within to relate to her own creative imagination.

While the lights and shadows in individuals vary greatly, a basic pattern of such a woman's psychology can be outlined. As a little girl she loves and admires her father, or her image of what her absent father must be. And apparently for good reason. He is courageous, intelligent and sensitive, a man of high ideals, a man of vision committed to his own search, a man who in many cases never found his place in the patriarchy. His vision of the perfect woman quite naturally took him into marriage with a woman who loved his vision, usually a 'father's daughter' whose dream for herself was cut short by the reality of marriage and family. Thus the *puer* man typically finds his mate in the *puella* woman.[3]

In such a household there is no place for the chaos of unruly children,

235

the 'filth' of the chthonic or earthy feminine, nor the energies of conscious sexuality. Ostensibly, the father may be 'the man around the house', but the wife and mother 'wears the pants'. Full of repressed sexuality and resentment, she deals stoically with a disappointing world and projects her unlived life on to her children.

The father, meanwhile, blessed with the comforting presence of his wife-mother, is then free to project his own unfulfilled feeling values – his young anima – on to his little girl. Together they build a Garden of Eden. The child is trapped in spiritual incest, even more dangerous than actual incest because neither he nor she has any reason to suspect that something is amiss. Called to be 'Daddy's little princess', the daughter is at once his spiritual mother, his beloved, his inspiratrice. With her he will have thoughts and feelings that never come up with anyone else. She instinctively knows how to act as buffer between him and a judgmental world; she instinctively knows how to connect him to his own inner reality. Indeed, this is the only world she really understands – this world where she acts as the connecting link between her father's ego and the collective unconscious. Feeding on his vision of Light, Beauty and Truth, her young psyche can plumb the depths of his anguish or soar to the heights of his dream. That dynamic interplay continues to be her life-source as a creative woman, and without it her life becomes empty.

If her father accepts her inner life, then they genuinely share the eternal world of the creative imagination. Its values become her reality. Quick to recognize the illusions of the temporal world, she sets her sights on what is authentic, often becoming a veritable Cassandra, outcast by both her peer group and her parents' friends. Her security lies in her commitment to *essence* (a commitment, incidentally, which may lead to anorexia because she either forgets to eat or her throat refuses to open to the food of a world of which she is not a part). Such a woman lives on the archetypal edge, where life is exciting, fraught with danger – all or nothing, perfect or impossible. She knows little about bread and butter living and does not suffer fools gladly.

If her father is not mature enough to value her for herself, but, consciously or unconsciously, forces her into becoming his star performer, then her trap is a very different one because it involves his

236

rejection of her reality. Unable to recognize her own responses, she simply relinquishes herself to trying to please Daddy.

Daughters of both types of men will be so-called anima women (good hooks for men's unconscious projections), though of a very different tempering. Both will have dreams where they appear, for instance, in well-lit glass solariums, in perfect blue apartments without kitchens, in plastic bags or coffins that threaten to suffocate them. Both will realize there is something between them and the world, something that cuts off their own feeling, a veil that is seldom penetrated. Both will strive to make life into a work of art, and vaguely realize they have not lived. Because of that primal relationship, the father's daughter walks a thin line precariously close to the collective unconscious, unable – like Rainer Maria Rilke, for example – to separate her personal angels and demons from the transpersonal.

And demons are as immediate to her as angels, because she lives so close to her father's shadow. Unless he has worked on himself, as in analysis, and gained some insight into his *puer* psychology, he is probably quite unaware of his ambivalence towards women. His bonding to his own mother may have created a Prince Charming, but a prince who is nevertheless dependent on women's approval. His chthonic shadow hates that dependence and hates the women who make him feel vulnerable. Unless he has worked hard on his own feeling values, he may function on a conscious level as an ascetic scholar, a priest, or even a carefree Don Juan, while his unconscious shadow is a cold, violent killer, intent on destroying any 'witch' who would seduce him into her power. Men who live close to the unconscious quite legitimately need to protect themselves from the seduction of the lamia, as the Romantic artists, many of them dead before forty, make painfully clear. The *puer*'s shadow, however, may murder not only witches but the femininity of his little daughter as well. On the one hand he may be mothering, nourishing, cherishing, while on the other creating a *femme fatale* whose attitude towards men is kill or be killed.

The *femme fatale* lives in an unconscious body: her femininity is unconscious, her sexuality is unconscious. Often promiscuous, she manipulates 'lovers' to prove her power as a woman, but her love is unrelated to her lust. Thus she may consciously love her father (or her father surrogate) and be committed to her own creativity through that incestuous bonding, and at the same time be lured into violent and dangerous adventures.

Her sexuality and femininity foundered on the reef of her primal relationship to her mother. The *puella* mother who has never taken up residence in her own body, and therefore fears her own chthonic nature, is not going to experience pregnancy as a quiet meditation with her unborn child, nor birth as a joyful bonding experience. Although she may go through the motions of natural childbirth, the psyche soma split in her is so deep that physical bonding between her and her baby daughter does not take place. Her child lives with a profound sense of despair, a despair which becomes conscious if in later years she does active imagination with her body and releases waves of grief and terror that resonate with the initial, primal rejection.

The body that appears in dreams wrapped in wire, encircled by a black snake or encumbered by a fish tail from the waist down, may be holding a death-wish too deep for tears. The security of the mother's body world is not present for her in the original matrix, nor is there reinforcement for her maturing body as she moves towards puberty, attempting to differentiate her own boundaries from those of her mother and the external world. Unable to establish these fundamental physical demarcations, she often literally does not know where she begins or where she ends in relation to Mater (mother). During her developmental years, when she might otherwise be consolidating a sense of her physical identity, she is instead responding to the unconscious rejection by her mother.

Gyn/Ecology

MARY DALY

Gyn/Ecology – The Metaethics of Radical Feminism

Written by a professor of theology, Mary Daly's *Gyn/Ecology* is one of the most furious and creative of feminist texts. Its unrelenting information and assertive flowing prose style crash through naïvité and ignorance about the true nature of patriarchy and its cruelty. If there is one book that forces the reader to finally see the reality of the gender imbalance, it is this one. The cultural nuances of the sex wars give way to the stark realities of a global culture whose history complacently includes the European witch-hunts, the burning of Indian widows, the hobbling of Chinese women, the clitoridectomy of African and Arabic women, and so on. The sheer awfulness of the information is made readable by her extraordinary writing style which has within it the mad joy of liberation.

Patriarchy is itself the prevailing religion of the entire planet, and its essential message is necrophilia. All of the so-called religions legitimating patriarchy are mere sects subsumed under its vast umbrella/canopy. They are essentially similar, despite the variations. All – from Buddhism and Hinduism to Islam, Judaism, Christianity, to secular derivatives such as Freudianism, Jungianism, Marxism, and Maoism – are infrastructures of the edifice of patriarchy. All are erected as parts of the male's shelter against anomie. And the symbolic message of all the sects of the religion which is patriarchy is this: Women are the dreaded anomie.[1] Consequently, women are the objects of male terror, the projected personifications of 'The Enemy', the real objects under attack in all the wars of patriarchy.

Women who are willing to make the Journey of becoming must indeed recognize the fact of possession by the structures of evil and by the controllers and legitimators of these structures. But the solution is hardly 'rebirth' (baptism) by the fathers in the name of male mating. Indeed, this 'rebirth' – whether it is accomplished by the officially acknowledged religious fathers or by the directors of derivative secular organizations (e.g., television, schools, publishers of children's books) – is the very captivity from which we are trying to escape, in order to find our own origins.

Radical feminism is not reconciliation with the father. Rather it is affirming our original birth, our original source, movement, surge of living. This finding of our original integrity is remembering our Selves. Athena remembers her mother and consequently remembers her Self. Radical feminism releases the inherent dynamic in the mother-daughter relationship towards friendship, which is strangled in the male-mastered system. Radical feminism means that mothers do *not* demand Self-sacrifice of daughters, and that daughters do not demand this of their mothers, as do sons in patriarchy. What both demand of each other is courageous moving which is mythic in its depths, which is spell-breaking and myth-making process. The 'sacrifice' that is required is not mutilation by men, but the discipline needed for acting/creating together on a planet which is under the Reign of Terror, the reign of the fathers and sons.

Women moving in this way are in the tradition of Great Hags. Significantly, Hags are commonly identified with Harpies and Furies. Harpies are mythic monsters represented as having the head of a woman and the body and claws of a vulture, and considered to be instruments of divine vengeance. As Harpies, Hags are workers of vengeance – not merely in the sense of re-venge, which is only reactionary – but as asserting the primal energy of our be-ing. The Furies were believed by the Greeks and Romans to be avenging deities. As Harpies and Furies, Feminists are agents for the Goddess Nemesis.

As Harpies and Furies, Feminists in the tradition of the Great Hags are beyond compromise. It is said of the Goddess Demeter after her daughter Korê (named 'Persephone' after being abducted by Hades and brought to the underworld) was stolen from her, that she compromised. She had stated flatly that she would not allow the earth to bear fruit again unless her daughter was returned to her. But, according to the patriarchal myth, when Zeus decided that Persephone should live with her husband (Hades) for three months of the year and pass the other nine months with her mother, *Demeter set aside her anger* and bade the soil be fertile. But Persephone had tasted of the pomegranate; she was *possessed* by her husband, and every year when the cold season arrived she went to join him in the deep shadows.[2] The myth expresses the essential tragedy of women after the patriarchal conquest. The male myth-makers presented an illusion of reunion between Demeter and Persephone-Korê. The compromise can be seen as forced upon Demeter, but it was fatal for her to undervalue the power of her own position and set aside her anger, just as it was fatal that she taught the kings of the earth her divine science and initiated them into her divine mysteries. The patriarchal Greek myth-makers (re-makers) constructed a typical phallocratic plot when they (through Zeus) seduced her into the apparently satisfactory – even triumphant – compromise. However, the fact that the daughter was *allowed* to return for a 'period of time' says everything about patriarchy.*

Those who live in the tradition of the Furies refuse to be tricked into setting aside our anger at this primordial mutilation, which is the ontological separation of mother from daughter, of daughter from mother, of sister from sister. Women choosing Hag-ocracy refuse to teach divine science to the kings of the earth, to initiate them into our mysteries. Hag-ocracy is the time/space of those who maintain a growing creative fury at this primal injustice – a fury which is the struggle of daughters to find our source, our stolen original divinity.

The history of the footbound women of China (which will be discussed at length in The Second Passage) provides us with a vivid and

---

* Women are constantly tempted to measure reality in terms of the measurements of Father Time, which are linear, clocked. This is a trap. Our gynocentric time/space is not measurable, bargainable. It is qualitative, not quantitative. Because we refuse to be possessed by patriarchal myth we live in a different kind of duration, which has multifarious rhythms. The fathers who control the Clockwork Society try to consume this, our Lifetime. The Time Keepers' Lie consists in claiming that 'free time' can be cut off neatly from sold or bargained time (the nine-to-five schedule, the constant availability demanded of the housewife). The Masters mask or deny the fact that this division is a fundamental fragmentation. This brokenness must be healed during alleged 'free time', when the wound-up captives of Father Time waste wounded energies 'unwinding'. Furious women must begin by seeing through the Time Keepers' Lie and daring to defy the Time Keepers' schedules. The more we do this, the more we 'find time' for our Selves. Hags' spirits soar out of the cells of the Clockwork Prison when we defy the Lie, leaving their 'frame of reference', de-riding their boundaries. Otherworld Journeyers are precisely time/space travellers, seeing through the senseless circles, the pointless processions of the hands on the Grand Fathers' clocks.

accurate image of the way in which women have been coerced into 'participating' in the phallocratic processions. The footbound daughter was *bound* to repeat the same procedure of mutilation upon her own daughter, and the daughter upon *her* daughter. To visualize the procession of generations of crippled mothers and daughters, hobbling on three-inch-long caricatures of feet, moving slowly, grotesquely, painfully in meaningless circles within the homes (prisons) of fathers and husbands – their owners – is to *see* the real state of women in patriarchy. To understand that this horror is still going on, assuming insidious forms of *mind-binding* and *spirit-binding* in every nation of this colonized planet, is to begin to comprehend the condition of women caught on the Wheel of Processions, clutched by the clockwork hands that circle the surface of the Time Keepers' clocks.

Furious women know that patriarchy is itself a continual resurrection of the past, a series of processions. No social revolution, however 'radical', that falls short of metapatriarchal movement can break the circles of repetition. Only Hags – that is, Furious women – can kick off spirit-bindings. This is possible, for mind/spirit has a resiliency that feet, once destroyed, can never have again. The bindings can be burned, Virginia Woolf knew this:

And let the daughters of educated men dance round the fire and heap armful upon armful of dead leaves upon the flames. And let their mothers lean from the upper windows and cry, 'Let it blaze! Let it blaze! For we have done with this "education"!'[3]

Keeping the fire burning, saying No to Processions, means facing something that is very hard to look at: Deadly Deception through male myth – the subject of the following chapters.

Menstruation – The Wise Wound

PENELOPE SHUTTLE and PETER REDGROVE
The Wise Wound

As a result of Penelope Shuttle's distress during and around her time of menstruation, she and her partner, Peter Redgrove, began some research. They found not a single book published on the subject. The female monthly cycle was so much the 'curse' that it was virtually denied by society at large, and if not denied, it was at least a target of disgust, disdain or derision.

They therefore wrote the *The Wise Wound* which gave the historical and cultural context to this almost universal repression, and which also drew on the latest insights of biological science. *The Wise Wound* was an integral part of the movement in which women could begin freely to acknowledge and understand their deep biological rhythms and experience – and feel proud of them. It was also a key text in exploring the relationship between physicality, psychology and culture; an area which still requires much research.

Both Penelope Shuttle and Peter Redgrove are distinguished poets and novelists.

We are suggesting that there is a structure to every woman's cycle, and that she can perceive this if she wishes. What that structure exactly is, will depend on the woman. If she is able to see it, and not close her consciousness to it, then she will be perceiving rhythms deeply rooted in her bodily experience – which science objectively confirms with its list of measurable bodily changes. Not to perceive this structure may be for many women to isolate themselves from processes which will occur anyway, and knowledge of which may very well bring balance and benefits. Even if she does not like the cycle, perhaps the only way out may be through it.

The point is that there is a *rhythm*, however one may divide it up in one's own personal experience. If mental experiences reflect, as they often seem to, bodily ones, then there are many possibilities of experience if one opens oneself to this rhythm. One is often asked or encouraged to detach oneself from them, by regarding them as an inconvenience or an illness. Detachment from the changes does of course ensure that they remain merely bodily ones, and may even force them to express themselves in the body-language of illness. Harmony with them, so far as is possible, can lead to a different form of independence: understanding of one's nature rather than repression of it. One might say that the difference is between a person who becomes independent of water by donning a heavy diving-suit, and someone who enjoys sailing and navigation through real knowledge of the tides and coast-lines.

The complete rhythm may be experienced as fourfold – or other-fold with more complex menstrual cycles, which many women have. Undeniably, however, the more complicated rhythms arise from a strong basic twofold beat. The normal menstrual cycle has *two* poles, or culminations. Ovulation, when the ripe egg is shed into the Fallopian tube; and menstruation, when the thick, built-up lining of the womb is shed, and its wall becomes thin and exquisitely sensitive, like a 'wound'. The latter process, shedding of the womb-wall, is confined to what we regard as the more evolved animals: humans and apes.

What is not usual is to give as emphatic a value to menstruation as to ovulation. Menstruation is usually regarded as the negative pole of the process, ovulation the positive one. Menstruation is customarily seen as merely an excretory process: a simple stripping-off of the walls of the womb because the 'disappointed egg' has not been fertilized: a kind of nosebleed of the womb, in which the blood-and-mucus attitudes are foremost, and not what else the experience might mean. One can see this in most encyclopaedia articles, in the *Britannica*, for instance.

It is a cultural attitude to favour the 'values of ovulation', of child-bearing, over those of menstruation, by discounting the latter experience. We can see this in dismissive expletives. A common attitude is that these 'bloody women' are second-class people because they bleed one week in four. That is, if they are not breeding. That frequent expletive 'bloody' is sometimes derived from the expression 'By Our Lady'. But we can see how shocking an unaccustomed attitude to menstruation may be if we think of the Virgin Mary menstruating. A Christian may think of her bearing her child with joy, but not of her period, or of her sexuality. Thus matronhood is separated from sexuality, the values of ovulation from – the other values.

So, in most accounts of the menstrual cycle, ovulation is regarded as the culmination, peak and purpose of the changes. It is rare to read such a statement as that of the psychologist Esther Harding, that 'the divine creative spark in man can either express itself in the creation of a human child or, alternatively, it can be assimilated into the individual himself, creating in him a spirit which is immortal' in a context, which she gives, of considering that the 'alternative' is in what she calls the *yin* or dark side of women, the menstrual pole of the cycle.

It is at ovulation that the woman may dedicate herself to carrying a child for the next ten common law months. To speak exclusively of ovulation is mentally to limit the role of women to this function. Menstruation is regarded, not only by physiologists and many doctors, but also by some feminists, as a sickness, a blank spot, a non-event that the woman must endure and would be better without, an evil time. This simply is not necessarily so. It is the time when the healthy woman may draw on abilities and capacities that are not related to the values of ovulation and childbearing, but that are instead related to that other side of her nature, of independence of thought and action. It is the exact counterpart, but in an opposite sense, of the ovulation. At ovulation she wishes to receive, accept, build, if she desires a child. But from menstruation there is a different set of energies available to her of receiving, accepting, building the child which is herself. If this is so, but she is not ready or willing to accept the possibility, then the turn or passage of change from one 'pole' to the other will be difficult, and if she wishes a child or wishes to 'prove' her fertility, then the appearance of the period will be disappointing. This may be because she is taught to look at herself as primarily the egg-producer, and has turned away from the interplay of the other side of her nature which is available to her at the menstrual 'pole' of her cycle. [. . .]

The new things that are brought into evolution by the menstrual cycle are caused by a shifting of hormonal action – which we have called 'plucking the menstruous fruit' – and these new things are, she confirms: 'Interest or continuous sexuality of a greater or lesser degree' and a build-up of the uterine wall in preparation for possible pregnancy. This build-up is so great that it 'cannot be reabsorbed whether or not the embryo implants: it must be shed'. And this too is like the exposing of a new inner skin as a snake sloughs into newness; mythically, like the plucking of a red apple, or in the Greek myth, the tasting or experiencing of the red pomegranate, womb-shaped fruit of many seeds. The entrance to the underworld, mined out, as it were, by menstruation, opens periodically to Persephone, where she is wedded to no human husband, but to her inner husband, Pluto, the god of the riches of the earth and the body, to whom she must always return, for he is herself.

Dr Sherfey also gives us the idea that the menstrual cycle could have been involved in the development of androgenic-sensitive structures that enhanced the sexual capacity of the female. Androgens are said to be the hormonal substances that stimulate masculine structures and behaviour, and embryology now tells us that the male embryo is to begin with anatomically female until foetal androgens begin to circulate. It appears that progesterone is strongly androgenic, and though during the period itself both progesterone and oestrogen levels decline sharply, androgens still circulate. Sherfey associates these facts with 'the marked development of the clitoral system' and that of skin erotism in the primates, together with sexual swelling or oedema, common before the period. On her theory, this would correspond to the 'other dimension' of sexuality at the period, which in a male-oriented society might be seen not as the natural possession of the woman, but be polarized into 'unnaturally' masculine behaviour, or be seen as the inner 'other husband' of the woman in her dreams and visions. What has not been usually acknowledged is that this 'other dimension' of sexuality is plainly a guide to extended experience, and might appear as such in dreams and visions. If this were the case, it would be natural that this 'other husband' would be projected on the woman's male companion, and this would tend to form his behaviour during the course of the evolution of masculine consciousness, which we suggest can be seen as a later development than that of the feminine. The woman not only forms the masculine in her womb from originally feminine structures, but also, on this hypothesis, inspires the man through her 'animus', her 'other dimension'. Of course, this would be a complex feedback process between two individuals, and within a social structure, and it is interesting as it has been pointed out as far back as Freud that what we see as 'characteristically masculine' behaviour does not obtain through the animal kingdom among males. Perhaps this is another way in which the menstrual rhythm operates in an evolutionary sense. Jung has noted the mutual animus–anima feedback and individuation in the figure known as the 'double pelican' known to the alchemists: in the ancient world the pelican was also thought to feed its young on blood it gashed from its own chest. On this view, *masculine conscious-ness originated with the woman's menstrual period*, as did specifically human sexuality.

Thus a further difference between human and other animals is that most animals have wombs which are comparatively thick-walled and entirely specialized for reproduction. After and during oestrus there is a thickening of the womb-wall, but this wall never becomes very thin since it is engaged in and specialized for either pregnancy itself, or for reabsorbing its own growth.

The human womb, as we have said, is not like this. Every month it sheds the lining it has built up for a possible pregnancy, and this shedding leaves the womb-wall raw, like a continuous wound. This means that the womb is intensely sensitive, just as the lining of the eye is sensitive, being lined with brain fibres – the retina – and exposed to light. The uterus is strongly supplied with consciously sensory nerves, but also with many filaments whose function is not clearly known to anatomy, as though these supplied an unconscious component – it is probable that all that the tissues of the body experience is in some manner accessible to our consciousness. The womb, particularly at menstruation, is like a sense organ, raw and very, very responsive. It is as though in animals other than the primates the womb is not thus a generalized sense organ, but a structure solely for making children. In the human, or so it appears, the womb has become an organ particularly open to stimulation through the genital organs, and this is why if there is intercourse during menstruation it can be exceptionally deep. Without practice, the rawly open womb may react with pain and irritation; and as it is immensely alive to all that goes on in the individual, if she is told that she is disgusting at that time, it writhes and cramps in anger and disgust. If the truth is told, however, and sexual stimulation is gentle and gradual, sex at menstruation can build up to an experience with completely different dimensions from that of sex at other times of the cycle, as for instance at the child-offering time, the ovulation, a fortnight earlier.

If the sexual experience is not offered, the desire is there still, and the womb seems to cramp in unsuccessful attempts at orgasmic experience, and the result is spasmodic dysmenorrhoea. The orgasm cures. An orgasm at this time causes an ejaculation of blood into the vagina from the cervix. Of course this ejaculatory capacity must also give sex at menstruation a different tone of experience. It is interesting in this connection that Epiphanius mentions a lost gospel of Eve, in which Eve is instructed by a man bleeding from the genitals. We believe that this is an emblem of the knowledge of oneself and one's lover to be gained at the period. The man of blood is Eve's 'true husband', the Moon. He recalls the Fisher King; guardian of the Grail, who is also wounded in the genitals.

Weideger remarks: 'As a menstruating species we are free from the constraint of sexual behaviour which is completely determined by the time of ovulation.' This is true, providing that we do not follow the tribal taboos which try to keep the woman in her role of continual pregnancy as must have been the condition of primitive species. Menstruation must have emerged as a permanent human possession, when the female *learned not to become pregnant*, and this was her emancipation towards the experience which a sexuality not geared to reproduction would give her. How this came about we do not know. There are persistent legends of magic drinks that give wisdom – *soma* from the Moon in India, *lygos* in Greece. One might guess that plants containing steroid substances related to human sex hormones may have been drunk as magic potions, which aborted the uterine lining and gave this new, magical experience of a particular sexual sensitivity, a particular dreamy quality of meditation, an independence from the men, a descent within. Many menstrual taboos of seclusion reflect a woman's desire to be alone at this time with her own body, to the present day.

Recovering the Female Body

THE BOSTON WOMEN'S HEALTH COLLECTIVE
Our Bodies Ourselves

Part of the feminist agenda, as well as the holistic agenda, is to come back into relationship with the body and to know and feel, rather than to ignore or repress, the earthy and sensuous reality of our lives. A minimal requirement for this is to understand and have control over its processes. Against the background of a male-dominated medical profession, groups of women came together in the 1960s to reclaim their bodies and their health.

The Boston Women's Health Book Collective emerged out of a small discussion group called 'Women and Their Bodies' at the Boston Women's Conference in 1969. The group's premise being 'We began to realize how little we knew about our bodies, so we decided to do further research, to prepare papers in groups and then to discuss our findings together.' The book that emerged was first published privately, but then because of demand was published commercially. As well as containing straightforward medical information, it was also full of previously unpublished emotional and psychological counsel.

For us, body education is core education. Our bodies are the physical bases from which we move out into the world: ignorance, uncertainty – even, at worst, shame – about our physical selves create in us an alienation from ourselves that keeps us from being the whole people that we should be.

We still work as a group: our current collective has been together for seven years. We are all white, middle class, and our ages range from twenty-nine to forty-five. Some of us are married, some of us are single, some have children and some do not: we are all working, or have worked, outside our homes. In short, we are both a very ordinary and a very special group, as women everywhere. We realize that poor and non-white women have greater difficulty in getting accurate information and adequate health care, and are most often mistreated in the ways we describe in this book. Learning about our womanhood from the inside out has allowed us to cross over some of the barriers of race, colour, income and class, and to feel a sense of identity with all women in the experience of being female.

How the experience changed us

We formed our group as individual women meeting together because we wanted to. Since most of us had patterned our lives around men, working together was a liberating experience. Like most women's groups we talked to each other about how it felt growing up female: this gave us a basis to discuss what we thought and felt about ourselves and how we wanted to change. At first it was rather scary admitting that we were not completely satisfied with our lives, standing back and taking a hard look at ourselves. Some of us were afraid that commitment to the women's movement and to the group would weaken our ties with men, children, jobs, life-styles: that we might lose control of our lives. We came to realize that this fear was unrealistic. No one could take from us what we did not want to give up.

Probably the most valuable thing we learned was to speak for ourselves and be ourselves. Many of us feared discussing personal details of our lives and relationships, we feared being ridiculed by others, but we soon learned that we had a lot in common. By facing up to our ambivalent feelings and being honest and open, we were able to build up more trusting relationships.

We discovered four cultural notions of femininity which we have in some sense shared: woman as inferior, passive, beautiful object, wife and mother. We realized how severely these notions had constricted us, how humanly limited we felt at being passive dependent creatures with no identities of our own. Gradually, with each other's support, we began to rediscover ourselves.

Rediscovering anger

As we were changing we found we were frequently feeling angry. This surprised us and embarrassed us. We had grown up feeling that we needed to love everyone and be loved by everyone. If we got angry with someone or they with us, we felt in some sense that we were failures.

We shared memories of our pasts. Nearly all of us had had a hard time expressing anger verbally or physically.

I have very few memories of fighting. Each time I did I felt guilty and embarrassed.

We did fight a lot at home, but I never made a public display of any anger or aggression. That was unladylike.

My husband has this habit of not listening to me when I talk. I get angry at him, but I don't tell him.

I seem to put up with a lot of nonsense from people. It is as if I am always being the accepting, forgiving and accommodating person.

We began to admit that we had felt angry during our lives but that we had been using the anger against ourselves in hating ourselves. There were many ways we had learned to cover up our anger. It had built up for so long inside us that we were afraid we would explode if we let it out. We realized that there are many aspects of our lives that make us angry. Until we know and feel our own oppression we are not motivated to try to create constructive alternative ways of being and living. Many have accused us of being shrill. Our mood is far more complex. Our critics hear only the anger, and anger separated from real issues is a distortion. The anger that is in us is a starting point for creative change and growth.[. . .]

Our feelings

Our feelings about our bodies are often negative.

I remember coming home from school every day and going over my body from head to toe. My forehead was too high, my hair too straight, my body too short, my teeth too yellow, and so on.

We are always making some comparison, we're never OK the way we are. We feel ugly, inadequate. And it's no wonder! The ideal woman is something very specific. She may change over time (for instance, small breasts are 'in' these days, large ones 'out'), yet there is always something to measure up to. This ideal is not what *we* created. Yet we are encouraged to change in countless ways so we can fulfil this image. We are discouraged from appreciating our uniqueness.

We are encouraged to feel as though our bodies are not ours. Our 'figure' is for a (potential) mate to admire. Our breasts are for 'the man in our lives', for our babies to suckle, for our doctors to examine. The same kind of 'hands-off' message is even stronger for our vaginas. Sometimes it's hard to like our bodies because we feel so far away from our physical selves.

Having my first child was the first experience in my life in which I felt my physical being was as important as my mind. I related to my total body. I became very unselfconscious. I felt my body was fantastic!

Experiences in the women's movement have drastically changed our thinking and feelings about our bodies.

Recently, as I became more aware of my body, I realized I had pretended some parts didn't exist, while others now seemed made of smaller parts. I also discovered mental and physical processes working together. I realized that when my chest pulled down and felt collapsed I felt unhappy or depressed. When I felt sad my chest would start to tighten. When I became aware of some of the connections, I could start to change. Gradually I felt a new kind of unity, wholeness in me, as my mental and physical selves became one self.

Until we began to prepare this material, many of us didn't know the names of parts of our anatomy. Some of us had learned bits and pieces of information, but it was not permissible to find out too much. The taboos were strongest in the areas of reproduction and sex, which is why our book concentrates on them.

The first month I was at college some of my friends were twittering about a girl down the hall. She was having a painful time trying to learn to put in a tampon. Finally someone helped her and found she was trying to put it in her anus.

Finding out about ourselves

Knowing the facts about our anatomy and physiology has been very exciting for us. It's exhilarating to discover that the material is not as difficult as we once thought. Knowing the language of doctors makes them less mysterious and frightening. We now feel more confident when asking questions. Sometimes a doctor has been startled to find us speaking 'his' language. 'How do you know that? Are you a medical student?' we heard again and again. 'A pretty girl like you shouldn't be concerned about that.' Some doctors are very cooperative in response to our questions. Yet many others appear outwardly pleased while continuing to 'manage' us with new tactics.* From sharing our experiences and knowledge we develop an awareness of difference as well as similarity. We start to have confidence in our knowledge, and that confidence helps us change our feelings about ourselves.

I used to wonder if my body was abnormal even though I didn't have any reason to believe it was. I had nothing to compare it with until I started to talk with other women. I don't feel any more that I might be a freak and not know it.

Since doing a lot of talking about our sexual organs, we have been encouraged to look inside our vaginas by the women's self-help movement. (See 'Self-Examination', p. 135.) Some of us have taken a while to get over our inhibitions about seeing or touching our genitals.

* Valerie Jorgensen, *The Gynaecologist and the Sexually Liberated Woman.*

When someone first said to me two years ago, 'You can feel the end of your own cervix with your finger,' I was interested but flustered. I had hardly ever put my finger in my vagina at all, and felt squeamish about touching myself there, in that place 'reserved' for lovers and doctors. It took me two months to get up my nerve to try it, and then one afternoon, pretty nervously, I squatted down in the bathroom and put my finger in deep, back into my vagina. There it was(!), feeling slippery and rounded, with an indentation at the centre through which, I realized, my menstrual flow came. It was both very exciting and beautifully ordinary at the same time. Last week I bought a plastic speculum so I can look at my cervix. Will it take as long this time?

We still have many bad feelings about ourselves that are hard to admit. We have not, of course, been able to erase decades of social influence in a few years. But we have learned to trust ourselves. We *can* take care of ourselves.

The Shamanic and Magical Traditions

Introduction

It is well known that mainstream organized religions have actively repressed the shamanic and magical traditions. The 'official' religions have been so powerful and so concerned with maintaining their power that they have virtually created monopolies of belief defining what could and could not be believed or practised. Natural tribal and animist spirituality has been persecuted, as has any independent spiritual inquiry. In fact, the control over belief has been so effective that the vast majority of people have been ignorant of any spiritual world-views beyond their local faith.

Nevertheless, often in secret, alternative avenues of spiritual research have been pursued. In the previous section on *Feminism and the Goddess* we saw how female spirituality and Wicca have enjoyed a renaissance during this century. Equally, for the first time in perhaps two thousand years, the twentieth century has seen a public rebirth of tribal shamanism and magic.

A central belief of both shamans and magicians is that the world is made of energy, that every object and living thing has its own energetic vibration, and that the human mind can manipulate this energy to produce tangible results. Mainstream religions have found this approach deeply threatening to their power base, mainly because it places authority in the hands of self-empowered practitioners. At worst it is considered the work of the Devil and his demons.

The religious freedom of the last two centuries, however, has allowed a more public study of these subjects and, as we come into a new millennium, the idea that the human mind can manipulate energy is no longer at all far-fetched. The shamanic and magical approaches are directly relevant to psychology and healing, suggesting insights and strategies. In fact, the idea that *energy follows thought* is the basis of many self-help and visualization techniques which are now popularly used, replacing more classic psychoanalytic and psychotherapeutic approaches.

The magical approach also encourages a much more engaged form of spirituality. The inner dimensions are not simply to be worshipped, but can be directly accessed and explored for education and transformation.

Smoking the Pipe of Peace

BLACK ELK
Black Elk Speaks

In 1930 the poet John Neihardt was researching what was called the 'Messiah craze' among American Indians in the 1880s, which ended with the defeat and massacre at Wounded Knee in 1890. Black Elk, a Sioux holy man, had been part of that movement and was second cousin to the movement's principal hero, Crazy Horse.

Neihardt met Black Elk, who was not interested in talking about history because he had received a prophetic vision. He recounted this vision to Neihardt, sharing with him the story and essence of Sioux spirituality and culture, so that the world in general might receive it. The translation rendered into English by the American poet was poetic prose at its finest. At publication in the 1930s the book did not do so well, but it was rediscovered in the 1960s and became a cult classic.

Black Elk Speaks:
My friend, I am going to tell you the story of my life, as you wish; and if it were only the story of my life I think I would not tell it; for what is one man that he should make much of his winters, even when they bend him like a heavy snow? So many other men have lived and shall live that story, to be grass upon the hills.

It is the story of all life that is holy and is good to tell, and of us two-leggeds sharing in it with the four-leggeds and the wings of the air and all green things; for these are children of one mother and their father is one Spirit.

This, then, is not the tale of a great hunter or of a great warrior, or of a great traveller, although I have made much meat in my time and fought for my people both as boy and man, and have gone far and seen strange lands and men. So also have many others done, and better than I. These things I shall remember by the way, and often they may seem to be the very tale itself, as when I was living them in happiness and sorrow. But now that I can see it all as from a lonely hilltop, I know it was the story of a mighty vision given to a man too weak to use it; of a holy tree that should have flourished in a people's heart with flowers and singing birds, and now is withered; and of a people's dream that died in bloody snow.

But if the vision was true and mighty, as I know, it is true and mighty yet; for such things are of the spirit, and it is in the darkness of their eyes that men get lost.

So I know that it is a good thing I am going to do; and because no good thing can be done by any man alone, I will first make an offering and send a voice to the Spirit of the World, that it may help me to be true. See, I fill this sacred pipe with the bark of the red willow; but before we smoke it, you must see how it is made and what it means. These four ribbons hanging here on the stem are the four quarters of the universe. The black one is for the west where the thunder beings live to send us rain; the white one for the north, whence comes the great white cleansing wind; the red one for the east, whence springs the light and where the morning star lives to give men wisdom; the yellow for the south, whence come the summer and the power to grow.

But these four spirits are only one Spirit after all, and this eagle feather here is for that One, which is like a father, and also it is for the thoughts of men that should rise high as eagles do. Is not the sky a father and the earth a mother, and are not all living things with feet or wings or roots their children? And this hide upon the mouthpiece here, which should be bison hide, is for the earth, from whence we came and at whose breast we suck as babies all our lives, along with all the animals and birds and trees and grasses. And because it means all this, and more than any man can understand, the pipe is holy.

There is a story about the way the pipe first came to us. A very long time ago, they say, two scouts were out looking for bison; and when they came to the top of a high hill and looked north, they saw something coming a long way off, and when it came closer they cried out, 'It is a woman', and it was. Then one of the scouts, being foolish, had bad thoughts and spoke them; but the other said: 'That is a sacred woman; throw all bad thoughts away.' When she came still closer, they saw that she wore a fine white buckskin dress, that her hair was very long and that she was young and very beautiful. And she knew their thoughts and said in a voice that was like singing: 'You do not know me, but if you want to do as you think, you may come.' And the foolish one went; but just as he stood before her, there was a white cloud that came and covered them. And the beautiful young woman came out of the cloud, and when it blew away the foolish man was a skeleton covered with worms.

Then the woman spoke to the one who was not foolish: 'You shall go home and tell your people that I am coming and that a big tepee shall be built for me in the centre of the nation.' And the man, who was very much afraid, went quickly and told the people, who did at once as they were told; and there around the big tepee they waited for the sacred woman. And after a while she came, very beautiful and singing, and as she went into the tepee this is what she sang:

With visible breath I am walking.
A voice I am sending as I walk.
In a sacred manner I am walking.
With visible tracks I am walking.
In a sacred manner I walk.

And as she sang, there came from her mouth a white cloud that was good to smell. Then she gave something to the chief, and it was a pipe with a bison calf carved on one side to mean the earth that bears and feeds us, and with twelve eagle feathers hanging from the stem to mean the sky and the twelve moons, and these were tied with a grass that never breaks. 'Behold!' she said. 'With this you shall multiply and be a good nation. Nothing but good shall come from it. Only the hands of the good shall take care of it and the bad shall not even see it.' Then she sang again and went out of the tepee; and as the people watched her going, suddenly it was a white bison galloping away and snorting, and soon it was gone.

This they tell, and whether it happened so or not I do not know; but if you think about it, you can see that it is true.

Now I light the pipe, and after I have offered it to the powers that are one Power, and sent forth a voice to them, we shall smoke together. Offering the mouthpiece first of all to the One above – so – I send a voice:

Hey hey! hey hey! hey hey! hey hey!

Grandfather, Great Spirit, you have been always, and before you no one has been. There is no other one to pray to but you. You yourself, everything that you see, everything has been made by you. The star nations all over the universe you have finished. The four quarters of the earth you have finished. The day, and in that day, everything you have finished. Grandfather, Great Spirit, lean close to the earth that you may hear the voice I send. You towards where the sun goes down, behold me; Thunder Beings, behold me! You where the White Giant lives in power, behold me! You where the sun shines continually, whence come the daybreak star and the day, behold me! You where the summer lives, behold me! You in the depths of the heavens, an eagle of power, behold! And you, Mother Earth, the only Mother, you who have shown mercy to your children!

Hear me, four quarters of the world – a relative I am! Give me the strength to walk the soft earth, a relative to all that is! Give me the eyes to see and the strength to understand, that I may be like you. With your power only can I face the winds.

Great Spirit, Great Spirit, my Grandfather, all over the earth the faces of living things are all alike. With tenderness have these come up out of the ground. Look upon these faces of children without number and with children in their arms, that they may face the winds and walk the good road to the day of quiet.

This is my prayer; hear me! The voice I have sent is weak, yet with earnestness I have sent it. Hear me!

It is finished. Hetchetu aloh!

Now, my friend, let us smoke together so that there may be only good between us.

Don Juan

CARLOS CASTANEDA

The Teachings of Don Juan: A Yaqui Way of Knowledge

In the summer of 1960 Carlos Castaneda, a young anthropology student, first met Don Juan, an elderly Yaqui Indian, and became his student in the ways of shamanism. When the first book of these teachings was published, the mixture of psychological metaphysics, weird happenings and the use of the organic hallucinogenic substances, had an instant appeal. For many people, *The Teachings of Don Juan* became a bible. Here was a spiritual path in which the inner world was explored in an eccentric, cavalier, humorous and psychedelic style – the very antithesis to the straight and square mainstream American religious culture.

Carlos Castaneda's books also set a modern trend for mystical books in which the reader could never be quite certain whether the story being told was truthful reportage or fiction. It also set the trend in which the sophisticated European-American is in actual fact a clumsy buffoon in contrast to the natural grace, wisdom and courage of the native teacher.

Saturday, 8 April 1962
In our conversations, Don Juan consistently used or referred to the phrase 'man of knowledge', but never explained what he meant by it. I asked him about it.

'A man of knowledge is one who has followed truthfully the hardships of learning,' he said. 'A man who has, without rushing or without faltering, gone as far as he can in unravelling the secrets of power and knowledge.'

'Can anyone be a man of knowledge?'

'No, not anyone.'

'Then what must a man do to become a man of knowledge?'

'He must challenge and defeat his four natural enemies.'

'Will he be a man of knowledge after defeating these four enemies?'

'Yes. A man can call himself a man of knowledge only if he is capable of defeating all four of them.'

'Then, can *anybody* who defeats these enemies be a man of knowledge?'

'Anybody who defeats them becomes a man of knowledge.'

'But are there any special requirements a man must fulfil before fighting with these enemies?'

'No. Anyone can try to become a man of knowledge; very few men actually succeed, but that is only natural. The enemies a man encounters on the path of learning to become a man of knowledge are truly formidable; most men succumb to them.'

'What kind of enemies are they, Don Juan?'

He refused to talk about the enemies. He said it would be a long time before the subject would make any sense to me. I tried to keep the topic alive and asked him if he thought *I* could become a man of knowledge. He said no man could possibly tell that for sure. But I insisted on knowing if there were any clues he could use to determine whether or not I had a chance of becoming a man of knowledge. He said it would depend on my battle against the four enemies – whether I could defeat them or would be defeated by them – but it was impossible to foretell the outcome of that fight.

I asked him if he could use witchcraft or divination to see the outcome of the battle. He flatly stated that the result of the struggle could not be foreseen by any means, because becoming a man of knowledge was a temporary thing. When I asked him to explain this point, he replied:

'To be a man of knowledge has no permanence. One is never a man of knowledge, not really. Rather, one becomes a man of knowledge for a very brief instant, after defeating the four natural enemies.'

'You must tell me, Don Juan, what kind of enemies they are.'

He did not answer. I insisted again, but he dropped the subject and started to talk about something else.

Sunday, 15 April 1962

As I was getting ready to leave, I decided to ask him once more about the enemies of a man of knowledge. I argued that I could not return for some time, and it would be a good idea to write down what he had to say and then think about it while I was away.

He hesitated for a while, but then began to talk.

'When a man starts to learn, he is never clear about his objectives. His purpose is faulty; his intent is vague. He hopes for rewards that will never materialize, for he knows nothing of the hardships of learning.

'He slowly begins to learn – bit by bit at first, then in big chunks. And his thoughts soon clash. What he learns is never what he pictured, or imagined, and so he begins to be afraid. Learning is never what one expects. Every step of learning is a new task, and the fear the man is experiencing begins to mount mercilessly, unyieldingly. His purpose becomes a battlefield.

'And thus he has tumbled upon the first of his natural enemies: Fear! A terrible enemy – treacherous, and difficult to overcome. It remains concealed at every turn of the way, prowling, waiting. And if the man, terrified in its presence, runs away, his enemy will have put an end to his quest.'

'What will happen to the man if he runs away in fear?'

'Nothing happens to him except that he will never learn. He will never become a man of knowledge. He will perhaps be a bully or a harmless, scared man; at any rate, he will be a defeated man. His first enemy will have put an end to his cravings.'

'And what can he do to overcome fear?'

'The answer is very simple. He must not run away. He must defy his fear, and in spite of it he must take the next step in learning, and the next, and the next. He must be fully afraid, and yet he must not stop. That is the rule! And a moment will come when his first enemy retreats. The man begins to feel sure of himself. His intent becomes stronger. Learning is no longer a terrifying task.

'When this joyful moment comes, the man can say without hesitation that he has defeated his first natural enemy.'

'Does it happen at once, Don Juan, or little by little?'

'It happens little by little, and yet the fear is vanquished suddenly and fast.'

'But won't the man be afraid again if something new happens to him?'

'No. Once a man has vanquished fear, he is free from it for the rest of his life because, instead of fear, he has acquired clarity – a clarity of mind which erases fear. By then a man knows his desires; he knows how to satisfy those desires. He can anticipate the new steps of learning, and a sharp clarity surrounds everything. The man feels that nothing is concealed.

'And thus he has encountered his second enemy: Clarity! That clarity of mind, which is so hard to obtain, dispels fear, but also blinds.

'It forces the man never to doubt himself. It gives him the assurance he can do anything he pleases, for he sees clearly into everything. And he is courageous because he is clear, and he stops at nothing because he is clear. But all that is a mistake; it is like something incomplete. If the man yields to this make-believe power, he has succumbed to his second enemy and will fumble with learning. He will rush when he should be patient, or he will be patient when he should rush. And he will fumble with learning until he winds up incapable of learning anything more.'

'What becomes of a man who is defeated in that way, Don Juan? Does he die as a result?'

'No, he doesn't die. His second enemy has just stopped him cold from trying to become a man of knowledge; instead, the man may turn into a buoyant warrior, or a clown. Yet the clarity for which he has paid so dearly will never change to darkness and fear again. He will be clear as long as he lives, but he will no longer learn, or yearn for, anything.'

'But what does he have to do to avoid being defeated?'

'He must do what he did with fear: he must defy his clarity and use it only to see, and wait patiently and measure carefully before taking new steps; he must think, above all, that his clarity is almost a mistake. And a moment will come when he will understand that his clarity was only a point before his eyes. And thus he will have overcome his second enemy, and will arrive at a position where nothing can harm him any more. This will not be a mistake. It will not be only a point before his eyes. It will be true power.

'He will know at this point that the power he has been pursuing for so long is finally his. He can do with it whatever he pleases. His ally is at his command. His wish is the rule. He sees all that is around him. But he has also come across his third enemy: Power!

'Power is the strongest of all enemies. And naturally the easiest thing to do is to give in; after all, the man is truly invincible. He commands;

he begins by taking calculated risks, and ends in making rules, because he is a master.

'A man at this stage hardly notices his third enemy closing in on him. And suddenly, without knowing, he will certainly have lost the battle. His enemy will have turned him into a cruel, capricious man.'

'Will he lose his power?'

'No, he will never lose his clarity or his power.'

'What then will distinguish him from a man of knowledge?'

'A man who is defeated by power dies without really knowing how to handle it. Power is only a burden upon his fate. Such a man has no command over himself, and cannot tell when or how to use his power.'

'Is the defeat by any of these enemies a final defeat?'

'Of course it is final. Once one of these enemies overpowers a man there is nothing he can do.'

'Is it possible, for instance, that the man who is defeated by power may see his error and mend his ways?'

'No. Once a man gives in he is through.'

'But what if he is temporarily blinded by power, and then refuses it?'

'That means his battle is still on. That means he is still trying to become a man of knowledge. A man is defeated only when he no longer tries, and abandons himself.'

'But then, Don Juan, it is possible that a man may abandon himself to fear for years, but finally conquer it.'

'No, that is not true. If he gives in to fear he will never conquer it, because he will shy away from learning and never try again. But if he tries to learn for years in the midst of his fear, he will eventually conquer it because he will never have really abandoned himself to it.'

'How can he defeat his third enemy, Don Juan?'

'He has to defy it, deliberately. He has to come to realize the power he has seemingly conquered is in reality never his. He must keep himself in line at all times, handling carefully and faithfully all that he has learned. If he can see that clarity and power, without his control over himself, are worse than mistakes, he will reach a point where everything is held in check. He will know then when and how to use his power. And thus he will have defeated his third enemy.

'The man will be, by then, at the end of his journey of learning, and almost without warning he will come upon the last of his enemies: Old age! This enemy is the cruellest of all, the one he won't be able to defeat completely, but only fight away.

'This is the time when a man has no more fears, no more impatient clarity of mind – a time when all his power is in check, but also the time when he has an unyielding desire to rest. If he gives in totally to his desire to lie down and forget, if he soothes himself in tiredness, he will have lost his last round, and his enemy will cut him down into a feeble old creature. His desire to retreat will overrule all his clarity, his power, and his knowledge.

'But if the man sloughs off his tiredness, and lives his fate through, he can then be called a man of knowledge, if only for the brief moment when he succeeds in fighting off his last, invincible enemy. That moment of clarity, power, and knowledge is enough.'

African Initiation

MALIDOMA SOMÉ
Of Water and the Spirit

Kidnapped as a child from the Dagara tribe in West Africa, Malidoma Somé was educated by Jesuits and went on to gain three master's degrees and two doctorates from the Sorbonne and Brandeis Universities. However, in his twenties he felt a deep need to return to his tribe where he was taken through the rites of passage and initiations of a Dagara shaman. As well as writing, he and his wife, Sobonfu, teach extensively in the United States and Europe giving Westerners direct experience of their material, in particular the healing that comes from group ritual and awareness of ancestral threads.

The sound of the *kuor*, a ceremonial drum, rose, speaking the words of the ritual that was to take place. It was usually high-pitched, but was punctuated now and then by a single bass note. The specific meaning of its rhythms was not immediately graspable, but its tones extended and intensified the sacredness of the moment. As if it were listening, the fire responded almost immediately by flashing its flames upward, changing its colour from orange to violet. Though the voice of the drum came from behind me, I could not tell if it was near or far. Its location was not important as long as its voice could be heard and its effect felt. Soon the circle opened from the south side. Five students entered, followed by the elders. The students were holding pots of paint which they set down beside the fire.

The elders positioned themselves at the corners of the four directions, and the coach examined the pots and their contents, pouring medicine into each of them. I had no clues as to what was going to happen tonight, and I was uneasy, realizing how powerfully last night's events had affected me. As I thought about my failure, I was afraid. If there was a continuity between experiences, if the success of one guaranteed the success of the other, then I was the least prepared initiate at the fire circle tonight.

The elder in the centre of the circle took one of the pots and began to paint on the coach's body with a brush. First he took some paint that shone red and made a series of lines on the coach's face, running from one ear to another. Then he added some lines that ran from one cheek to the other, above and below the nose. He added a circle around the mouth.

The symbolism of the patterns of the face paint was indecipherable to me, though I sensed that the lines had meaning. As the elder painted the coach, he spoke all the while in primal language, the language elders learn as a tool to fulfil their responsibilities. Primal language is the language of the spirit, and of creation. When uttered under certain circumstances it has the power to manifest what is uttered. Primal language is also dangerous because of the potential it has to be lethal. I still remember the first time I heard Grandfather speak it during my childhood. He used it as a retaliatory weapon against a vulture who had defecated on his bald head. He faced the tree where the bird was sitting, uttered a few sentences, and the poor thing came crashing to the ground. When I rushed over to grab it, it was ash. Because of the potency of primal language, only certain elders are given custody of it.

As I watched the elder paint, I also intuited that there was a connection between what he said and the almost mechanical precision of his drawing. The way the brush ran looked almost magical. It was a dance that responded to the way the drum spoke. The dancing of the brush also responded to the dancing of the flames. I became aware that there was a connection between the rhythm of the drum, the dance of the fire, and the manner in which meaning was inscribed on the coach's face. Upon completion, the pattern on his face was a combination of colours: white, red, green, blue and yellow.

The elder then moved on to the coach's chest, drawing a long vertical white line that ran from below the neck to the navel. Then he drew a series of yellow horizontal lines that crossed the vertical line from east to west. These lines on the chest made the coach look like he was carrying his bones outside his body. The painted patterns became even more complicated when the elder started painting on the legs.

I stopped paying attention to the painting as my attention was drawn to what the coach and the elder were saying to each other. It began as a murmur, as if they were merely communicating practical information to each other. Soon they seemed to be reciting prayers as part of the ritual. Their language was not primal language, nor was it the common tongue. As they spoke, the drum intensified. The fire grew bigger and roared louder as the old man busied himself on the coach, transforming him into a phantasm.

When the elder was finished, he threw his brush into the fire, which bucked and roared. The other elders then entered the circle and in a flash had painted the five students who had helped them carry the paint pots. Then each student came and painted one of us with whatever he had at hand. One of them approached me with a potful of green paint. I shut my eyes. He ran the brush upward and downward, right to left, all over my body. The paint was warm. I wondered if it would ever come off.

When I opened my eyes the circle looked like a wonderland. The fire was alive in a magnificent way. It had ceased to be fire and become a luminescent circle of dynamism, the window into a marvellous world populated by Lilliputians. They were suspended in the middle of it, singing a curious melody. I watched these beings, magnetized by their unceasing motion. They were suspended in mid-air. I realized that they appeared small only because they were far away, yet I also knew that this was happening in the fire right there in front of me. The song that rose from the fire did not necessarily come from the floating people, but seemed to emanate from everywhere and everything. Soon the luminescent circle of the fire grew bigger and bigger. I could not tell what exactly was happening, but I did not care. It felt great.

Everybody began singing one of those songs you suddenly know the words to, as if you had learned it in a previous life. I lost the analytical part of my mind and was drawn irresistibly into participation. I sang full-throated, clapped my hands, and danced. I could not see the other people, but I knew everybody was there. I could perceive their presence by a different sensory apparatus than the usual five senses. Soon I experienced myself in the same way, as if I were invisible, yet all the more concrete, cogent, powerful, and inalienable. This feeling was wonderful. Never before had I experienced something so real, so true, and so befitting a human being.

When invited into the dynamic circle of fire, we did not hesitate. I do not recall who made the invitation, but I don't think it was an elder. Rather, the invitation came from the Angels who floated in it. The land in the middle of the fire was a vast natural place with trees that burned but were not consumed. The fire they burned with was as bright and pure as the purest gold in the world – and I was in the middle of it.

The grass was also in flames, golden and non-burning. I came to a river – flowing golden liquid like fresh lava running down a hill. The river made me experience an indescribable relief a thousand times more powerful than any earthly sensation. When I jumped into it in a moment of excess and foolishness, the effect produced by my contact with the water was so powerful that I blacked out.

When I awoke, the night was far gone. I could tell this by the position of the shepherd star, which had already risen high in the sky. Dawn was close. I was lying, wet and cold, on the bank of a familiar village river some three kilometres from where we had the painting ceremony at dusk. I was more exhausted and surprised than frightened. I stood up and started the trek back to the initiation camp while images crowded my mind.

One thing I noticed: although it was still pitch-black night, I did not hesitate about where I was going for one single moment. Somehow I felt as if I were being mechanically drawn towards the camp by an irresistible force that I did not mind having around me.

When I finally arrived, dawn was only a few moments away. The few students I saw were sound asleep. Nyangoli and Touri were not on their foliage couches, and I thought they must have been left behind in the wondrous experience of the night. When I lay down on the cold leaves, I could not sleep and I did not try to. Instead, I watched the sky above me. As I gazed at it, I felt an immense nostalgia, as if voices from afar were calling to me.

The voices seemed to emanate from each of the tiny stars that lit the sky. A feeling of sadness and pain I cannot put into words overtook me, and I surrendered to it gently as if it were natural to feel what I felt. As to what had really happened to me during the course of the night, my mind never once tried to analyse it. The proximity of the silent darkness spoke comforting words to my heart, and I felt the friendliness of the trees and the grass surrounding the camp. This

invisible presence of the stillness resurrected an intense sense of home
and comfort within me.

Old Song
Do not seek too much fame,
but do not seek obscurity.
Be proud.
But do not remind the world of your deeds.
Excel when you must,
but do not excel the world.
Many heroes are not yet born,
many have already died.
To be alive to hear this song is a victory.

Traditional, West Africa

The Qabalah

DION FORTUNE
The Mystical Qabalah

Dion Fortune is considered to be the most important woman writer and thinker to emerge from the magical revival in England at the turn of the nineteenth century. She was a member of the Hermetic Order of the Golden Dawn, whose members included W. B. Yeats. She brought to the occult an understanding of psychology which she had studied at London University. She founded the Society of the Inner Light and had her study centre in Glastonbury. Many commentators think that her *The Mystical Qabalah* is the best introductory text to the practice of Qabalah, the esoteric and magical tradition of Judaism. This may seem paradoxical as Dion Fortune was not Jewish, but it illustrates the permeable boundaries of the holistic approach.

1. Speaking of the method of the Qabalah, one of the ancient Rabbis says that an angel coming down to earth would have to take on human form in order to converse with men. The curious symbol-system known to us as the Tree of Life is an attempt to reduce to diagrammatic form every force and factor in the manifested universe and the soul of man; to correlate them one to another and reveal them spread out as on a map so that the relative positions of each unit can be seen and the relations between them traced. In brief, the Tree of Life is a compendium of science, psychology, philosophy, and theology.

2. The student of the Qabalah goes to work in exactly the opposite way to the student of natural science; the latter builds up synthetic concepts; the former analyses abstract concepts. It goes without saying, however, that before a concept can be analysed it must first be assembled. Someone must have thought out the principles that are resumed in the symbol which is the object of meditation of the Qabalist. Who then were the first Qabalists who built up the whole scheme?

The Rabbis are unanimous upon this point, they were angels. In other words, it was beings of another order of creation than humanity who gave the Chosen People their Qabalah.

3. To the modern mind this may seem as absurd a statement as the doctrine that babies are found under gooseberry bushes; but if we study the many mystical systems of comparative religion we find that all the illuminati are in agreement upon this point. All men and women who have had practical experience of the spiritual life tell us that they are taught by Divine beings. We shall be very foolish if we altogether disregard such a cloud of witnesses, especially those of us who never have had any personal experience of the higher states of consciousness.

4. There are some psychologists who will tell us that the Angels of the Qabalists and the Gods and Manus of other systems are our own repressed complexes; there are others with less limited outlook who will tell us that these Divine beings are the latent capacities of our own higher selves. To the devotional mystic this is not a point of any great moment; he gets his results, and that is all he cares about; but the philosophical mystic, in other words the occultist, thinks the matter out and arrives at certain conclusions. These conclusions, however, can only be understood when we know what we mean by reality and have a clear line of demarcation between the subjective and the objective. Anyone who is trained in philosophical method knows that this is asking a good deal.

5. The Indian schools of metaphysics have most elaborate and intricate systems of philosophy which attempt to define these ideas and render them thinkable; and though generations of seers have given their lives to the task, the concepts still remain so abstract that it is only after a long course of discipline, called Yoga in the East, that the mind is able to apprehend them at all.

6. The Qabalist goes to work in a different way. He does not attempt to make the mind rise up on the wings of metaphysics into the rarefied air of abstract reality; he formulates a concrete symbol that the eye can see, and lets it represent the abstract reality that no untrained human mind can grasp.

7. It is exactly the same principle as algebra. Let X represent the unknown quantity, let Y represent the half of X, and let Z represent something we know. If we begin to experiment with Y, to find out its relation to Z, and in what proportions, it soon ceases to be entirely unknown; we have learned something at any rate about it; and if we are sufficiently skilful we may in the end be able to express Y in terms of Z, and then we shall begin to understand X.

8. There are a great many symbols which are used as objects of meditation; the Cross in Christendom; the God-forms in the Egyptian system; phallic symbols in other faiths. These symbols are used by the uninitiated as a means of concentrating the mind and introducing into it certain thoughts, calling up certain associated ideas, and stimulating certain feelings. The initiate, however, uses a symbol-system differently; he uses it as an algebra by means of which he will read the secrets of unknown potencies; in other words, he uses the symbol as a means of guiding thought out into the Unseen and Incomprehensible.

9. And how does he do this? He does it by using a composite symbol; a symbol which is an unattached unit would not serve his purpose. In contemplating such a composite symbol as the Tree of Life he observes that there are definite relations between its parts. There are some parts of which he knows something; there are others of which he can intuit something, or, more crudely, make a guess, reasoning from first principles. The mind leaps from one known to another known and in so doing traverses certain distances, metaphorically speaking; it is like a traveller in the desert who knows the situation of two oases and makes a forced march between them. He would never have dared to push out into the desert from the first oasis if he had not known the location of the second; but at the end of his journey he not only knows much more about the characteristics of the second oasis, but he has also observed the country lying between them. Thus, making forced marches from oasis to oasis, backwards and forwards across the desert, he gradually explores it; nevertheless, the desert is incapable of supporting life.

10. So it is with the Qabalistic system of notation. The things it renders are unthinkable – and yet the mind, tracking from symbol to symbol,

manages to think about them; and although we have to be content to see in a glass darkly, yet we have every reason to hope that ultimately we shall see face to face and know even as we are known; for the human mind grows by exercise, and that which was at first as unthinkable as mathematics to the child who cannot manage his sums, finally comes within the range of our realization. By thinking about a thing, we build concepts of it.

11. It is said that thought grew out of language, not language out of thought. What words are to thought, symbols are to intuition. Curious as it may seem, the symbol precedes the elucidation; that is why we declare that the Qabalah is a growing system, not a historic monument. There is more to be got out of the Qabalistic symbols today than there was in the time of the old dispensation because our mental content is richer in ideas. How much more, for instance, does the Sephirah Yesod, wherein work the forces of growth and reproduction, mean to the biologist than to the ancient rabbi? Everything that has to do with growth and reproduction is resumed in the Sphere of the Moon. But this Sphere, as represented upon the Tree of Life, is set about with Paths leading to other Sephiroth; therefore the biological Qabalist knows that there must be certain definite relationships between the forces subsumed in Yesod and those represented by the symbols assigned to these Paths. Brooding over these symbols, he gets glimpses of relationships that do not reveal themselves when the material aspect of things is considered; and when he comes to work these out in the material of his studies he finds that therein are hidden important clues; and so upon the Tree, one thing leads to another, explanation of hidden causes arising out of the proportions and relations of the various individual symbols composing this mighty synthetic glyph.

12. Each symbol, moreover, admits of interpretation upon the different planes, and through its astrological associations can be related to the gods of any pantheon, thus opening up vast new fields of implication in which the mind ranges endlessly, symbol leading on to symbol in an unbroken chain of associations; symbol confirming symbol as the many-branching threads gather themselves together into a synthetic glyph once more, and each symbol capable of interpretation in terms of whatever plane the mind may be functioning upon.

13. This mighty, all-embracing glyph of the soul of man and of the universe, by virtue of its logical association of symbols, evokes images in the mind; but these images are not randomly evolved, but follow along well-defined association-tracks in the Universal Mind. The symbol of the Tree is to the Universal Mind what the dream is to the individual ego – it is a glyph synthetized from subconsciousness to represent the hidden forces.

14. The universe is really a thought-form projected from the mind of God. The Qabalistic Tree might be likened to a dream-picture arising from the subconsciousness of God and dramatizing the subconscious content of Deity. In other words, if the universe is the conscious end-product of the mental activity of the Logos, the Tree is the symbolic representation of the raw material of the Divine consciousness and of the processes whereby the universe came into being.

15. But the Tree applies not only to the Macrocosm but to the Microcosm which, as all occultists realize, is a replica in miniature. It is for this reason that divination is possible. That little-understood and much-maligned art has for its philosophical basis the System of Correspondences represented by symbols. The correspondences between the soul of man and the universe are not arbitrary, but arise out of developmental identities. Certain aspects of consciousness were developed in response to certain phases of evolution, and therefore embody the same principles; consequently they react to the same influences. A man's soul is like a lagoon connected with the sea by a submerged channel; although to all outward seeming it is land-locked, nevertheless its water level rises and falls with the tides of the sea because of the hidden connection. So it is with human consciousness, there is a subconscious connection between each individual soul and the world-soul deep hidden in the most primitive depths of subconsciousness, and in consequence we share in the rise and fall of the cosmic tides.

16. Each symbol upon the Tree represents a cosmic force or factor. When the mind concentrates upon it, it comes into touch with that force; in other words, a surface channel, a channel in consciousness, has been made between the conscious mind of the individual and a

particular factor in the world-soul, and through this channel the waters of the ocean pour into the lagoon. The aspirant who uses the Tree as his meditation-symbol establishes point by point the union between his soul and the world-soul. This results in a tremendous access of energy to the individual soul; it is this which endows it with magical powers.

17. But just as the universe must be ruled by God, so must the many-sided soul of man be ruled by its god – the spirit of man. The Higher Self must dominate its universe or there will be unbalanced force; each factor will rule its own aspect, and they will war among themselves. Then do we have the rule of the Kings of Edom, whose kingdoms are unbalanced force.

18. Thus do we see in the Tree a glyph of the soul of man and the universe, and in the legends associated with it the history of the evolution of the soul and the Way of Initiation.

Energy Therapy

PHYLLIS KRYSTAL
Cutting the Ties That Bind

Phyllis Krystal was trained as a psychotherapist in the Jungian and Eriksonian schools and is also a disciple of Sai Baba. Her work integrates a psychotherapeutic approach with a fundamental magical technique. The basic concept of *Cutting the Ties That Bind* is that people are sometimes too closely connected – for example, children and parents, or ex-lovers. The connection is not purely psychological, but there are also threads of energy which connect the two people together. A healthy separation therefore requires not only a mature attitude but also the cutting of these energetic bonds.

After the person is relaxed, I suggest that we both imagine a triangle erected between us, explaining its function if that has not already been done. I have the person take a place at point B on the base, with me at the other end at point A, joined by a line representing the mutual trust we have for each other as working partners. Then we both visualize an antenna reaching up our spines, out from the top of each of our heads, meeting at a point in space at the apex of the triangle, which we call the High C, High Consciousness or God-self. The High C is the innate wisdom within all of us, where we are all one.

We then take time to ask that each of us be guided from that mutual High C, so that the right questions and directions will come to the one who is directing and that the person in the relaxed state will receive and be ready to handle whatever he needs to see, feel, know or experience at that particular time.

This method has proved to be foolproof over the years and we have never had occasion when someone with whom we were working got out of his depth, or was faced with any memory, fault or old trauma that was too much for him to handle.

I then explain that the person is not to worry if this first time he sees nothing, as in that event I can easily slip into the reverie state myself and describe what I see, and then direct him according to how I am guided from within. Even if that is difficult, I make it clear that I can, if so directed, take over, watch and describe the impressions I am receiving and do whatever I am prompted to do to help on his inner level. This seems to take all the anxiety and pressure off those who may be worried that they will not be able to visualize.

Next, I ask the person to visualize the two circles of the Figure Eight which are already familiar from the two-week daily practice periods, and then invite into the circle opposite the one he is in the parent from whom he is about to separate. I tell him to explain to the parent that the ritual about to be performed will free both of them so that each will be able to live his own life as a separate individual and will no longer be pulled this way and that by the actions of the other via the cords which still bind them together. I then encourage the person to see if he can see the ties between him and his parent, and to tell me at which parts of the body on each person the cords are attached. Most people seem to be able to visualize this fairly easily and some are really shocked at what they see. I warn the person not to be disturbed since what he sees will show us how best to help the relationship.

It is not at all unusual for the parent of the opposite sex to be joined to the child between the sex organs, telling us a great deal about their relationship and showing us where they will need to work if they ever hope to have a good relationship with someone of the opposite sex.

Some people find only one link while others discover several, depending on the closeness, either positive or negative, of the relationship. We have had a few cases where the connection was so strong that the two were like Siamese twins. In these situations, it was impossible for the person desiring to be free to see clearly and it was out of the question to expect him to perform the 'surgery' himself. In this case the person directing the session must be willing to perform the operation for him, urging him to participate as much as possible.

When the ties have been located, I ask for a description of the size and texture and, here again, I have heard literally hundreds of different descriptions, all symbolic of the relationship and often astonishingly revealing. There have been velvet ribbons, nylon thread, fishing lines, wire, rope, chains, metal bars, and many, many other types of cords.

When the nature of the ties has been determined, I tell him to ask to be shown the appropriate instrument with which to sever or detach the bonds, and again the selection is surprisingly varied. Scissors, all kinds of knives such as kitchen and hunting knives, swords, and daggers, light rays, laser beams, fire, acid, saws, to mention but a few, are forthcoming.

I usually suggest that the first cut be made in the middle of the bond and then each end removed from each person's body where it is attached. Frequently I have to help remove the end from the person doing the detaching if it happens to be on a part of the body which is hard for him to reach or is too sensitive for him to dare to tackle on his own with any confidence of success.

As each end is removed, I suggest placing the right hand (if the person is right handed, otherwise the left hand) over the place where it was removed on either body, with the other hand behind it to create a force field. Then we ask that a healing force flow down from the High C into his hands and into the wound left by the cutting.

The ties are then placed in a pile at the feet of the person working and, when they have all been detached, he asks to be shown the best method of destroying them, thus preventing them from returning to continue the old pattern.

Most people choose to burn or bury, dissolve with acid, or hurl the bonds into the sea or a fast-flowing river. Frequently, people are so anxious to be finished with such ties that they cannot think of enough to do to be sure they are definitely destroyed, often deciding to bury the fire in which they have burned them and then jumping up and down on the site to erase all evidence of it. This has, at times, developed into something like an Indian war dance, which I then suggest should become an expression of the person's relief at being finally free. I encourage them to let go and express this freedom in any way they choose.

After they are satisfied that everything has been done to erase all trace of the old ties, I suggest they thank the parent from whom they have just been separated for providing the means for them to enter the world in a human body, and thus be able to learn whatever was necessary in this life.

Next the person performs a ritual in which he asks forgiveness from the parent and forgives the parent for any hurts that have been inflicted on him, consciously or unconsciously. This is often very hard for the person to do, especially in a case where there are hard feelings between him and the parent. It is essential that the forgiving be done as it is part of the process of becoming detached and whole. Lack of forgiveness can forge the links all over again in a negative way.

I usually start by having the person first ask the parent for forgiveness, as this part of the ritual seems to be, for most people, slightly easier: many people suffer from a load of guilt and this presents the person with an opportunity to relieve himself of the burden. I suggest that he allow specific things to come to mind for which he would like forgiveness and either to verbalize them or silently mention them, one at a time. If he chooses to be silent, I ask him to let me know when he has finished, to the best of his knowledge. I also tell him that anything more coming up later can always be handled at that time. We find that this opportunity to ask forgiveness is most welcome and frees the person from the haunting sense of guilt and regret which people are so often left with, particularly after the parent has passed on.

The next step is to forgive the parent for any hurts or wrongs inflicted, either consciously or unconsciously, on the one seeking release. This is by far the harder task for most people and, in some cases, they find it impossible to attempt.

At such times, I suggest that even though the person cannot find it in his heart to forgive this parent, he can ask the High C, or God-force within him, to send forgiveness from the top of the triangle between us down through himself and across to the parent. This is almost always acceptable even by those who know they need to forgive but cannot bring themselves to do so on their own. Again, I suggest that they allow specific episodes to enter their minds where forgiveness of the parent is needed to set them both free from the negative emotions which bind people just as strongly as positive ones.

Finally, the parent is asked to leave the scene and go on his way to lead his own life, now free from the constant emotional tug of the child. This request does not necessarily mean that there will be no further contact between them; indeed, most people find that, on the contrary, the relationship becomes much less emotionally charged and more satisfactory.

We always suggest an appropriate parting, preferably with a blessing. Sometimes it is indicated that a triangle be visualized between the parent and child connecting them both to the High C instead of to one another. We have been shown that this visualization is the most helpful thing anyone can do for another person, and we call it 'running the triangle'. We often do this ourselves when we receive a call for help (even before the person has been told anything about it) to connect him to the High C as quickly as possible.

One further step is taken to complete the release. This is a cleansing process, which is designed to wash away all old conditioning and habit patterns.

Soul Retrieval

Soul Retrieval – Mending the Fragmented Self

A student and then professor at the Foundation for Shamanic Studies under the direction of Michael Harner, Sandra Ingerman wrote the major text for a form of therapy which merges contemporary psychological insight with a classic shamanic technique. According to shamanic lore, when a person is psychologically or physically abused they lose, or have stolen from them, a fragment of their own soul. To recover this fragment, the shaman or tribal healer needs to journey, in a trance state, into the underworld of the collective unconscious where, often after facing certain challenges, the fragment is brought back and returned to the client.

On the title page of her book, Sandra Ingerman is very clear: *The shamanic way of healing using soul retrieval presented in this book should not be considered an exclusive method of confronting psychological and/or medical problems. It should be viewed as an adjunct to orthodox medical or psychological treatment.*

A serious phenomenon I see when searching for souls is that sometimes a soul has actually been stolen by another person. I often hear incest survivors who know nothing about shamanism say, 'My father stole my soul', or 'My uncle stole my soul.' Similarly, people who have been caught in abusive relationships frequently claim, 'My lover stole my soul.'

For lack of a better word in the English language, I use the word *thief* for a person who steals a soul. But I use this word without judgement or blame. Soul stealing is often done out of ignorance rather than intent to harm. Soul theft is a hard concept for many of us to grasp. Why would someone commit what amounts to grand larceny on a human level? How can we explain this? And how can we take a compassionate stance on the issue of soul stealing?

In most cases of soul stealing the thief is also a victim of soul theft.

Through contemporary psychology, we have discovered that people who abuse usually were abused themselves. Likewise, soul stealing is generational; therefore, doing a soul retrieval for a person whose soul has been stolen may end family karma. Bringing back the soul and educating the client about the concept of soul theft and loss prevents this behaviour from being passed down to future generations.

But why steal another person's soul? One reason is power. The thief might envy the person's power and might attempt to take that power for personal use, putting the thief in the position of power over the victim. It is sad but all too common for a person who feels powerless to deal with this feeling by moving into a power-over stance. For example, if a father feels powerless because he's unable to create wholeness in his own life, he might move into stealing the soul of his young, defenceless child by raping or beating the child or his wife. In this way he is saying, 'I am more powerful than you.' Yet he is creating a false sense of self.

In our society the word *power* is understood by most of us as *power over* another person. The two words seem to go together. Because people generally have no concept of what personal power means, most of my clients, especially women, have no understanding of how to avoid giving their personal power away to another person. This lack of understanding of power goes hand in hand with soul stealing. A person who is willing to give away his or her personal power to another becomes vulnerable to soul theft. Children, who usually don't know how to protect themselves physically, are especially susceptible to having their souls stolen.

Another reason for soul stealing is the mistaken belief that one person's essence, vitality, and power can be used by someone else. For example, I worked with a woman whose soul was stolen at the age of three months by her mother. Her mother saw such light and energy in the baby that she felt that if she could have just a part of this child, it would restore her own vitality. A common pattern I see is that clients who had a part of their souls taken at an early age tend to be chronically ill as children. They lose part of their vitality and therefore don't have the power or the will to fight off illness. After the soul retrieval it's not unusual for a client to rattle off a long list of childhood illnesses.

The same scene appears repeatedly in my journeys. To protect themselves in the psychic battle with a parent, children surrender their will. What I see is a child who has given up – hunched over, turned in, and despondent. The effects of soul theft at an early age are manifested similarly in these clients as adults. Often, through these life experiences, they have become very protective of their energy and vitality and look very 'pulled in'. It's almost as if they have a need to hide their 'light' or vitality so that no one will try to take it away again. I also find that a common complaint among these clients is a lack of hope and will in their lives.

The belief that we can use another person's light, power, energy, or essence for our own good is a misunderstanding. Certainly, you can reflect an individual's light and power, but you cannot use them as a source of your own energy. Each one of us must reach inside ourselves to find our own power sources.

Restoring Angela's light

When Angela came to see me for a soul retrieval, she complained that she was always withdrawn. She didn't feel able to take a stand in the world or to get ahead by demonstrating her talents. She also felt that she had issues of abandonment to work through. Her history revealed that at age four, she had been hospitalized with pneumonia. From what Angela now knew of psychology, she suspected she was carrying around feelings of abandonment from that time. She assumed she must have felt abandoned and scarred by the separation from her parents.

I begin my journey by going to the Lower World – through my tree trunk, into my tunnel, and out into the pine forest where my power animal resides. I tell him about Angela and ask him if there is any information or anything I can do that will be helpful to her.

Together we move through time and space to the Middle World. A white house with a picket fence stands before us. We open the gate and go through the front door, wandering through the living room, which is cluttered with lots of things. As we walk through, I can smell something sweet baking in the oven. It is a nice, sunny afternoon, and lots of light streams through the windows.

I follow the smell into the kitchen, my power animal walking beside me. To one seeing with ordinary vision, the kitchen scene that I observe is that of a happy bond between mother and daughter. There is three- or four-year-old Angela with her blonde curls and green dress on the floor playing with her stuffed bear. Angela's mom is lovingly mixing cookie batter. But looking with the strong eye, a psychic battle is going on. Angela's mother, worn out by the drudgery of cooking, cleaning, and raising children, is tired and despondent. Angela, by contrast, has such life force and energy, and a strong will.

Angela stubbornly resists her mother's attempt to attach a psychic cord to her, to use some of the child's energy for herself. She loves her mom, but unconsciously she knows her mother wants her life or light. She struggles against her mom, but finally, she can no longer endure. The psychic desire of the adult is too much for this child to withstand.

Angela collapses psychically and lets her soul go to her mother. Again, to an observer with ordinary vision, all things in the kitchen seem the same. To one seeing what is being hidden, Angela is now different: her essence has been taken from her. Soon after this event, Angela becomes ill with pneumonia and fights for her life in the hospital.

I stand in the kitchen observing all that is happening. I go to Angela's mother. She is a nice woman, who looks like a typical mom. She does love Angela. She is not jealous of her child as I sometimes see with parents; she is just exhausted by her life.

I say to her, 'Angela needs her soul back.' She looks up at me, startled; she has been caught. I keep talking. 'Angela cannot lead a healthy, productive life as long as you hold on to her soul. If you really love Angela, please give it back.'

She starts to cry and wipes her tears with her stained apron. She says, 'I'm sorry. Of course you can have it back.' She gives me Angela's soul, and in return I give her a beautiful gold ball that immediately brightens her up. Light essence is exchanged for light essence.

I returned to ordinary reality with Angela's soul and blew it into her. After I welcomed her home, we talked about the experience. What I saw from my journey was how, after losing her soul at age three or four, she had turned inward and become self-protective so that no one else could steal whatever light she had left. And so she associated showing herself, her talents, her light to the world with someone's wanting to take them from her. I explained to Angela that she was now old enough to protect herself without having to hide who she was; she could be whoever she wanted to be. If she felt herself becoming drained in someone else's presence, she could simply visualize herself surrounded by white light, or she could 'put' herself into a blue egg that would protect her. (This latter is a technique taught to me by a Chumash medicine woman I met at a gathering in the San Francisco Bay Area many years ago. A group of us were discussing different methods we had for protecting ourselves from other people's energies. This medicine woman shared with us that she visualizes herself into a blue egg. I tried it myself, and for years the method has been serving me well when I feel some outside energy trying to get into my field.)

Another way Angela could protect herself and hold on to her energy and light would be by calling her own power animal to her. She decided to learn how to journey for herself. Upon leaving her tunnel in the Lower World, she found a great white bear who told her she would remain with her. The bear encouraged Angela to be herself and open up to let her light and power shine through. She now had the tools she needed to do this in a safe way.

Angela felt that she now needed to nurture this four-year-old part of herself, to let her know she wouldn't be abandoned again and that she could be herself. Though she now felt light and expansive, she began to cry, remembering how hard it had been to protect herself for so many years. Angela now could breathe deeper into her body without its contracting into a fear space; this made her feel free and also a little overwhelmed at the same time.

The night after Angela's soul retrieval session, she called me, feeling troubled. She said that the feelings she was experiencing in her body were not comfortable for her. There was too much energy in her body. I asked her if she felt raw, and she replied that this was exactly how she felt. I explained to her that this was a common experience. For years, out of fear, she had contracted and hadn't let energy pass through her body. To protect herself she had to block her feelings, which cut her off from any life force.

Now she was open, and life force was pulsating through her. It felt raw, she reported, as if her nervous system were on fire. I let her know I felt this was a good sign, and I shared with her the tried-and-true method that I use with myself and others to work through such feelings. I discovered this method on my own years ago when I was running too much energy through my body. I told her just to say the following words to herself: 'I ask to get in touch with my higher consciousness. I ask higher consciousness to let in only as much energy as my body can handle at this present time.' For Angela, this technique worked within minutes.

Depending on how blocked we have been, we sometimes have to moderate the amount of energy and information coming through. A person's constitution, which is often dependent on diet and physical exercise, determines how much energy he or she can handle. Angela allowed the feeling of being alive to pulsate through her body a little more each week. She was no longer overwhelmed by the feelings but learned how to moderate them. She began to enjoy experiencing the raw power of the earth.

Tantra and Sexual Ecstasy

MARGO ANAND

The Art of Sexual Ecstasy

Margo Anand is the most well-known practitioner and teacher of Tantra in the West. Whereas Western religious culture has tended to be frightened of the physical body in general and of sexual pleasure in particular, the Eastern approach of Tantra not only demonstrates techniques for increasing sexual pleasure, but shows how sexual ecstasy is a gateway to God and a deepening spirituality. This is also completely in tune with Freud's and Reich's ideas that true health is accompanied by a healthy flow and release of libido.

There were several scholastic Tantric texts available in the 1960s, but Margo Anand's presentation was accessible, practical and brought it more clearly into the mainstream.

In Tantra, when the male and female polarities merge, a new dimension becomes available – the sense of the sacred. When the sacredness of sexual union is felt, it is possible to experience your connection to the life force itself, the source of creation. This connection lifts your consciousness beyond the physical plane into a field of power and energy much greater than your own. Then you feel linked, through your partner, to everything that lives and loves. You feel that you are a part of the great dance of existence; you feel one with it.

Introducing a sacred dimension to sexual loving allows both partners to acknowledge that they possess divine qualities. By this I mean that they recognize their true potential as infinite and unlimited. In Tantra you discover that by honouring the god or goddess in your partner, you can see beyond the limitations of personality and, by seeing the divine in the other person, perceive the same potential in yourself. The other person becomes a reflection of your own godlike nature. That is why Tantric partners greet each other by saying, 'I honour you as an aspect of myself.' This means, 'You are one with me, and your consciousness is a reflection of mine.' This may seem far-fetched to you now, but you may come to see it as an effective device for moving beyond the self-imposed and self-limiting images by which people tend to confine themselves.

Tantra views sexual union not only as sacred, but as an art. Interestingly, the Sanskrit root of the word *art* means 'suitably united'. To become Tantrikas, practitioners of Tantra, lovers were required to be versed in a multiplicity of skills, such as conversation, dance, ceremony, massage, flower arrangement, costumes and make-up, music, hygiene, breathing, and meditation, among others.

When we learn the erotic arts in this way, a deep healing of our sexuality takes place. The sex act is not a hurried and tense affair, fraught with the dangers of disease (transmitted by partners who do not take time for thorough preparations), but a safe and healthy exchange between partners who respect and know each other intellectually, emotionally, and sensually before they enter into sexual union. This is what is urgently needed today: a playful, loving, and comprehensive perspective on sex that makes it safe and ecstatic at the same time. A modern resurrection of Tantra can offer these alternatives, reducing the carelessness that contributes to sexually transmitted diseases.

According to Tantra, sex is first a matter of energy, and Tantra views energy as the movement of life. Within the human body, energy is continuously in motion. For example, the nucleus and electrons of an atom have characteristic vibratory movements and rhythms. The same goes for the molecules, cells, and organs of the human body. Each cell in the body pulsates rhythmically, and so do the heart, diaphragm, intestines, lungs, brain, and many other physiological components. The vibrations from these rhythmic movements generate bioelectrical currents that stream continuously through the whole body. They also generate energy fields that surround the body, and our moods and emotions generate specific vibrations that alter these energy fields as well.

Tantra sees each human being as an organism that is part of a larger whole – the surrounding environment, the planet Earth, nature itself – in which rhythm and vibration are the unifying factors. They are also the factors that influence the relationship of one person to another. So Tantra teaches lovers how to harmonize their energies and be on the same wavelength, creating a measurable resonance between their energy fields. In Tantra the art of creating such a resonance is equivalent to what we call foreplay. [. . .]

When I was living in Paris, I became friends with a man named Rampal who was acclaimed as a great psychotherapist and a gifted 'magician' in the science of Tantra.

Rampal was hardly a sex symbol in the ordinary sense. During the war, while working in the Resistance, he suffered a wound to his lower spine. Nerves had been severed. Doctors told him that he would never be able to walk again. The government gave him a hundred per cent disability pension.

But he refused to remain a cripple. Instead he turned to the Tantric traditions in an attempt to heal himself, using ancient visualization and meditation techniques to project the image of an 'energy body' parallel to his physical form that healed his shattered nervous system. He succeeded. After some years he was able to walk with only a slight limp and, confounding medical opinion that his wounds had rendered him permanently impotent, began to make love normally and fathered two sons.

On hearing that I was studying the Tantric scriptures, Rampal invited me to his home for a practical demonstration. When I arrived, the first thing I noticed was a Tibetan painting, a *tanka*, hanging in the waiting room, depicting an awesome deity sitting with crossed legs in the lotus position. Sitting on his lap, with her legs wrapped around him, was a very sexy woman. They were naked and clearly in a state of ecstasy. The painting aroused my curiosity. If this was a meditation, I thought, I wanted to learn it.

Rampal welcomed me into his study. He had an appearance of effortless elegance and nobility, wearing a casual pale yellow silk shirt and navy pants. Although it was in the middle of the city, the room felt quiet and protected. As we spoke, I told him that I wanted to experience the secrets he had learned. In response he asked me to try a simple experiment: to stand across the room, opposite him, with my feet parallel – about eighteen inches apart – to bend my knees slightly, let my mouth fall open, and begin to breathe deeply.

'As you continue to breathe deeply, let your genital muscles relax,' he said in a low voice that seemed to come from his belly. Rampal announced no goal and offered no theory about what he was doing. Even though his instructions were intimate, his tone was casual. Nobody had talked to me that way before.

'Now let the connection between us intensify through the eyes,' he told me. His eyes were an intense, luminescent green.

Soon I was inhaling fully, exhaling deeply and evenly, keeping my mouth open, and bending my knees while relaxing the rest of my body and gazing at him. What would he ask me to do next?

'As you inhale, rock your pelvis gently back,' said Rampal. 'As you exhale, let it rock forward, as if you were giving yourself to me.' I did so and felt a surge of energy combined with vulnerability, such as one may feel in the presence of a new lover. Despite the physical distance between us, a sense of intimacy was growing through our steady gaze. I felt deeply connected to him, yet independent and grounded in myself.

Rampal next suggested that as I inhaled and rocked back, I should become aware of the energy that was developing in my pelvis and let it move up, as if it were rising through my body in a tube – the Inner Flute. Upon exhaling, I should reverse the flow, letting the energy descend as my pelvis rocked forward. I did as he instructed and began to feel highly aroused, even though we had not touched.

Rampal then asked me to walk slowly towards him while continuing the exercise. I felt like a tightrope walker about to have an orgasm while poised above a canyon. When I reached him, he gently touched points in my shoulders and back, as if to adjust my posture.

Even though I felt a little awkward and inexperienced, I sensed his acceptance of me and was able to relax even further. As I exhaled, I felt a strong vibrancy, like an electrical current, stream through my body. Then Rampal sat down cross-legged on the floor and placed a small pillow on his lap. He invited me to sit on the pillow with my legs around him.

We were both fully dressed. His manner was not at all seductive. Instead I felt as if we were both paying homage to the energy that I was experiencing, as if we were celebrating the power that we shared.

As I sat on his lap, he told me that Buddhists call this position *yab yum* – the union of mother and father. I recalled the painting I had seen in Rampal's waiting room and felt excited to find myself imitating the woman's pose, as if I were being initiated into an ancient mystery.

Rampal was behaving in an ordinary and matter-of-fact manner. I wanted to move and express my excitement, but he kept saying in his deep, quiet voice, 'Keep the energy inside; breathe into it softly. Stay focused on it; relax into it.'

We sat breathing together for some minutes. After a while, he said, 'Now that you are relaxed, tighten your genital muscles as you inhale. Tighten them as a dancer would tighten her thigh muscles before springing into the air. Inhale deeply and tighten. Feel the energy moving up the spine as you do so.' I did it. 'Now,' he went on, 'gently relax the genital muscles as you exhale. Let go. Let yourself fly.'

As we sat there, breathing and rocking and gazing together, I was learning to 'hold my horses' while relaxing into their stride. After a while we fell into a subtle rhythm. I had a sense of being lifted up, independent of my will – of floating. I was not 'doing' it – it was happening to me naturally. 'Let it continue,' Rampal whispered. 'Breathe through the mouth, more deeply now, all the way down to your sex centre.'

I felt as if my lungs had become a bellows stoking my inner fire. Rampal was breathing with me, moving with me, as if he were inside me. I felt tremendously excited. Some part of me rebelled against the control, the waiting that this practice imposed on my arousal. Why hold back? Surely there was much to be said in defence of wild, spontaneous lovemaking. But I already knew that way. I had experienced it many times.

As if reading my thoughts, Rampal suggested, 'Instead of keeping the excitement and energy in your sexual centre, allow it to move upward as you inhale, towards your brain. Feel, as you inhale, that you are drinking me in, taking my energy into you, inhaling my soul.'

I felt that my energy was a growing sphere, pushing against the limits of my physical body, then expanding beyond it.

'As you exhale, relax the genitals,' I heard Rampal say. 'Feel that you are opening your gates. Offer your energy; offer your spirit . . . Yes, that's it.' The energy was subtle yet so vibrant that it was almost tangible, as if I were being enveloped in a luminous egg that had existed unnoticed within my body and that was expanding and surrounding us as we breathed and gazed into each other's eyes.

Looking at him so intensely was threatening at first. Would he not see the ragged edges of my soul, the secret fears and self-doubt? But as I opened myself to Rampal's love and surrendered to his gentle guidance, our energies blended and went aflame. It was as if a protective filter between us had been removed, a filter that I ordinarily used to keep things under control and to protect my sense of separateness.

Now, surrounded by the egg of light, Rampal also seemed luminous. On some level of reality, this man was no longer Rampal and I was no longer Margo. We had become a delicious dance between breath, energy, and light.

Women are peonies, spring
    flowers, lotuses and bowers.
Women are pomegranates,
    peaches, melons and pearls.
Women are receptacles, crucibles,
    vessels and worlds.
Women are the fruit of life, the
    nourishing force of Nature.

> Yuan Shih Yeh-Ting Chi,
> Tao Tsung-Ti

Mystic and Esoteric Religion

Introduction

For anyone who wishes directly to explore spiritual realities, the standard fare of the world's great religions – especially in the West – is hardly appealing. The general advice of the monolithic religions is to behave well, perform the rituals and trust the priestly hierarchy. They tend to be suspicious of people who would like to conduct their own investigation.

The gift of an open society is that we can do precisely this, and conduct our own inquiry. There is in fact a great deal of literature on mystical experience and its methods written by religious practitioners who have very little interest in teaching dogma or theology. Their concern has been to find ways of directly experiencing the divine inner reality and how to experience it fully in everyday life.

To a casual reader approaching the subject for the first time what becomes clear almost immediately is that, no matter what the spiritual tradition, the mystic experience is in fact a universal experience and is not dependent upon any one local culture or belief. For many this is a healing revelation. Mystics always describe the same experience. There is essentially no difference between the Muslim, Christian, Hindu, Jewish, tribal or Buddhist mystic. They experience and share the same reality.

Though they teach different practical approaches and methods, and the symbols and metaphors change, the inner landscape remains the same. In gnostic Christianity, in the Qabalah of Judaism, in the Sufi tradition of Islam, in esoteric Buddhism, in Tantra, the same lessons are taught: we exist in a great chain of being that flows from the rocks out to galaxies. God, the Source, Spirit, is incomprehensible. The essential dynamic of the universe is purposeful, intelligent and benevolent. All form has an inner dynamic of energy and consciousness. All human beings are evolving into a transcendent consciousness. Whether it matters to us or not, we are always an intimate part of this.

The Characteristics of Mysticism

EVELYN UNDERHILL
Mysticism

Evelyn Underhill was a Christian mystic and poet who is credited with helping to establish mystical theology as a respectable discipline among intellectuals. She disliked the occult and magical approach, but by arguing with it so seriously she also gave it a new credibility.

Many decades on, the same argument is still being debated: should one seek to surrender gracefully to the divine, or should one seek wilfully to know and engage with the energies and forms of the inner world? From a holistic perspective, it is a false argument as the two approaches are not mutually exclusive. Especially with the insights from quantum science, it seems clear that the mystical and magical can be integrated.

The spiritual history of man reveals two distinct and fundamental attitudes towards the unseen; and two methods whereby he has sought to get in touch with it. For our present purpose I will call these methods the 'way of magic' and the 'way of mysticism'. Having said this, we must at once add that although in their extreme forms these methods are sharply contrasted, their frontiers are far from being clearly defined: that, starting from the same point, they often confuse the inquirer by using the same language, instruments, and methods. Hence, much which is really magic is loosely and popularly described as mysticism. They represent as a matter of fact the opposite poles of the same thing: the transcendental consciousness of humanity. Between them lie the great religions, which might be described under this metaphor as representing the ordinarily habitable regions of that consciousness. Thus, at one end of the scale, pure mysticism 'shades off' into religion – from some points of view seems to grow out of it. No deeply religious man is without a touch of mysticism; and no mystic can be other than religious, in the psychological if not in the theological sense of the word. At the other end of the scale, as we shall see later, religion, no less surely, shades off into magic.

The fundamental difference between the two is this: magic wants to get, mysticism wants to give – immortal and antagonistic attitudes, which turn up under one disguise or another in every age of thought. Both magic and mysticism in their full development bring the whole mental machinery, conscious and unconscious, to bear on their undertaking: both claim that they give their initiates powers unknown to ordinary men. But the centre round which that machinery is grouped, the reasons of that undertaking, and the ends to which those powers are applied differ enormously. In mysticism the will is united with the emotions in an impassioned desire to transcend the sense-world, in order that the self may be joined by love to the one eternal and ultimate Object of love; whose existence is intuitively perceived by that which we used to call the soul, but now find it easier to refer to as the 'cosmic' or 'transcendental' sense. This is the poetic and religious temperament acting upon the plane of reality. In magic, the will unites with the intellect in an impassioned desire for supersensible knowledge. This is the intellectual, aggressive, and scientific temperament trying to extend its field of consciousness, until it includes the supersensual world: obviously the antithesis of mysticism, though often adopting its title and style.

It will be our business later to consider in more detail the characteristics and significance of magic. Now it is enough to say that we may class broadly as magical all forms of self-seeking transcendentalism. It matters little whether the apparatus which they use be the incantations of the old magicians, the congregational prayer for rain of orthodox Churchmen, or the consciously self-hypnotizing devices of 'New Thought': whether the end proposed be the evocation of an angel, the power of transcending circumstance, or the healing of disease. The object is always the same: the deliberate exaltation of the will, till it transcends its usual limitations and obtains for the self or group of selves something which it or they did not previously possess. It is an individualistic and acquisitive science: in all its forms an activity of the intellect, seeking Reality for its own purposes, or for those of humanity at large.

Mysticism, whose great name is too often given to these super-sensual activities, has nothing in common with this. It is non-individualistic. It implies, indeed, the abolition of individuality; of that hard separateness, that 'I, Me, Mine' which makes of man a finite isolated thing. It is essentially a movement of the heart, seeking to transcend the limitations of the individual standpoint and to surrender itself to ultimate Reality; for no personal gain, to satisfy no transcendental curiosity, to obtain no other-worldly joys, but purely from an instinct of love. By the word *heart*, of course, we here mean not merely 'the seat of the affections', 'the organ of tender emotion', and the like: but rather the inmost sanctuary of personal being, the deep root of its love and will, the very source of its energy and life. The mystic is 'in love with the Absolute' not in any idle or sentimental manner, but in that vital sense which presses at all costs and through all dangers towards union with the object beloved. Hence, while the practice of magic – like the practice of science – does not necessarily entail passionate emotion, though of course it does and must entail interest of some kind, mysticism, like art, cannot exist without it. We must feel, and feel acutely, before we want to act on this hard and heroic scale.

We see, then, that these two activities correspond to the two eternal passions of the self, the desire of love and the desire of knowledge: severally representing the hunger of heart and intellect for ultimate truth. The third attitude towards the super-sensual world, that of transcendental philosophy, hardly comes within the scope of the present inquiry; since it is purely academic, while both magic and mysticism are practical and empirical. Such philosophy is often wrongly called mysticism, because it tries to make maps of the countries which the mystic explores. Its performances are useful, as diagrams are useful, so long as they do not ape finality; remembering that the only final thing is personal experience – the personal and costly exploration of the exalted and truth-loving soul.

What then do we really mean by mysticism? A word which is impartially applied to the performances of mediums and the ecstasies of the saints, to 'menticulture' and sorcery, dreamy poetry and mediaeval art, to prayer and palmistry, the doctrinal excesses of Gnosticism, and the tepid speculations of the Cambridge Platonists – even, according to William James, to the higher branches of intoxication* – soon

* See *Varieties of Religious Experience*, p. 387, 'The Drunken Consciousness is a bit of the Mystic Consciousness.'

ceases to have any useful meaning. Its employment merely confuses the inexperienced student, who ends with a vague idea that every kind of super-sensual theory and practice is somehow 'mystical'. Hence the need of fixing, if possible, its true characteristics: and restating the fact that Mysticism, in its pure form, is the science of ultimates, the science of union with the Absolute, and nothing else, and that the mystic is the person who attains to this union, not the person who talks about it. Not to *know about*, but to *Be*, is the mark of the real initiate.

The difficulty lies in determining the point at which super-sensual experience ceases to be merely a practical and interesting extension of sensual experience – an enlarging, so to speak, of the boundaries of existence – and passes over into that boundless life where Subject and Object, desirous and desired, are *one*. No sharp line, but rather an infinite series of gradations separate the two states. Hence we must look carefully at all the pilgrims on the road; discover, if we can, the motive of their travels, the maps which they use, the luggage which they take, the end which they attain.

Now we have said that the end which the mystic sets before him is conscious union with a living Absolute. That Divine Dark, that Abyss of the Godhead, of which he sometimes speaks as the goal of his quest, is just this Absolute, the Uncreated Light in which the universe is bathed, and which – transcending, as it does, all human powers of expression – he can only describe to us as *dark*. But there is – must be – contact 'in an intelligible where' between every individual self and this Supreme Self, this Ultimate. In the mystic this union is conscious, personal, and complete. 'He enjoys,' says St John of the Cross, 'a certain contact of the soul with the Divinity; and it is God Himself who is then felt and tasted.'* More or less according to his measure, he has touched – or better, been touched by – the substantial Being of Deity, not merely its manifestation in life. This it is which distinguishes him from the best and most brilliant of other men, and makes his science, in Patmore's words, 'the science of self-evident Reality'. Gazing with him into that unsearchable ground whence the World of Becoming comes forth 'eternally generated in an eternal Now', we may see only

---

* Llama de Amor Viva, II. 26.

the icy darkness of perpetual negations: but he, beyond the coincidence of opposites, looks upon the face of Perfect Love.

As genius in any of the arts is – humanly speaking – the final term of a power of which each individual possesses the rudiments, so mysticism may be looked upon as the final term, the active expression, of a power latent in the whole race: the power, that is to say, of so perceiving transcendent reality. Few people pass through life without knowing what it is to be at least touched by this mystical feeling. He who falls in love with a woman and perceives – as the lover really does perceive – that the categorical term 'girl' veils a wondrous and unspeakable reality: he who, falling in love with nature, sees the landscape 'touched with light divine' – a charming phrase to those who have not seen it, but a scientific statement to the rest – he who falls in love with the Holy, or as we say 'undergoes conversion': all these have truly known for an instant something of the secret of the world.

. . . Ever and anon a trumpet sounds
From the hid battlements of Eternity,
Those shaken mists a space unsettle, then
Round the half-glimpsèd turrets slowly wash again.

At such moments 'Transcendental Feeling, welling up from another "Part of the Soul" whispers to Understanding and Sense that they are leaving out something. What? Nothing less than the secret plan of the universe. And what is that secret plan? The other "Part of the Soul" indeed comprehends it in silence as it is, but can explain it to the Understanding only in the symbolical language of the interpreter, Imagination – in Vision.'*

Here, in this spark or 'part of the soul' where the spirit, as religion says, 'rests in God who made it', is the fountain alike of the creative imagination and the mystic life. Now and again something stings it into consciousness, and man is caught up to the spiritual level, catches a glimpse of the 'secret plan'. Then hints of a marvellous truth, a unity whose note is ineffable peace, shine in created things; awakening in

* J. A. Stewart, *The Myths of Plato*, p. 40.

the self a sentiment of love, adoration, and awe. Its life is enhanced, the barrier of personality is broken, man escapes the sense-world, ascends to the apex of his spirit, and enters for a brief period into the more extended life of the All.

The Mystic Experience

WILLIAM JAMES
The Varieties of Religious Experience

Given as a series of lectures at Edinburgh University at the turn of the last century, William James's book was for many an extraordinary breath of fresh air blowing into the cobwebbed scholasticism of theology and religion. Originally an academic psychologist, but from a family of mystics (his father was a Swedenborgian), he looked at the actual religious experience of the individual. He was interested in pragmatic reality and not in spiritual theory. As such his approach was pragmatic and fully present to the real world. It stole intellectual and ideological power away from the overwhelming religious belief systems to look at the underlying experiences that had started the whole thing off. Being concerned with the primacy of experience, he was therefore equal-handed with the different faiths, giving none priority.

Religion, therefore, as I now ask you arbitrarily to take it, shall mean for us *the feelings, acts, and experiences of individual men in their solitude, so far as they apprehend themselves to stand in relation to whatever they may consider the divine.* Since the relation may be either moral, physical, or ritual, it is evident that out of religion in the sense in which we take it, theologies, philosophies, and ecclesiastical organizations may secondarily grow. In these lectures, however, as I have already said, the immediate personal experiences will amply fill our time, and we shall hardly consider theology or ecclesiasticism at all. [...]

Over and over again in these lectures I have raised points and left them open and unfinished until we should have come to the subject of Mysticism. Some of you, I fear, may have smiled as you noted my reiterated postponements. But now the hour has come when mysticism must be faced in good earnest, and those broken threads wound up together. One may say truly, I think, that personal religious experience has its root and centre in mystical states of consciousness; so for us, who in these lectures are treating personal experience as the exclusive subject of our study, such states of consciousness ought to form the vital chapter from which the other chapters get their light. Whether my treatment of mystical states will shed more light or darkness, I do not know, for my own constitution shuts me out from their enjoyment almost entirely, and I can speak of them only at second-hand. But though forced to look upon the subject so externally, I will be as objective and receptive as I can; and I think I shall at least succeed in convincing you of the reality of the states in question, and of the paramount importance of their function.

First of all, then, I ask, What does the expression 'mystical states of consciousness' mean? How do we part off mystical states from other states?

The words 'mysticism' and 'mystical' are often used as terms of mere reproach, to throw at any opinion which we regard as vague and vast and sentimental, and without a base in either facts or logic. For some writers a 'mystic' is any person who believes in thought-transference, or spirit-return. Employed in this way the word has little value: there are too many less ambiguous synonyms. So, to keep it useful by restricting it, I will do what I did in the case of the word 'religion', and simply propose to you four marks which, when an experience has them, may justify us in calling it mystical for the purpose of the present lectures. In this way we shall save verbal disputation, and the recriminations that generally go therewith.

1. *Ineffability* – The handiest of the marks by which I classify a state of mind as mystical is negative. The subject of it immediately says that it defies expression, that no adequate report of its contents can be given in words. It follows from this that its quality must be directly experienced; it cannot be imparted or transferred to others. In this peculiarity mystical states are more like states of feeling than like states of intellect. No one can make clear to another who has never had a certain feeling, in what the quality or worth of it consists. One must have musical ears to know the value of a symphony; one must have been in love one's self to understand a lover's state of mind. Lacking the heart or ear, we cannot interpret the musician or the lover justly, and are even likely to consider him weak-minded or absurd. The mystic

finds that most of us accord to his experiences an equally incompetent treatment.

2. *Noetic quality* – Although so similar to states of feeling, mystical states seem to those who experience them to be also states of knowledge. They are states of insight into depths of truth unplumbed by the discursive intellect. They are illuminations, revelations, full of significance and importance, all inarticulate though they remain; and as a rule they carry with them a curious sense of authority for aftertime.

These two characters will entitle any state to be called mystical, in the sense in which I use the word. Two other qualities are less sharply marked, but are usually found. These are:

3. *Transiency* – Mystical states cannot be sustained for long. Except in rare instances, half an hour, or at most an hour or two, seems to be the limit beyond which they fade into the light of common day. Often, when faded, their quality can but imperfectly be reproduced in memory; but when they recur it is recognized; and from one recurrence to another it is susceptible of continuous development in what is felt as inner richness and importance.

4. *Passivity* – Although the oncoming of mystical states may be facilitated by preliminary voluntary operations, as by fixing the attention, or going through certain bodily performances, or in other ways which manuals of mysticism prescribe; yet when the characteristic sort of consciousness once has set in, the mystic feels as if his own will were in abeyance, and indeed sometimes as if he were grasped and held by a superior power. This latter peculiarity connects mystical states with certain definite phenomena of secondary or alternative personality, such as prophetic speech, automatic writing, or the mediumistic trance. When these latter conditions are well pronounced, however, there may be no recollection whatever of the phenomenon, and it may have no significance for the subject's usual inner life, to which, as it were, it makes a mere interruption. Mystical states, strictly so-called, are never merely interruptive. Some memory of their content always remains, and a profound sense of their importance. They modify the inner life of the subject between the times of their recurrence. Sharp divisions in this region are, however, difficult to make, and we find all sorts of gradations and mixtures.

These four characteristics are sufficient to mark out a group of states of consciousness peculiar enough to deserve a special name and to call for careful study. Let it then be called the mystical group.

Our next step should be to gain acquaintance with some typical examples. Professional mystics at the height of their development have often elaborately organized experiences and a philosophy based thereupon. But you remember what I said in my first lecture: phenomena are best understood when placed within their series, studied in their germ and in their over-ripe decay, and compared with their exaggerated and degenerated kindred. The range of mystical experience is very wide, much too wide for us to cover in the time at our disposal. Yet the method of serial study is so essential for interpretation that if we really wish to reach conclusions we must use it. I will begin, therefore, with phenomena which claim no special religious significance, and end with those of which the religious pretensions are extreme.

The simplest rudiment of mystical experience would seem to be that deepened sense of the significance of a maxim or formula which occasionally sweeps over one. 'I've heard that said all my life,' we exclaim, 'but I never realized its full meaning until now.' 'When a fellow-monk,' said Luther, 'one day repeated the words of the Creed: "I believe in the forgiveness of sins", I saw the scripture in an entirely new light; and straightway I felt as if I were born anew. It was as if I had found the door of paradise thrown wide open.'[1] This sense of deeper significance is not confined to rational propositions. Single words,[2] and conjunctions of words, effects of light on land and sea, odours and musical sounds, all bring it when the mind is tuned aright. Most of us can remember the strangely moving power of passages in certain poems read when we were young, irrational doorways as they were through which the mystery of fact, the wildness and the pang of life, stole into our hearts and thrilled them. The words have now perhaps become mere polished surfaces for us; but lyric poetry and music are alive and significant only in proportion as they fetch these vague vistas of a life continuous with our own, beckoning and inviting, yet ever eluding our pursuit. We are alive or dead to the eternal inner message of the arts according as we have kept or lost this mystical susceptibility.

A more pronounced step forward on the mystical ladder is found in an extremely frequent phenomenon, that sudden feeling, namely, which

309

sometimes sweeps over us, of having 'been here before', as if at some indefinite past time, in just this place, with just these people, we were already saying just these things. As Tennyson writes:

Moreover, something is or seems
That touches me with mystic gleams,
Like glimpses of forgotten dreams –

Of something felt, like something here;
Of something done, I know not where;
Such as no language may declare.[3]

Sir James Crichton-Browne has given the technical name of 'dreamy states' to these sudden invasions of vaguely reminiscent consciousness.[4] They bring a sense of mystery and of the metaphysical duality of things, and the feeling of an enlargement of perception which seems imminent but which never completes itself. In Dr Crichton-Browne's opinion they connect themselves with the perplexed and scared disturbances of self-consciousness which occasionally precede epileptic attacks. I think that this learned alienist takes a rather absurdly alarmist view of an intrinsically insignificant phenomenon. He follows it along the downward ladder, to insanity; our path pursues the upward ladder chiefly. The divergence shows how important it is to neglect no part of a phenomenon's connections, for we make it appear admirable or dreadful according to the context by which we set it off.

Somewhat deeper plunges into mystical consciousness are met with in yet other dreamy states. Such feelings as these which Charles Kingsley describes are surely far from being uncommon, especially in youth:

When I walk the fields, I am oppressed now and then with an innate feeling that everything I see has a meaning, if I could but understand it. And this feeling of being surrounded with truths which I cannot grasp amounts to indescribable awe sometimes ... Have you not felt that your real soul was imperceptible to your mental vision, except in a few hallowed moments?[5]

Gnostic Christianity

ELAINE PAGELS
The Gnostic Gospels

In 1945 a red earthenware jar was found buried beneath the soil near Nag Hammadi in Upper Egypt. In it were several Coptic manuscripts dating from around AD 350, based upon much earlier texts. Translating the first manuscript, Professor Gilles Quispel was incredulous and startled as he read the first lines: 'These are the secret words which the living Jesus spoke, and which the twin, Judas Thomas, wrote down.' The Nag Hammadi manuscripts provided a completely new interpretation of Jesus and early Christianity. In particular they represented the beliefs of a Christian sect, the Gnostics, which had virtually disappeared or been repressed by orthodoxy and the Catholic Church.

It was *The Gnostic Gospels*, by Barnard's Elaine Pagels, which brought this information accessibly and elegantly to the public.

Thomas said to him, 'Lord, we do not know where you are going; how can we know the way?' Jesus said to him, 'I am the way, the truth, and the life; no one comes to the Father, but by me.'[1]

The Gospel of John, which contains this saying, is a remarkable book that many Gnostic Christians claimed for themselves and used as a primary source for Gnostic teaching.[2] Yet the emerging Church, despite some orthodox opposition, included John within the New Testament. What makes John acceptably 'orthodox'? Why did the Church accept John while rejecting such writings as the *Gospel of Thomas* or the *Dialogue of the Saviour*? In considering this question, remember that anyone who drives through the United States is likely to see billboards proclaiming this saying from John – billboards signed by any of the local churches. Their purpose is clear: by indicating that one finds God only through Jesus, the saying, in its contemporary context, implies that one finds Jesus only through the Church. Similarly, in the first centuries of this era, Christians concerned to strengthen the institutional Church could find support in John.

Gnostic sources offer a different religious perspective. According to the *Dialogue of the Saviour*, for example, when the disciples asked Jesus the same question ('What is the place to which we shall go?') he answered, 'the place which you can reach, stand there!'[3] The *Gospel of Thomas* relates that when the disciples asked Jesus where they should go, he said only, 'There is light within a man of light, and it lights up the whole world. If he does not shine, he is darkness.'[4] Far from legitimizing any institution, both sayings direct one instead to oneself – to one's inner capacity to find one's own direction, to the 'light within'.

The contrast sketched above is, of course, somewhat simplistic. Followers of Valentinus themselves demonstrated – convincingly – that many sayings and stories in John could lend themselves to such interpretation. But Christians like Irenaeus apparently decided that, on balance, the gospel of John (especially, perhaps, when placed in sequence after Matthew, Mark, and Luke) could serve the needs of the emerging institution.

As the Church organized politically, it could sustain within itself many contradictory ideas and practices as long as the disputed elements supported its basic institutional structure. In the third and fourth centuries, for example, hundreds of Catholic Christians adopted ascetic forms of self-discipline, seeking religious insight through solitude, visions, and ecstatic experience. (The terms 'monk' and 'monastic' come from the Greek word *monachos*, meaning 'solitary', or 'single one', which the *Gospel of Thomas* frequently uses to describe the Gnostic.) Rather than exclude the monastic movement, the church moved, in the fourth century, to bring the monks into line with episcopal authority. The scholar Frederik Wisse has suggested that the monks who lived at the monastery of St Pachomius, within sight of the cliff where the texts were found, may have included the Nag Hammadi texts within their devotional library.[5] But in 367, when Athanasius, the powerful Archbishop of Alexandria, sent an order to purge all 'apocryphal books' with 'heretical' tendencies, one (or several) of the monks may have hidden the precious manuscripts in the jar and buried it on the cliff of the Jabal al-Tārif, where Muhammad 'Alī found it 1,600 years later.

Furthermore, as the Church, disparate as it was internally, increasingly became a political unity between 150 and 400, its leaders tended to treat their opponents – an even more diverse range of groups – as if they, too, constituted an *opposite* political unity. When Irenaeus denounced the heretics as 'Gnostics',[6] he referred less to any specific doctrinal agreement among them (indeed, he often castigated them for the variety of their beliefs) than to the fact that they all resisted accepting the authority of the clergy, the creed, and the New Testament canon.

What – if anything – did the various groups that Irenaeus called 'Gnostic' have in common? Or, to put the question another way, what do the diverse texts discovered at Nag Hammadi have in common? No simple answer could cover all the different groups that the orthodox attack, or all the different texts in the Nag Hammadi collection. But I suggest that the trouble with Gnosticism, from the orthodox viewpoint, was not only that Gnostics often disagreed with the majority on such specific issues as those we have explored so far – the organization of authority, the participation of women, martyrdom: the orthodox recognized that those they called 'Gnostics' shared a fundamental religious perspective that remained antithetical to the claims of the institutional Church.

For orthodox Christians insisted that humanity needs a way beyond its own power – a divinely given way – to approach God. And this, they declared, the Catholic Church offered to those who would be lost without it: 'Outside the Church there is no salvation.' Their conviction was based on the premise that God created humanity. As Irenaeus says, 'In this respect God differs from humanity; God makes, but humanity is made.'[7] One is the originating agent, the other the passive recipient; one is 'truly perfect in all things',[8] omnipotent, infinite, the other an imperfect and finite creature. The philosopher Justin Martyr says that when he recognized the great difference between the human mind and God, he abandoned Plato and became a Christian philosopher. He relates that before his conversion an old man challenged his basic assumption, asking, 'What affinity, then, is there between us and God? Is the soul also divine and immortal, and a part of that very regal mind?' Speaking as a disciple of Plato, Justin answered without hesitation, 'Certainly.'[9] But when the old man's further questions led him to doubt that certainty, he says he realized that the human mind could not find God within itself and needed instead to be enlightened by divine revelation – by means of the Scriptures and the faith proclaimed in the Church.

But some Gnostic Christians went so far as to claim that humanity created God – and so, from its own inner potential, discovered for itself the revelation of truth. This conviction may underlie the ironic comment in the *Gospel of Philip*:

God created humanity; [but now human beings] create God. That is the way it is in the world – human beings make gods, and worship their creation. It would be appropriate for the gods to worship human beings![10]

The Gnostic Valentinus taught that humanity itself manifests the divine life and divine revelation. The church, he says, consists of that portion of humanity that recognizes and celebrates its divine origin.[11] But Valentinus did not use the term in its contemporary sense, to refer to the human race taken collectively. Instead, he and his followers thought of *Anthropos* (here translated 'humanity') as the underlying nature of that collective entity, the archetype, or spiritual essence, of human being. In this sense, some of Valentinus' followers, 'those ... considered more skilful'[12] than the rest, agreed with the teacher Colorbasus, who said that when God revealed himself, He revealed himself in the form of *Anthropos*. Still others, Irenaeus reports, maintained that

the primal father of the whole, the primal beginning, and the primal incomprehensible, is called *Anthropos* ... and that this is the great and abstruse mystery, namely, that the power which is above all others, and contains all others in its embrace, is called *Anthropos*.[13]

For this reason, these Gnostics explained, the Saviour called himself 'Son of Man' (that is, Son of *Anthropos*).[14] The Sethian Gnostics, who called the creator Ialdabaoth (a name apparently derived from mystical Judaism but which here indicates his inferior status), said that for this reason, when the creator,

Ialdabaoth, becoming arrogant in spirit, boasted himself over all those who were below him, and explained, 'I am father, and God, and above me there is no one', his mother, hearing him speak thus, cried out against him: 'Do not lie, Ialdabaoth; for the father of all, the primal *Anthropos*, is above you; and so is *Anthropos*, the son of *Anthropos*.'[15]

In the words of another Valentinian, since human beings created the whole language of religious expression, so, in effect, humanity created the divine world: '. . . and this [*Anthropos*] is really he who is God over all.'

Many Gnostics, then, would have agreed in principle with Ludwig Feuerbach, the nineteenth-century psychologist, that 'theology is really anthropology' (the term derives, of course, from *anthropos*, and means 'study of humanity'). For Gnostics, exploring the *psyche* became explicitly what it is for many people today implicitly – a religious quest.

The Hermetic Tradition

CAITLIN AND JOHN MATTHEWS
The Western Way II

Along with R. J. Stewart and Geoffrey Ashe, the husband-and-wife team of Caitlín Matthews and John Matthews have been pioneers in the renaissance of the Celtic and Western mystical traditions. Together and separately, they have authored around one hundred books in the field and they are also practitioners, leading workshops and running their own school. In their classic *The Western Way* they clearly delineated the two major threads of the Western esoteric tradition: the Celtic tradition and the Hermetic tradition of the Middle Eastern and Mediterranean mystery schools.

Between the Orphic mysteries and their partial revival in the Renaissance there is a long gap, not only in time but in understanding. In part this was bridged by the figure of the magician [. . .] and the Alchemist [. . .] The magician, in particular, is related to the earlier mystery schools, while the Alchemist draws upon a far wider range of sources, including Arabic metaphysics and Christian mysticism. The single force which unites all these elements is the body of teaching attributed to Hermes Trismegistos, 'Thrice Greatest' Hermes, whose doctrines stand at the very heart of the Western Way. [. . .]

Of what, then, does Hermes' *Corpus Hermeticum* consist? Basically it is a series of exchanges, purporting to be between pupil and master, or between Hermes Trismegistos and his 'sons' (i.e. disciples) of various names. They are often repetitive and cover much of the same ground in varying degrees of complexity. The first, and perhaps the best known, is the *Poimandres*, a description of the creation cast in the form of a dream. The (here unnamed) adept falls asleep and is visited by Poimandres (Mind of the Sovereignty) who explains to him all that he has wished to know concerning 'the things that are, (how to) understand their nature, and get knowledge of God'.

When he had thus spoken, forthwith all things changed in aspect before me, and were opened out in a moment. And I beheld a boundless view: all was changed into light, a mild and joyous light; and I marvelled when I saw it . . .

There follows a description of the creation, a mingling of light and dark from which comes forth 'a holy Word . . . and methought this Word was the voice of the Light'. When the seeker desires to understand what he has seen, Poimandres tells him: 'That light . . . is I, even Mind, the first God . . . and the Word which came forth from the Light is the son of God.'
When the dreamer asks how this may be, he is told:

Learn my meaning . . . by looking at what you yourself have in you; for in you too, the word is son, and the mind is father of the word. They are not separate one from the other; for life is the union of word and mind. (ibid)

Again and again this message is affirmed: there is a god within which gives life to the body and inspiration of all that we do: events in the sphere of incarnation reflect those in the heavenly sphere. It is this emphasis on unity rather than disharmony which marks out the Hermetic mysteries: unity of all things, of God with man, of higher with lower, of divine with mundane. It finds its clearest expression in the *Emerald Tablet of Hermes* with its famous injunction 'as above, so below', so often quoted and so little understood by occultists throughout the ages. [. . .]
Whatever one chooses to believe there is no getting away from the fact that the *Emerald Tablet* is one of the most profound and important documents to have come down to us. It has been said more than once that it contains the sum of all knowledge – for those able to understand it.
The *Tablet* outlines a doctrine of signatures and correspondences which reflect the mind of the Creator. The Greek word from which we derive cosmos means 'order', and we live in an ordered creation through which we are able to move at will yet always find a point of recognition. This is because the cosmos is the product of a single act of generation which has set a signature upon everything. In the finite world in which we attempt to bind ourselves this is scarcely recognized

by anyone; yet the youngest mystery school initiate would have known it once, no matter how many different gods he worshipped. [. . .]

It is on this doctrine of unity that the foundation of Hermeticism rests. We have grown used to a dualistic tendency in Western philosophy since Zoroaster, but in the Orphic and Hermetic schools the emphasis was on balance, polarity, the coming together of elements into a unique whole. This is why the Gnostic Hermes is represented as being the uniting principle in the system of the ogdoads. As one ancient text has it: 'One is the All . . . and if the All did not contain the All, the All would be nothing.' Once again we hear the echo of the divine interaction between God (the One) and creation (Matter, the All). It is not just incidental that Hermes' symbol is a staff with twin serpents of wisdom and understanding coiled about it. As in the Qabala, where the central pillar holds those of left and right in balance, here too the principle is the same.

The mysteries were always intended to be understood in a threefold fashion: with the spirit, the mind and the senses. Such a threefold division has continued to be recognized in Western esoteric practice ever since. Sacred words, uttered in temple or lodge, echo through three worlds: the divine, the intellectual and the physical, bringing all three together in a *rapprochement* which causes them to vibrate harmoniously one with the other.

The universe (or God) is always willing to respond to an harmonious note emitted by those in tune with the infinite Word of creation. To find that note within the self has ever been the most important action of the mystery seeker. Initiation leads towards just this point; study and self-observation, discipline and obedience, self-abdication: all acts of the adept are aimed first at realizing the divine harmonic within himself and then in tuning this to include the whole of the creation in which he stands.

The elements of creation may well be divided and scattered, as the myths of the Titans and the rending of gods like Dionysius and Osiris suggest, but what has been divided can be joined again – in the story of Isis and Osiris even the absence of the phallus did not prevent the creation of the divine child, Horus, the uniting principle which ushered in a new age of peace and harmony.

In this sense the passions of Christ, Baldur, Tammuz, of all the saviour gods, can be seen as a wholly natural process in which matter seeks out its component parts and reunites to form the whole which was the original design of the cosmos. God is lonely for the children that are lost to him, the fragments of himself created so that he could know himself. We should not be surprised, therefore, to find him sending forth his beloved Son – the nearest aspect of himself – into matter to seek out those lost ones.

Christ and Hermes with all of the shepherd gods, are come to gather in their flocks. But they cannot do so unaided. We must be willing to co-operate, to harmonize with them as we do whenever we celebrate the mysteries. Thus the glorious anamnesis of the Eucharist, the love-feast of the Agathadaimon, are aimed at giving us a glimpse outside the walls of our chaotic, fractured universe at the peace and tranquillity which can be ours – if we wish it to be.

This, then, is the Hermetic reality: the maintaining of a divine unity within the mundane sphere, which in turn raises that sphere to divine heights. As above so below, always. God imprints everything at the moment of creation with a divine signature, the DNA of the cosmos, which makes every rose a rose, every man a man, every beast a beast. And this signature contains the very essence of the creator, his message to all that he has caused to have being: like to like, very like to very like, the One and the All contained in each other. As a seventeenth-century Hermeticist put it:

The Sun and the Moon I see above me influence me neither for good nor bad, but the Sun and Moon and Planets (with) which God's providence has adorned the heaven *in me*, which also is the seat of the Almighty, these have the power to rule and reform me according to their course ordained by God.

Yoga

B. K. S. IYENGAR
Light on Yoga

B. K. S. Iyengar started teaching yoga in 1936, and in 1952 the world-famous violinist, Yehudi Menuhin, became his student and began to introduce him around the world. If one single person has been pivotal in bringing yoga to the West it is Iyengar through his students and through his classic book *Light on Yoga*. As well as introducing people to the popularly known physical stretches and techniques of breath, Iyengar also introduces people to the teachings of the *Bhagavad Gita* and the Yoga Sutras of Patanjali. Here is a mystical belief system that is grounded in the physical body and teaches practical techniques for a healthy body and mind.

If a man's reason succumbs to the pull of his senses he is lost. On the other hand, if there is rhythmic control of breath, the senses instead of running after external objects of desire turn inwards, and man is set free from their tyranny. This is the fifth stage of Yoga, namely, pratyāhāra, where the senses are brought under control.

When this stage is reached, the sādhaka goes through a searching self examination. To overcome the deadly but attractive spell of sensual objects, he needs the insulation of adoration (bhakti) by recalling to his mind the Creator who made the objects of his desire. He also needs the lamp of knowledge of his divine heritage. The mind, in truth, is for mankind the cause of bondage and liberation; it brings bondage if it is bound to the objects of desire and liberation when it is free from objects. There is bondage when the mind craves, grieves or is unhappy over something. The mind becomes pure when all desires and fears are annihilated. Both the good and the pleasant present themselves to men and prompt them to action. The yogi prefers the good to the pleasant. Others driven by their desires, prefer the pleasant to the good and miss the very purpose of life. The yogi feels joy in what he is. He knows how to stop and, therefore, lives in peace. At first he prefers that which is bitter as poison, but he perseveres in his practice knowing well that in the end it will become as sweet as nectar. Others hankering for the union of their senses with the objects of their desires, prefer that which at first seems sweet as nectar, but do not know that in the end it will be as bitter as poison.

The yogi knows that the path towards satisfaction of the senses by sensual desires is broad, but that it leads to destruction and that there are many who follow it. The path of Yoga is like the sharp edge of a razor, narrow and difficult to tread, and there are few who find it. The yogi knows that the paths of ruin or of salvation lie within himself.

According to Hindu philosophy, consciousness manifests in three different qualities. For man, his life and his consciousness, together with the entire cosmos, are the emanations of one and the same prakṛti (cosmic matter or substance) – emanations that differ in designation through the predominance of one of the guṇās. These guṇās (qualities or attributes) are:

1. Sattva (the illuminating, pure or good quality) which leads to clarity and mental serenity.
2. Rajas (the quality of mobility or activity) which makes a person active and energetic, tense and wilful, and
3. Tamas (the dark and restraining quality) which obstructs and counteracts the tendency of rajas to work and of sattva to reveal.

Tamas is a quality of delusion, obscurity, inertia and ignorance. A person in whom it predominates is inert and plunged in a state of torpor. The quality of sattva leads towards the divine and tamas towards the demonic, while in between these two stands rajas.

The faith held, the food consumed, the sacrifices performed, the austerities undergone and the gifts given by each individual vary in accordance with his predominating guṇa.

He that is born with tendencies towards the divine is fearless and pure. He is generous and self-controlled. He pursues the study of the Self. He is non-violent, truthful and free from anger. He renounces the fruits of his labour, working only for the sake of work. He has a tranquil mind, with malice towards none and charity towards all, for he is free from craving. He is gentle, modest and steady. He is illumined, clement and resolute, being free from perfidy and pride.

A man in whom rajō-guṇa predominates has inner thirst and is affectionate. As he is passionate and covetous, he hurts others. Being full of lust and hatred, envy and deceit, his desires are insatiable. He is unsteady, fickle and easily distracted as well as ambitious and acquisitive. He seeks the patronage of friends and has family pride. He shrinks from unpleasant things and clings to pleasant ones. His speech is sour and his stomach greedy.

He that is born with demonic tendencies is deceitful, insolent and conceited. He is full of wrath, cruelty and ignorance. In such people there is neither purity, nor right conduct, nor truth. They gratify their passions. Bewildered by numerous desires, caught in the web of delusion, these addicts of sensual pleasures fall into hell.

The working of the mind of persons with different predominating guṇās may be illustrated by their different ways of approach towards a universal commandment like 'Thou shalt not covet.' A man in whom tamō-guṇa predominates might interpret it thus: 'Others should not covet what is mine, no matter how I obtained it. If they do, I shall destroy them.' The rajō-guṇa type is a calculating self interested person who would construe the commandment as meaning: 'I will not covet others' goods lest they covet mine.' He will follow the letter of the law as a matter of policy, but not the true spirit of the law as a matter of principle. A person of sattvika temperament will follow both the letter and the spirit of the precept as a matter of principle and not of policy, as a matter of eternal value. He will be righteous for the sake of righteousness alone, and not because there is a human law imposing punishment to keep him honest.

The yogi who is also human is affected by these three guṇās. By his constant and disciplined study (abhyāsa) of himself and of the objects which his senses tend to pursue, he learns which thoughts, words and actions are prompted by tamas and which by rajas. With unceasing effort he weeds out and eradicates such thoughts as are prompted by tamas and he works to achieve a sattvika frame of mind. When the sattva-guṇa alone remains, the human soul has advanced a long way towards the ultimate goal.

Like unto the pull of gravity is the pull of the guṇās. As intensive research and rigorous discipline are needed to experience the wonder of weightlessness in space, so also a searching self-examination and the discipline furnished by Yoga is needed by a sādhaka to experience union with the Creator of space when he is freed from the pull of the guṇās.

Once the sādhaka has experienced the fulness of creation or of the Creator, his thirst (tṛṣṇa) for objects of sense vanishes and he looks at them ever after with dispassion (vairāgya). He experiences no disquiet in heat or cold, in pain or pleasure, in honour or dishonour and in virtue or vice. He treats the two imposters – triumph and disaster – with equanimity. He has emancipated himself from these pairs of opposites. He has passed beyond the pull of the guṇās and has become a guṇātīta (one who has transcended the guṇās). He is then free from birth and death, from pain and sorrow and becomes immortal. He has no self identity as he lives experiencing the fulness of the Universal Soul. Such a man, scorning nothing, leads all things to the path of perfection.

Dhāraṇā

When the body has been tempered by āsanas, when the mind has been refined by the fire of prāṇāyāma and when the senses have been brought under control by pratyāhāra, the sādhaka reaches the sixth stage called dhāraṇā. Here he is concentrated wholly on a single point or on a task in which he is completely engrossed. The mind has to be stilled in order to achieve this state of complete absorption.

The mind is an instrument which classifies, judges and co-ordinates the impressions from the outside world and those that arise within oneself.

Mind is the product of thoughts which are difficult to restrain for they are subtle and fickle. A thought which is well guarded by a controlled mind brings happiness. To get the best out of an instrument, one must know how it works. The mind is the instrument for thinking and it is therefore necessary to consider how it functions. Mental states are classified in five groups. The first of these is the kṣipta state, where the mental forces are scattered, being in disarray and in a state of neglect. Here the mind hankers after objects, the ragō-guṇa being dominant. The second is the vikṣipta state, where the mind is agitated and distracted. Here there is a capacity to enjoy the fruits of one's efforts, but the desires are not marshalled and controlled. Then in the mūḍha state the mind is foolish, dull and stupid. It is confounded and at a loss to know what it wants and here the tamō-guṇa predominates. The fourth state of the mind is the ekāgra (eka = one; agra = foremost) state, where the mind is closely attentive and the mental faculties are concentrated on a single object or focussed on one point only, with the sattva-guṇa prevailing. The ekāgra person has superior intellectual powers and knows exactly what he wants, so he uses all his powers to achieve his purpose. At times the ruthless pursuit of the desired object, irrespective of the cost to others, can create great misery, and it often happens that even if the desired object is achieved it leaves behind a bitter taste.

Arjuna, the mighty bowman of the epic Mahābhārata, provides us with an example of what is meant by dhāraṇā. Once Droṇa, the preceptor of the royal princes, organized an archery contest to test their proficiency. They were called upon one by one to describe the target, which was pointed out to them. It was a nesting bird. Some princes described the grove of trees, others the particular tree or the bough on which the nest stood. When Arjuna's turn came, he described first the bird. Then he saw only its head, and lastly he could see nothing but the shining eye of the bird, which was the centre of the target chosen by Droṇa.

There is danger, however, of an ekāgra person becoming supremely egotistical. Where the senses start roaming unchecked, the mind follows suit. They cloud a man's judgement and set him adrift like a battered ship on a storm-tossed sea. A ship needs ballast to keep her on an even keel and the helmsman needs a star to steer her by. The ekāgra person needs bhakti (adoration of the Lord) and concentration on divinity to keep his mental equilibrium so that he goes on always in the right direction. He will not know happiness until the sense of 'I' and 'mine' disappears.

The last mental state is that of niruddha, where the mind (manas), intellect (buddhi) and ego (ahamkāra) are all restrained and all these faculties are offered to the Lord for His use and in His service. Here

324

there is no feeling of 'I' and 'mine'. As a lens becomes more luminous when great light is thrown upon it and seems to be all light and undistinguishable from it, so also the sādhaka who has given up his mind, intellect and ego to the Lord, becomes one with Him, for the sādhaka thinks of nothing but Him, who is the creator of thought.

Without ekāgratā or concentration one can master nothing. Without concentration on Divinity, which shapes and controls the universe, one cannot unlock the divinity within oneself or become a universal man.

Conscious Dying

SOGYAL RINPOCHE
The Tibetan Book of Living and Dying

Born in Tibet, Sogyal Rinpoche went into exile with the Chinese occupation of his country. Educated at Delhi and Cambridge universities, he is one of the foremost interpreters of Tibetan Buddhism in the modern world. He is the founder of Rigpa, an international network of centres and groups dedicated to a contemporary Buddhist approach.

The most valuable and powerful of all practices I have found in caring for the dying, one which I have seen an astonishing number of people take to with enthusiasm, is a practice from the Tibetan tradition called *phowa* (pronounced 'po-wa'), which means the transference of consciousness.

Phowa for dying people has been performed by friends, relatives, or masters, quite simply and naturally, all over the modern world – in Australia, America, and Europe. Thousands of people have been given the chance to die serenely because of its power. It gives me joy to make the *heart* of the *phowa* practice now available to anyone who wishes to use it.

I want to emphasize that this is a practice that anyone at all can do. It is simple, but it is also the most essential practice we can do to prepare for our own death, and it is the main practice I teach my students for helping their dying friends and relatives, and their loved ones who have already died.

Practice one

First make sure you are comfortable, and assume the meditative posture. If you are doing this practice as you are coming close to death, just sit as comfortably as you are able, or practise lying down.

Then bring your mind home, release, and relax completely.

1. In the sky in front of you, invoke the embodiment of whatever truth you believe in, in the form of radiant light. Choose whichever divine being or saint you feel close to. If you are a Buddhist, invoke a buddha with whom you feel an intimate connection. If you are a practising Christian, feel with all your heart the vivid, immediate presence of God, the Holy Spirit, Jesus, or the Virgin Mary. If you don't feel linked with any particular spiritual figure, simply imagine a form of pure golden light in the sky before you. The important point is that you consider the being you are visualizing or whose presence you feel *is* the embodiment of the truth, wisdom, and compassion of all the buddhas, saints, masters, and enlightened beings. Don't worry if you cannot visualize them very clearly, just fill your heart with their presence and trust that they are there.

2. Then focus your mind, heart, and soul on the presence you have invoked, and pray:

Through your blessing, grace, and guidance, through the power of the light
   that streams from you:
May all my negative karma, destructive emotions, obscurations, and
   blockages be purified and removed,
May I know myself forgiven for all the harm I may have thought and done,
May I accomplish this profound practice of phowa, *and die a good and*
   peaceful death,
And through the triumph of my death, may I be able to benefit all other
   beings, living or dead.

3. Now imagine that the presence of light you have invoked is so moved by your sincere and heartfelt prayer that he or she responds with a loving smile and sends out love and compassion in a stream of rays of light from his or her heart. As these touch and penetrate you, they cleanse and purify all your negative karma, destructive emotions, and obscurations, which are the causes of suffering. You see and feel that you are totally immersed in light.

4. You are now completely purified and completely healed by the light

streaming from the presence. Consider that your very body, itself created by karma, now dissolves completely into light.

5. The body of light you are now soars up into the sky and merges, inseparably, with the blissful presence of light.

6. Remain in that state of oneness with the presence for as long as possible.

Practice two

1. To do this practice even more simply, begin as before by resting quietly, and then invoke the presence of the embodiment of truth.

2. Imagine your consciousness as a sphere of light at your heart, which flashes out from you like a shooting star, and flies into the heart of the presence in front of you.

3. It dissolves and merges with the presence.

Through this practice you are investing your mind in the wisdom mind of the Buddha or enlightened being, which is the same as surrendering your soul into the nature of God. Dilgo Khyentse Rinpoche says this is like casting a pebble into a lake; think of it plummeting down into the water, deeper and deeper. Imagine that through the blessing your mind is transformed into the wisdom mind of this enlightened presence.

Practice three

The most essential way to do the practice is this: simply merge your mind with the wisdom mind of the pure presence. Consider: 'My mind and the mind of the Buddha are one.'

Choose whichever one of these versions of the *phowa* feels more comfortable, or has most appeal for you at any particular moment. Sometimes the most powerful practices can be the most simple. But whichever one you choose, remember that it is essential to take the time now to become familiar with this practice. How else will you have the confidence to do it for yourself or others at the moment of death? My master Jamyang Khyentse wrote, 'If you meditate and practise in this manner always, at the moment of death it will come easier.'

In fact you should be so familiar with the practice of *phowa* that it becomes a natural reflex, your second nature. If you have seen the film *Gandhi*, you will know that when he was shot, his immediate response was to call out: 'Ram . . . Ram!' which is, in the Hindu tradition, the sacred name of God. Remember that we never know how we will die, or if we will be given the time to recall any kind of practice at all. What time will we have, for example, if we smash our car into a truck at 100 mph on the freeway? There won't be a second then to think about how to do *phowa*, or to check the instructions in this book. Either we are familiar with the *phowa* or we are not. There is a simple way to gauge this: just look at your reactions when you are in a critical situation or in a moment of crisis, such as an earthquake, or in a nightmare. Do you respond with the practice or don't you? And if you do, how stable and confident is your practice?

I remember a student of mine in America who went out riding one day. The horse threw her; her foot got stuck in the stirrup, and she was dragged along the ground. Her mind went blank. She tried desperately to recall some practice, but nothing at all would come. She grew terrified. What was good about that terror was that it made her realize that her practice had to become her second nature. This was the lesson she had to learn; it is the lesson, in fact, we all have to learn. Practise *phowa* as intensively as you can, until you can be sure you will react with it to any unforeseen event. This will make certain that whenever death comes, you will be as ready as you can be.

Using the essential phowa *practice to help the dying*

How can we use this practice to help someone who is dying?

The principle and the sequence of the practice are exactly the same; the only difference is that you visualize the Buddha or spiritual presence above the head of the dying person:

Imagine that the rays of light pour down on to the dying person, purifying his or her whole being, and then he or she dissolves into light and merges into the spiritual presence.

Do this practice throughout your loved one's illness, and especially (and most important) when the person is breathing their last breath, or as soon as possible after breathing stops and before the body is touched or disturbed in any way. If the dying person knows you are going to do this practice for them, and knows what it is, it can be a great source of inspiration and comfort.

Sit quietly with the dying person, and offer a candle or light in front of a picture or statue of Buddha or Christ or the Virgin Mary. Then do the practice for them. You can be doing the practice quietly, and the person need not even know about it; on the other hand, if he or she is open to it, as sometimes dying people are, share the practice and explain how to do it.

People often ask me: 'If my dying relative or friend is a practising Christian and I am a Buddhist, is there any conflict?' How could there be? I tell them: You are invoking the truth, and Christ and Buddha are both compassionate manifestations of truth, appearing in different ways to help beings.

I strongly suggest to doctors and nurses that they can also do *phowa* for their dying patients. Imagine how marvellously it could change the atmosphere in a hospital if those who were ministering to the dying were also doing this practice.

The Book of Changes

RICHARD WILHELM (TRANSLATION)
The I Ching

First published in English in 1952, with an introduction by Carl Jung, Richard Wilhelm's version of *The I Ching* was probably the most important book in bringing into Western awareness a whole stream of Chinese philosophy, including the terms Tao, Yin and Yang, and Chi.

By throwing stalks or coins, inquirers of *The I Ching* are directed to one of sixty-four hexagrams in the book, each of which gives the readers both reflection and counsel on how to lead their lives. The counsel is phrased in evocative and symbolic language, and the advice is both pragmatic and ethical. Part of Chinese culture for over three thousand years, *The I Ching* transcended its status simply as an oracle when moral values were attached to its pronouncements. It became one of the five classics of Confucianism, and provided a common source for both Confucian and Taoist philosophy.

Of far greater significance than the use of the Book of Changes as an oracle is its other use, namely, as a book of wisdom. Lao-tse[1] knew this book, and some of his profoundest aphorisms were inspired by it. Indeed, his whole thought is permeated with its teachings. Confucius[2] too knew the Book of Changes and devoted himself to reflection upon it. He probably wrote down some of his interpretative comments and imparted others to his pupils in oral teaching. The Book of Changes as edited and annotated by Confucius is the version that has come down to our time.

If we inquire as to the philosophy that pervades the book, we can confine ourselves to a few basically important concepts. The underlying idea of the whole is the idea of change. It is related in the Analects[3] that Confucius, standing by a river, said: 'Everything flows on and on like this river, without pause, day and night.' This expresses the idea of change. He who has perceived the meaning of change fixes his attention no longer on transitory individual things but on the immutable, eternal law at work in all change. This law is the tao[4] of Lao-tse, the course of things, the principle of the one in the many. That it may become manifest, a decision, a postulate, is necessary. This fundamental postulate is the 'great primal beginning' of all that exists, *t'ai chi* – in its original meaning, the 'ridgepole'. Later Chinese philosophers devoted much thought to this idea of a primal beginning. A still earlier beginning, *wu chi*, was represented by the symbol of a circle. Under this conception, *t'ai chi* was represented by the circle divided into the light and the dark, yang and yin, ☯.[5]

This symbol has also played a significant part in India and Europe. However, speculations of a gnostic-dualistic character are foreign to the original thought of the *I Ching*; what it posits is simply the ridgepole, the line. With this line, which in itself represents oneness, duality comes into the world, for the line at the same time posits an above and a below, a right and left, front and back – in a word, the world of the opposites.

These opposites became known under the names yin and yang and created a great stir, especially in the transition period between the Ch'in and Han dynasties, in the centuries just before our era, when there was an entire school of yin-yang doctrine. At that time, the Book of Changes was much in use as a book of magic, and people read into the text all sorts of things not originally there. This doctrine of yin and yang, of the female and the male as primal principles, has naturally also attracted much attention among foreign students of Chinese thought. Following the usual bent, some of these have predicated in it a primitive phallic symbolism, with all the accompanying connotations.

To the disappointment of such discoverers it must be said that there is nothing to indicate this in the original meaning of the words yin and yang. In its primary meaning yin is 'the cloudy', 'the overcast', and yang means actually 'banners waving in the sun',[6] that is, something 'shone upon', or bright. By transference the two concepts were applied to the light and dark sides of a mountain or of a river. In the case of a mountain the southern is the bright side and the northern the dark side, while in the case of a river seen from above, it is the northern side that is bright (yang), because it reflects the light, and the southern side that is in shadow (yin). Thence the two expressions were carried over into the Book of Changes and applied to the two alternating primal states of being. It should be pointed out, however, that the terms yin and yang do not occur in this derived sense either in the actual text of the book or in the oldest commentaries. Their first occurrence is in the Great Commentary, which already shows Taoistic influence in some parts. In the Commentary on the Decision the terms used for the opposites are 'the firm' and 'the yielding', not yang and yin.

However, no matter what names are applied to these forces, it is certain that the world of being arises out of their change and interplay. Thus change is conceived of partly as the continuous transformation of the one force into the other and partly as a cycle of complexes of phenomena, in themselves connected, such as day and night, summer and winter. Change is not meaningless – if it were, there could be no knowledge of it – but subject to the universal law, tao.

The second theme fundamental to the Book of Changes is its theory of ideas. The eight trigrams are images not so much of objects as of states of change. This view is associated with the concept expressed in the teachings of Lao-tse, as also in those of Confucius, that every event in the visible world is the effect of an 'image', that is, of an idea in the unseen world. Accordingly, everything that happens on earth is only a reproduction, as it were, of an event in a world beyond our sense perception; as regards its occurrence in time, it is later than the supra-sensible event. The holy men and sages, who are in contact with those higher spheres, have access to these ideas through direct intuition and are therefore able to intervene decisively in events in the world. Thus man is linked with heaven, the supra-sensible world of ideas, and with earth, the material world of visible things, to form with these a trinity of the primal powers.

This theory of ideas is applied in a twofold sense. The Book of Changes shows the images of events and also the unfolding of conditions *in statu nascendi*. Thus, in discerning with its help the seeds of things to come, we learn to foresee the future as well as to understand the past. In this way the images on which the hexagrams are based serve as patterns for timely action in the situations indicated. Not only is adaptation to the course of nature thus made possible, but in the Great Commentary (pt. II, chap. II), an interesting attempt is made to trace back the origin of all the practices and inventions of civilization to such ideas and archetypal images. Whether or not the hypothesis can be made to apply in all specific instances, the basic concept contains a truth.[7]

The third element fundamental to the Book of Changes is the judgements. The judgements clothe the images in words, as it were; they indicate whether a given action will bring good fortune or misfortune, remorse or humiliation. The judgements make it possible for a man to make a decision to desist from a course of action indicated by the situation of the moment but harmful in the long run. In this way he makes himself independent of the tyranny of events. In its judgements, and in the interpretations attached to it from the time of Confucius on, the Book of Changes opens to the reader the richest treasure of Chinese wisdom; at the same time it affords him a comprehensive view of the varieties of human experience, enabling him thereby to shape his life of his own sovereign will into an organic whole and so to direct it that it comes into accord with the ultimate tao lying at the root of all that exists.

Tibetan Buddhism

CHÖGYAM TRUNGPA
Cutting Through Spiritual Materialism

Chögyam Trungpa was the eleventh descendant in the line of Trungpa
tülkus. These were important teachers of the Kagyü lineage – one of the four
main schools of Tibetan Buddhism and renowned for its strong emphasis
on meditation practice. He was also an adherent of the non-sectarian
ecumenical movement within Tibetan Buddhism, which aspired to bring
together and make available all the valuable teachings of the different
schools, free of sectarian rivalry. Already installed as the head of the Surm-
ang monasteries in eastern Tibet, Chögyam Trungpa was forced to flee the
country in 1959, at the age of twenty.

In 1967 he moved to Scotland, where he founded the Samye Ling meditation centre, the first Tibetan Buddhist practice centre in the West. Under
his guidance and leadership many centres were set up around the world,
especially in the United States. His most well-known book *Cutting Through
Spiritual Materialism* was given as a series of lectures in Boulder, Colorado.

So we try to fit things into pigeonholes, try to fit the situation to our
expectations, and we cannot surrender any part of our anticipation to
all. If we search for a guru or teacher, we expect him to be saintly,
peaceful, quiet, a simple and yet wise man. When we find that he does
not match our expectations, then we begin to be disappointed, we
begin to doubt.

In order to establish a real teacher-student relationship it is necessary
for us to give up all our preconceptions regarding that relationship
and the condition of opening and surrender. 'Surrender' means opening
oneself completely, trying to get beyond fascination and expectation.

Surrender also means acknowledging the raw, rugged, clumsy and
shocking qualities of one's ego, acknowledging them and surrendering
them as well. Generally, we find it very difficult to give out and
surrender our raw and rugged qualities of ego. Although we may hate

ourselves, at the same time we find our self-hatred a kind of occupation. In spite of the fact that we may dislike what we are and find that self-condemnation painful, still we cannot give it up completely. If we begin to give up our self-criticism, then we may feel that we are losing our occupation, as though someone were taking away our job. We would have no further occupation if we were to surrender everything; there would be nothing to hold on to. Self-evaluation and self-criticism are, basically, neurotic tendencies which derive from our not having enough confidence in ourselves, 'confidence' in the sense of seeing what we are, knowing what we are, knowing that we can afford to open. We *can* afford to surrender that raw and rugged neurotic quality of self and step out of fascination, step out of preconceived ideas.

We must surrender our hopes and expectations, as well as our fears, and march directly into disappointment, work with disappointment, go into it and make it our way of life, which is a very hard thing to do. Disappointment is a good sign of basic intelligence. It cannot be compared to anything else: it is so sharp, precise, obvious and direct. If we can open, then we suddenly begin to see that our expectations are irrelevant compared with the reality of the situations we are facing. This automatically brings a feeling of disappointment.

Disappointment is the best chariot to use on the path of the dharma. It does not confirm the existence of our ego and its dreams. However, if we are involved with spiritual materialism, if we regard spirituality as a part of our accumulation of learning and virtue, if spirituality becomes a way of building ourselves up, then of course the whole process of surrendering is completely distorted. If we regard spirituality as a way of making ourselves comfortable, then whenever we experience something unpleasant, a disappointment, we try to rationalize it: 'Of course this must be an act of wisdom on the part of the guru, because I know, I'm quite certain the guru doesn't do harmful things. Guruji is a perfect being and whatever Guruji does is right. Whatever Guruji does is for me, because he is on my side. So I can afford to open. I can safely surrender. I know that I am treading on the right path.' Something is not quite right about such an attitude. It is, at best, simple-minded and naive. We are captivated by the awesome, inspiring, dignified and colourful aspect of 'Guruji'. We dare not contemplate any other way. We develop the conviction that whatever we experience is part of our spiritual development. 'I've made it, I have experienced it, I am a self-made person and I know everything, roughly, because I've read books and they confirm my beliefs, my rightness, my ideas. Everything coincides.'

We can hold back in still another way, not really surrendering because we feel that we are very genteel, sophisticated and dignified people. 'Surely we can't give ourselves to this dirty, ordinary street-scene of reality.' We have the feeling that every step of the path we tread should be a lotus petal and we develop a logic that interprets whatever happens to us accordingly. If we fall, we create a soft landing which prevents sudden shock. Surrendering does not involve preparing for a soft landing: it means just landing on hard, ordinary ground, on rocky, wild countryside. Once we open ourselves, then we land on *what is*.

Traditionally, surrendering is symbolized by such practices as prostration, which is the act of falling on the ground in a gesture of surrender. At the same time we open psychologically and surrender completely by identifying ourselves with the lowest of the low, acknowledging our raw and rugged quality. There is nothing that we fear to lose once we identify ourselves with the lowest of the low. By doing so, we prepare ourselves to be an empty vessel, ready to receive the teachings.

In the Buddhist tradition, there is this basic formula: 'I take refuge in the Buddha, I take refuge in the dharma, I take refuge in the sangha.' I take refuge in the Buddha as the example of surrender, the example of acknowledging negativity as a part of our make-up and opening to it. I take refuge in the dharma–dharma, the 'law of existence', life as it is, I am willing to open my eyes to the circumstances of life as they are. I am not willing to view them as spiritual or mystical, but I am willing to see the situations of life as they really are. I take refuge in the sangha. 'Sangha' means 'community of people on the spiritual path', 'companions'. I am willing to share my experience of the whole environment of life with my fellow pilgrims, my fellow searchers, those who walk with me; but I am not willing to lean on them in order to gain support. I am only willing to walk along with them. There is a very dangerous tendency to lean on one another as we tread the path. If a group of people leans one upon the other, then if one should happen to fall down, everyone falls down. So we do not lean on anyone else. We just walk with each other, side by side, shoulder to shoulder, working with each other, going with each other. This approach to surrendering, this idea of taking refuge is very profound.

The wrong way to take refuge involves seeking shelter – worshipping mountains, sun gods, moon gods, deities of any kind simply because they would seem to be greater than we. This kind of refuge-taking is similar to the response of the little child who says, 'If you beat me, I'll tell my mommy,' thinking that his mother is a great, archetypically powerful person. If he is attacked, his automatic recourse is to his mother, an invincible and all-knowing, all-powerful personality. The child believes his mother can protect him, in fact that she is the only person who can save him. Taking refuge in a mother- or father-principle is truly self-defeating; the refuge-seeker has no real basic strength at all, no true inspiration. He is constantly busy assessing greater and smaller powers. If we are small, then someone greater can crush us. We seek refuge because we cannot afford to be small and without protection. We tend to be apologetic: 'I am such a small thing, but I acknowledge your great quality. I would like to worship and join your greatness, so will you please protect me?'

Surrendering is not a question of being low and stupid, nor of wanting to be elevated and profound. It has nothing to do with levels and evaluation. Instead, we surrender because we would like to communicate with the world 'as it is'. We do not have to classify ourselves as learners or ignorant people. We know where we stand, therefore we make the gesture of surrendering, of opening, which means communication, link, direct communication with the object of our surrendering. We are not embarrassed about our rich collection of raw, rugged, beautiful and clean qualities. We present everything to the object of our surrendering. The basic act of surrender does not involve the worship of an external power. Rather it means working together with inspiration, so that one becomes an open vessel into which knowledge can be poured.

Thus openness and surrendering are the necessary preparation for working with a spiritual friend. We acknowledge our fundamental richness rather than bemoan the imagined poverty of our being. We know we are worthy to receive the teachings, worthy of relating ourselves to the wealth of the opportunities for learning.

338

Zazen

SHUNRYU SUZUKI
Zen Mind, Beginner's Mind

In 1958, at the age of fifty-three, Shunryu Suzuki of the Soto Zen lineage journeyed to the United States for a short trip. He was so impressed by the seriousness and intelligence with which he was greeted that he stayed until his death, thirteen years later. Under his guidance the United States' first Zen Center was opened, in San Francisco, and several more followed including the Tassajara Zen Mountain Center. Everything at Tassajara was done with awareness, including the cooking and the two Tassajara cookbooks were hugely influential in the philosophy and move towards wholefoods.

Beyond consciousness – '*To realize pure mind in your delusion is practice. If you try to expel the delusion it will only persist the more. Just say, "Oh, this is just delusion", and do not be bothered by it.*'

We should establish our practice where there is no practice or enlightenment. As long as we practise zazen in the area where there is practice and enlightenment, there is no chance to make perfect peace for ourselves. In other words, we must firmly believe in our true nature. Our true nature is beyond our conscious experience. It is only in our conscious experience that we find practice and enlightenment or good and bad. But whether or not we have experience of our true nature, what exists there, beyond consciousness, actually exists, and it is there that we have to establish the foundation of our practice.

Even to have a good thing in your mind is not so good. Buddha sometimes said, 'You should be like this. You ought not to be like that.' But to have what he says in your mind is not so good. It is a kind of burden for you, and you may not actually feel so good. In fact to harbour some ill will may even be better than to have some idea in your mind of what is good or of what you ought to do. To have some

339

mischievous idea in your mind is sometimes very agreeable. That is true. Actually, good and bad is not the point. Whether or not you make yourself peaceful is the point, and whether or not you stick to it.

When you have something in your consciousness you do not have perfect composure. The best way towards perfect composure is to forget everything. Then your mind is calm, and it is wide and clear enough to see and feel things as they are without any effort. The best way to find perfect composure is not to retain any idea of things, whatever they may be – to forget all about them and not to leave any trace or shadow of thinking. But if you try to stop your mind or try to go beyond your conscious activity, that will only be another burden for you. 'I have to stop my mind in my practice, but I cannot. My practice is not so good.' This kind of idea is also the wrong way of practice. Do not try to stop your mind, but leave everything as it is. Then things will not stay in your mind so long. Things will come as they come and go as they go. Then eventually your clear, empty mind will last fairly long.

So to have a firm conviction in the original emptiness of your mind is the most important thing in your practice. In Buddhist scriptures we sometimes use vast analogies in an attempt to describe empty mind. Sometimes we use an astronomically great number, so great it is beyond counting. This means to give up calculating. If it is so great that you cannot count it, then you will lose your interest and eventually give up. This kind of description may also give rise to a kind of interest in the innumerable number, which will help you to stop the thinking of your small mind.

But it is when you sit in zazen that you will have the most pure, genuine experience of the empty state of mind. Actually, emptiness of mind is not even a state of mind, but the original essence of mind which Buddha and the Sixth Patriarch experienced. 'Essence of mind', 'original mind', 'original face', 'Buddha nature', 'emptiness' – all these words mean the absolute calmness of our mind.

You know how to rest physically. You do not know how to rest mentally. Even though you lie in your bed your mind is still busy; even if you sleep your mind is busy dreaming. Your mind is always in intense activity. This is not so good. We should know how to give up our thinking mind, our busy mind. In order to go beyond our thinking faculty, it is necessary to have a firm conviction in the emptiness of your mind. Believing firmly in the perfect rest of our mind, we should resume our pure original state.

Dogen-zenji said, 'You should establish your practice in your delusion.' Even though you think you are in delusion, your pure mind is there. To realize pure mind in your delusion is practice. If you have pure mind, essential mind in your delusion, the delusion will vanish. It cannot stay when you say, 'This is delusion!' It will be very much ashamed. It will run away. So you should establish your practice in your delusion. To have delusion is practice. This is to attain enlightenment before you realize it. Even though you do not realize it, you have it. So when you say, 'This is delusion', that is actually enlightenment itself. If you try to expel the delusion it will only persist the more, and your mind will become busier and busier trying to cope with it. That is not so good. Just say, 'Oh, this is just delusion', and do not be bothered by it. When you just observe the delusion, you have your true mind, your calm, peaceful mind. When you start to cope with it you will be involved in delusion.

So whether or not you attain enlightenment, just to sit in zazen is enough. When you try to attain enlightenment, then you have a big burden on your mind. Your mind will not be clear enough to see things as they are. If you truly see things as they are, then you will see things as they should be. On the one hand, we should attain enlightenment – that is how things should be. But on the other hand, as long as we are physical beings, in reality it is pretty hard to attain enlightenment – that is how things actually are in this moment. But if we start to sit, both sides of our nature will be brought up, and we will see things both as they are and as they should be. Because we are not good right now, we want to be better, but when we attain the transcendental mind, we go beyond things as they are and as they should be. In the emptiness of our original mind they are one, and there we find our perfect composure.

Usually religion develops itself in the realm of consciousness, seeking to perfect its organization, building beautiful buildings, creating music, evolving a philosophy, and so forth. These are religious activities in the conscious world. But Buddhism emphasizes the world of unconsciousness. The best way to develop Buddhism is to sit in zazen – just to sit, with a firm conviction in our true nature. This way is much better than to read books or study the philosophy of Buddhism.

Of course it is necessary to study the philosophy – it will strengthen your conviction. Buddhist philosophy is so universal and logical that it is not just the philosophy of Buddhism, but of life itself. The purpose of Buddhist teaching is to point to life itself existing beyond consciousness in our pure original mind. All Buddhist practices were built up to protect this true teaching, not to propagate Buddhism in some wonderful mystic way. So when we discuss religion, it should be in the most common and universal way. We should not try to propagate our way by wonderful philosophical thought. In some ways Buddhism is rather polemical, with some feeling of controversy in it, because the Buddhist must protect his way from mystic or magical interpretations of religion. But philosophical discussion will not be the best way to understand Buddhism. If you want to be a sincere Buddhist, the best way is to sit. We are very fortunate to have a place to sit in this way. I want you to have a firm, wide, imperturbable conviction in your zazen of just sitting. Just to sit, that is enough.

Zen food for body and mind

Rock and Water
Wind and Tree
Bread Dough Rising

Vastly all
Are patient with me

Bread makes itself, by your kindness, with your help, with imagination running through you, with dough under hand, you are breadmaking itself, which is why breadmaking is so fulfilling and rewarding.

A recipe doesn't belong to anyone. Given to me, I give it to you. Only a guide, only a skeletal framework. You must fill in the flesh according to your nature and desire. Your life, your love will bring these words into full creation. This cannot be taught. You already know. So please cook, love, feel, create.

The Tassajara Bread Book, Edward Espe Brown,
Shambhala Publications, Boulder, 1970

The Hippy's Enlightenment

RAM DASS
Be Here Now

If there was a bible for all the hippies who later became the backbone of the American holistic movement, it was Ram Dass's *Be Here Now*. Ram Dass was in fact Dr Richard Alpert, a very successful academic who became involved with the psychedelic drug culture before travelling to India where he met a guru who truly blew his mind. He dropped all his academic work; he dropped his name; and he became a living icon bridging the modern Western world with the teachings of Eastern mysticism. His great popularity is based in his sense of humour, humility and his openness about the internal psychological struggles that he, too, experiences.

In 1961, the beginning of March, I was at perhaps the highest point of my academic career. I had just returned from being a visiting professor at the University of California at Berkeley: I had been assured of a permanent post that was being held for me at Harvard, if I got my publications in order. I held appointments in four departments at Harvard – the Social Relations Department, the Psychology Department, the Graduate School of Education, and the Health Service (where I was a therapist); I had research contracts with Yale and Stanford. In a worldly sense, I was making a great income and I was a collector of possessions.

I had an apartment in Cambridge that was filled with antiques and I gave very charming dinner parties. I had a Mercedes-Benz sedan and a Triumph 500 CC motorcycle and a Cessna 172 airplane and an MG sports car and a sailboat and a bicycle. I vacationed in the Caribbean where I did scuba-diving. I was living the way a successful bachelor professor is supposed to live in the American world of 'he who makes it'. I wasn't a genuine scholar, but I had gone through the whole academic trip. I had gotten my Ph.D.; I was writing books. I had research contracts. I taught courses in Human Motivation, Freudian

Theory, Child Development. But what all this boils down to is that I was really a very good game player.

My lecture notes were the ideas of other men, subtly presented, and my research was all within the Zeitgeist – all that which one was supposed to research about.

In 1955 I had started doing therapy and my first therapy patient had turned me on to pot. I had not smoked regularly after that, but only sporadically, and I was still quite a heavy drinker. But this first patient had friends and they had friends and all of them became my patients. I became a 'hip' therapist, for the hip community at Stanford. When I'd go to the parties, they'd all say 'Here comes the shrink' and I would sit in the corner looking superior. In addition, I had spent five years in psychoanalysis at a cool investment of something like $26,000.

Before 6 March, which was the day I took Psylocybin, one of the psychedelics, I felt something was wrong in my world, but I couldn't label it in any way so as to get hold of it. I felt that the theories I was teaching in psychology didn't make it, that the psychologists didn't really have a grasp of the human condition, and that the theories I was teaching, which were theories of achievement and anxiety and defence mechanisms and so on, weren't getting to the crux of the matter.

My colleagues and I were nine-to-five psychologists: we came to work every day and we did our psychology, just like you would do insurance or auto mechanics, and then at five we went home and were just as neurotic as we were before we went to work. Somehow, it seemed to me, if all of this theory were right, it should play more intimately into my own life. I understood the requirement of being 'objective' for a scientist, but this is a most naive concept in social sciences as we are finding out. And whatever the psychoanalysis did (and it did many things, I'm sure) I still was a neurotic at the end of those five years of psychoanalysis. Even my therapist thought so, because when I stopped analysis to go to Harvard, he said, 'You are too sick to leave analysis.' Those were his final words. But because I had been trained in Freudian theory, I knew his game well enough to enjoy this terribly sophisticated, competitive relationship with my analyst, and I would say to him, 'Well in Freud's 1906 paper, don't you recall he said this, and when I'm saying this you should be interpreting . . .' For this I was paying $20 an hour!

Something was wrong. And the something wrong was that I just didn't know, though I kept feeling all along the way that somebody else must know even though I didn't. The nature of life was a mystery to me. All the stuff I was teaching was just like little molecular bits of stuff but they didn't add up to a feeling anything like wisdom. I was just getting more and more knowledgeable. And I was getting very good at bouncing three knowledge balls at once. I could sit in a doctoral exam, ask very sophisticated questions and look terribly wise. It was a hustle. [. . .]

And this fellow, Bhagwan Dass, comes up, runs to this man and throws himself on the ground, full-face doing 'dunda pranam', and he's stretched out so his face is down on the ground, full-length and his hands are touching the feet of this man, who is sitting cross-legged. And he's crying and the man is patting him on the head and I don't know what's happening.

I'm standing on the side and thinking 'I'm not going to touch his feet. I don't have to. I'm not required to do that.' And every now and then this man looks up at me and he twinkles a little. But I'm so uptight that I couldn't care less. Twinkle away, man!

Then he looks up at me – he speaks in Hindi, of which I understand maybe half, but there is a fellow who's translating all the time, who hangs out with him, and the Guru says to Bhagwan Dass, 'You have a picture of me?'

Bhagwan Dass nods, 'Yes.'

'Give it to him,' says the man, pointing at me.

'That's very nice,' I think, giving me a picture of himself, and I smile and nod appreciatively. But I'm still not going to touch his feet!

Then he says, 'You came in a big car?' Of course that's the one thing I'm really uptight about.

'Yeah.'

So he looks at me and he smiles and says, 'You give it to me?'

I started to say, 'Wha . . .' and Bhagwan Dass looks up – he's lying there – and he says, 'Maharaji (meaning "great king"), if you want it you can have it – it's yours.'

And I said, 'No – now wait a minute – you can't give away David's car like that. That isn't our car . . .' and this old man is laughing. In fact, everyone is laughing . . . except me.

Then he says, 'You made much money in America?'

'Ah, at last he's feeding my ego,' I think.

So I flick through all of my years as a professor and years as a smuggler and all my different dramas in my mind and I said, 'Yeah.'

'How much you make?'

'Well,' I said, 'at one time' – and I sort of upped the figure a bit, you know, my ego – '$25,000.'

So they all converted that into rupees which was practically half the economic base of India, and everybody was terribly awed by this figure, which was complete bragging on my part. It was phony – I never made $25,000. And he laughed again. And he said,

'You'll buy a car like that for me?'

And I remember what went through my mind. I had come out of a family of fund-raisers for the United Jewish Appeal, Brandeis, and Einstein Medical School, and I had never seen hustling like this. He doesn't even know my name and already he wants a $7,000 vehicle.

And I said, 'Well, maybe . . .' The whole thing was freaking me so much.

And he said, 'Take them away and give them food.' So we were taken and given food – magnificent food – we were together still, and saddhus brought us beautiful food and then we were told to rest. Some time later we were back with the Maharaji and he said to me, 'Come here. Sit.'

So I sat down and he looked at me and he said, 'You were out under the stars last night.'

'Um-hum.'

'You were thinking about your mother.'

'Yes.' ('Wow,' I thought, 'that's pretty good. I never mentioned that to anybody.')

'She died last year.'

'Um-hum.'

'She got very big in the stomach before she died.'

. . . Pause . . . 'Yes.'

He leaned back and closed his eyes and said, 'Spleen. She died of spleen.'

Well, what happened to me at that moment, I can't really put into words. He looked at me in a certain way at that moment, and two things happened – it seemed simultaneous. They do not seem like cause and effect.

The first thing that happened was that my mind raced faster and faster to try to get leverage – to get a hold on what he had just done. I went through every super CIA paranoia I've ever had:

'Who is he?' 'Who does he represent?'

'Where's the button he pushes where the file appears?' and 'Why have they brought me here?'

None of it would gel.

It was just too impossible that this could have happened this way. The guy I was with didn't know all that stuff, and I was a tourist in a car, and the whole thing was just too far out. My mind went faster and faster and faster.

Up until then I had two categories for 'psychic experiences'. One was 'they happened to somebody else and they haven't happened to me, and they were terribly interesting and we certainly had to keep an open mind about it'. That was my social science approach. The other one was, 'well, man, I'm high on LSD. Who knows how it really is? After all, under the influence of a chemical, how do I know I'm not creating the whole thing?' Because, in fact, I had taken certain chemicals where I experienced the creation of total realities. The greatest example I have of this came about through a drug called JB 318, which I took in a room at Millbrook. I was sitting on the third floor and it seemed like nothing was happening at all. And into the room walked a girl from the community with a pitcher of lemonade and she said, would I like some lemonade, and I said that would be great, and she poured the lemonade, and she poured it and she kept pouring and the lemonade went over the side of the glass and fell to the floor and it went across the floor and up the wall and over the ceiling and down the wall and under my pants which got wet and it came back up into the glass – and when it touched the glass the glass disappeared and the lemonade disappeared and the wetness in my pants disappeared and the girl disappeared and I turned around to Ralph Metzner and I said,

347

'Ralph, the most extraordinary thing happened to me', and Ralph disappeared!

I was afraid to do anything but just sit. Whatever this is, it's not nothing. Just sit. Don't move, just sit!

So I had had experiences where I had seen myself completely create whole environments under psychedelics, and therefore I wasn't eager to interpret these things very quickly, because I, the observer, was, at those times, under the influence of the psychedelics.

But neither of these categories applied in this situation, and my mind went faster and faster and then I felt like what happens when a computer is fed an insoluble problem; the bell rings and the red light goes on and the machine stops. And my mind just gave up. It burned out its circuitry . . . its zeal to have an explanation. I needed something to get closure at the rational level and there wasn't anything. There just wasn't a place I could hide in my head about this.

And at the same moment, I felt this extremely violent pain in my chest and a tremendous wrenching feeling and I started to cry. And I cried and I cried and I cried. And I wasn't happy and I wasn't sad. It was not that kind of crying. The only thing I could say was it felt like I was home. Like the journey was over. Like I had finished.

Well, I cried and they finally sort of spooned me up and took me to the home of devotee, K. K. Sah, to stay overnight. That night I was very confused. A great feeling of lightness and confusion.

Modern Prophesy

Introduction

In this final section, I want to look at one element of the holistic culture which can embarrass holists.

There is always a certain interesting tension between those holists who are comfortable with spirituality and those who are wary of it. That tension can turn into downright disdain when it comes to prophesy and channelling. Nevertheless, they are powerful strands of the movement.

Prophesy can of course be terribly embarrassing – especially around the idea of a 'New Age'. Historically, it seems to be the nature of mystical prophets to exclaim that our time is a special time and that God has special plans for us right now. In fact, adherents of the idea 'New Age' are bound to be embarrassed if they look back through history and see that, decade by decade, there has always been some group of crackpots claiming a new age, earth changes, catastrophe and revelation from God, gods or aliens.

Yet, if my understanding of our newly emerging holistic culture is true, and it is a reflection of the information revolution, then the change is as dramatic as that from hunter-gatherer to farmer, or from stone to iron – all new ages. But beyond the socio-economic and cultural change there is a mystic viewpoint which seeks to bring in a cosmic perspective. There are mystics who feel that in some way humanity is coming of age. Emerging out of a tribal and insular experience of identity, humanity is becoming self-conscious of itself as a total species. This goes hand-in-hand with electronic communications networking and profound revelations about the nature of matter, biology, psychology and cosmology. Some new, deep linking is taking place; some mass expansion of consciousness which allows for a deepening experience of love and cosmic and holistic awareness.

And then there is the whole business of channelled material. Channelled material is writing done while the author is in an altered state of consciousness and some other persona is actually doing the communicating. That other persona might be an aspect of the author's own psyche or perhaps, as is often claimed, a genuinely separate being.

Whatever you think of the phenomenon, there is a huge amount of channelled material published – and some of it is terrible. Much of it is mediocre, but some of it is brilliant. In fact many holistic writers, such as myself, believe that the best mystic writing of this century has in fact been channelled. One example of channelled writing has already appeared in this anthology, Alice Bailey writing on healing. I also offer here two other examples of channelled material which, whatever you may think of channelling, have been extremely influential and stand as excellent writing in their own right. This anthology would not be complete without them and, as Francis Bacon wrote several centuries ago, 'There is a superstition in avoiding superstition.'

The Evolution of Human Consciousness

PIERRE TEILHARD DE CHARDIN
The Phenomenon of Man

A biologist and palaeontologist, Pierre Teilhard de Chardin was also a Jesuit father. He is one of the most quoted figures in New Age thinking because of his vision and theory about the natural evolution of the human species. In this vision, he regards human society not as an irrelevant cul-de-sac of nature, but as a divinely intended natural phenomenon. From his perspective, the modern age and modern society are indications of a divine providence that is working out perfectly.

The illumination

The consciousness of each of us is evolution looking at itself and reflecting upon itself.

With that very simple view, destined, as I suppose, to become as instinctive and familiar to our descendants as the discovery of a third dimension in space is to a baby, a new light – inexhaustibly harmonious – bursts upon the world, radiating from ourselves.

Step by step, from the early earth onwards, we have followed *going upwards* the successive advances of consciousness in matter undergoing organization. Having reached the peak, we can now turn round and, *looking downwards*, take in the pattern of the whole. And this second check is decisive, the harmony is perfect. From any other point of view, there is always a 'snag': something clashes, for there is no natural place – no genetic place – for human thought in the landscape. Whereas here, from top to bottom, from our souls and *including* our souls, the lines stretch in both directions, untwisted and unbroken. From top to bottom, a triple unity persists and develops: unity of structure, unity of mechanism and unity of movement. [...]

The social phenomenon is the culmination and not the attenuation of the biological phenomenon. [. . .]

A certain sort of common sense[1] tells us that with man biological evolution has reached its ceiling: in reflecting upon itself, life has become stationary. But should we not rather say that it leaps forward? Look at the way in which, as mankind technically patterns its multitudes, *pari passu* the psychic tension within it increases, with the consciousness of time and space and the taste for, and power of, discovery. This great event we accept without surprise. Yet how can one fail to recognize this revealing association of technical organization and inward spiritual concentration as the work of the same great force (though in proportions and with a depth hitherto never attained), the very force which brought us into being? How can we fail to see that after rolling us on individually – all of us, you and me – upon our own selves, it is still the same cyclone (only now on the social scale) which is still blowing over our heads, driving us together into a contact which tends to perfect each one of us by linking him organically to each and all of his neighbours?

'Through human socialization, whose specific effect is to involute upon itself the whole bundle of reflexive scales and fibres of the earth, it is the very axis of the cosmic vortex of interiorization which is pursuing its course': replacing and extending the two preliminary postulates stated above (the one concerning the primacy of life in the universe, the other the primacy of reflection in life) this is the third option – the most decisive of all – which completes the definition and clarification of my scientific position as regards the phenomenon of man.

This is not the place to show in detail how easily and coherently this organic interpretation of the social phenomenon explains, or even in some directions allows us to predict, the course of history. Let it merely be stated that, if above the elementary hominization that culminates in each individual, there is really developing above us another hominization, a collective one of the whole species, then it is quite natural to observe, parallel with the socialization of humanity, the same three psycho-biological properties rising upwards on the earth that the individual step to reflection originally produced.

a. Firstly the power of invention, so rapidly intensified at the present time by the rationalized collaboration of all the forces of research that it is already possible to speak of a human rebound of evolution.

b. Next, capacity for attraction (or repulsion), still operating in a chaotic way throughout the world but rising so rapidly around us that (whatever be said to the contrary) economics will soon count for very little in comparison with the ideological and the emotional factors in the arrangement of the world.

c. Lastly and above all, the demand for irreversibility. This emerges from the still somewhat hesitating zone of individual aspirations, so as to find categorical expression in consciousness and through the voice of the species. Categorical in the sense that, if an isolated man can succeed in imagining that it is possible physically, or even morally, for him to contemplate a complete suppression of himself – confronted with a total annihilation (or even simply with an insufficient preservation) destined for the fruit of his evolutionary labour – mankind, in its turn, is beginning to realize once and for all that its only course would be to go on strike. For the effort to push the earth forward is much too heavy, and the task threatens to go on much too long, for us to continue to accept it, unless we are to work in what is incorruptible.

These and other assembled pointers seem to me to constitute a serious scientific proof that (in conformity with the universal law of centro-complexity) the zoological group of mankind – far from drifting biologically, under the influence of exaggerated individualism, towards a state of growing granulation; far from turning (through space-travel) to an escape from death by sidereal expansion; or yet again far from simply declining towards a catastrophe or senility – the human group is in fact turning, by planetary arrangement and convergence of all elemental terrestrial reflections, towards a second critical pole of reflection of a collective and higher order; towards a point beyond which (precisely because it is critical) we can see nothing directly, but a point through which we can nevertheless prognosticate the contact between thought, born of involution upon itself of the stuff of the universe, and that transcendent focus we call Omega, the principle which at one and the same time makes this involution irreversible and moves and gathers it in.

The Gnostic Man

SRI AUROBINDO
The Life Divine

Sri Aurobindo was a seer, poet and Indian nationalist. He merged the classic teachings of Hinduism with a contemporary cosmology and psychology. In his scheme humanity was evolving into a new type of being, the Gnostic Man. He founded an ashram in Pondicherry and was also instrumental in founding the one New Age community in India, Auroville.

But here we are still on earth, and yet it is supposed that the ego personality is extinguished and replaced by a universalized spiritual individual who is a centre and power of the transcendent Being. It might be deduced that this gnostic or supra-mental individual is a self without personality, an impersonal Purusha. There could be many gnostic individuals but there would be no personality, all would be the same in being and nature. This, again, would create the idea of a void or blank of pure being from which an action and function of experiencing consciousness would arise, but without a construction of differentiated personality such as that which we now observe and regard as ourselves on our surface. But this would be a mental rather than a supra-mental solution of the problem of a spiritual individuality surviving ego and persisting in experience. In the supermind conscious-ness personality and impersonality are not opposite principles; they are inseparable aspects of one and the same reality. This reality is not the ego but the being, who is impersonal and universal in his stuff of nature, but forms out of it an expressive personality which is his form of self in the changes of Nature.

Impersonality is in its source something fundamental and universal; it is an existence, a force, a consciousness that takes on various shapes of its being and energy; each such shape of energy, quality, power or force, though still in itself general, impersonal and universal, is taken by the individual being as material for the building of his personality.

Thus impersonality is in the original undifferentiated truth of things the pure substance of nature of the Being, the Person; in the dynamic truth of things it differentiates its powers and lends them to constitute by their variations the manifestation of personality. Love is the nature of the lover, courage the nature of the warrior; love and courage are impersonal and universal forces or formulations of the cosmic Force, they are the spirit's powers of its universal being and nature. The Person is the Being supporting what is thus impersonal, holding it in himself as his, his nature of self; he is that which is the lover and warrior. What we call the personality of the Person is his expression in nature-status and nature-action, he himself being in his self-existence, originally and ultimately, much more than that; it is the form of himself that he puts forth as his manifested already developed natural being or self in nature. In the formed limited individual it is his personal expression of what is impersonal, his personal appropriation of it, we may say, so as to have a material with which he can build a significant figure of himself in manifestation. In his formless unlimited self, his real being, the true Person or Purusha, he is not that, but contains in himself boundless and universal possibilities; but he gives to them, as the divine Individual, his own turn in the manifestation so that each among the Many is a unique self of the one Divine. The Divine, the Eternal, expresses himself as existence, consciousness, bliss, wisdom, knowledge, love, beauty, and we can think of him as these impersonal and universal powers of himself, regard them as the nature of the Divine and Eternal; we can say that God is Love, God is Wisdom, God is Truth or Righteousness: but he is not himself an impersonal state or abstract of states or qualities; he is the Being, at once absolute, universal and individual. If we look at it from this basis, there is, very clearly, no opposition, no incompatibility, no impossibility of a co-existence or one-existence of the Impersonal and the Person; they are each other, live in one another, melt into each other, and yet in a way can appear as if different ends, sides, obverse and reverse of the same Reality. The gnostic being is of the nature of the Divine and therefore repeats in himself this natural mystery of existence.

A supra-mental gnostic individual will be a spiritual Person, but not a personality in the sense of a pattern of being marked out by a settled combination of fixed qualities, a determined character; he cannot be that since he is a conscious expression of the universal and the transcendent. But neither can his being be a capricious impersonal flux throwing up at random waves of various form, waves of personality as it pours through Time. Something like this may be felt in men who have no strong centralizing Person in their depths but act from a sort of confused multi-personality according to whatever element in them becomes prominent at the time; but the gnostic consciousness is a consciousness of harmony and self-knowledge and self-mastery and would not present such a disorder. There are, indeed, varying notions of what constitutes personality and what constitutes character. In one view personality is regarded as a fixed structure of recognizable qualities expressing a power of being; but another idea distinguishes personality and character, personality as a flux of self-expressive or sensitive and responsive being, character as a formed fixity of Nature's structure. But flux of nature and fixity of nature are two aspects of being neither of which, nor indeed both together, can be a definition of personality. For in all men there is a double element, the unformed though limited flux of being or Nature out of which personality is fashioned and the personal formation out of that flux. The formation may become rigid and ossify or it may remain sufficiently plastic to change constantly and develop; but it develops out of the formative flux, by a modification or enlargement or remoulding of the personality, not, ordinarily, by an abolition of the formation already made and the substitution of a new form of being – this can only occur in an abnormal turn or a supernormal conversion. But besides this flux and this fixity there is also a third and occult element, the Person behind of whom the personality is a self-expression; the Person puts forward the personality as his role, character, *persona*, in the present act of his long drama of manifested existence. But the Person is larger than his personality, and it may happen that this inner largeness overflows into the surface formation; the result is a self-expression of being which can no longer be described by fixed qualities, normalities of mood, exact lineaments, or marked out by any structural limits. But neither is it a mere indistinguishable, quite amorphous and unseizable flux: though its acts of nature can be characterized but not itself, still it can be distinctively felt, followed in its action, it can be recognized, though it cannot easily be described; for it is a power of being rather than a structure. The ordinary restricted personality can be grasped by a description of the characters stamped on its life and thought and action, its very definite surface building and expression of self; even if we may miss whatever was not so expressed, that might seem to detract little from the general adequacy of our understanding, because the element missed is usually little more than an amorphous raw material, part of the flux, not used to form a significant part of the personality. But such a description would be pitifully inadequate to express the Person when its Power of Self within manifests more amply and puts forward its hidden daemonic force in the surface composition and the life. We feel ourselves in presence of a light of consciousness, a potency, a sea of energy, can distinguish and describe its free waves of action and quality, but not fix itself; and yet there is an impression of personality, the presence of a powerful being, a strong, high or beautiful recognizable Someone, a Person, not a limited creature of Nature but a Self or Soul, a Purusha. The gnostic Individual would be such an inner Person unveiled, occupying both the depths – no longer self-hidden – and the surface in a unified self-awareness; he would not be a surface personality partly expressive of a larger secret being, he would be not the wave but the ocean: he would be the Purusha, the inner conscious Existence self-revealed, and would have no need of a carved expressive mask or *persona*.

Lessons in Reality

ANONYMOUS
A Course in Miracles

Working as a clinical psychologist in a hospital, with no belief in either metaphysics or God or Jesus, the author began to hear a voice in her head. This voice, which she was clear was not an aspect of her own psyche, began to dictate an extraordinary book. It was divided into three sections: a general introduction for students; the workbook itself – a daily lesson and exercise for 365 days; and a primer for students who wanted to move on to teaching the material. Even its antagonists have had to recognize its wisdom and deep insights. Its tone is in many ways devotional and Christian, and it has provided the most important bridge between Christians and mystical holists.

Some of the ideas the workbook presents you will find hard to believe, and others may seem to be quite startling. This does not matter. You are merely asked to apply the ideas as you are directed to do. You are not asked to judge them at all. You are asked only to use them. It is their use that will give them meaning to you, and will show you that they are true.

Remember only this; you need not believe the ideas, you need not accept them, and you need not even welcome them. Some of them you may actively resist. None of this will matter, or decrease their efficacy. But do not allow yourself to make exceptions in applying the ideas the workbook contains, and whatever your reactions to the ideas may be, use them. Nothing more than that is required.

Part I

Lesson 1

'Nothing I see in this room [on this street, from this window, in this place] means anything.'

Now look slowly around you, and practise applying this idea very specifically to whatever you see:

'This table does not mean anything.'
'This chair does not mean anything.'
'This hand does not mean anything.'
'This foot does not mean anything.'
'This pen does not mean anything.'

Then look farther away from your immediate area, and apply the idea to a wider range:

'That door does not mean anything.'
'That body does not mean anything.'
'That lamp does not mean anything.'
'That sign does not mean anything.'
'That shadow does not mean anything.'

Notice that these statements are not arranged in any order, and make no allowance for differences in the kinds of things to which they are applied. That is the purpose of the exercise. The statement should merely be applied to anything you see. As you practise the idea for the day, use it totally indiscriminately. Do not attempt to apply it to everything you see, for these exercises should not become ritualistic. Only be sure that nothing you see is specifically excluded. One thing is like another as far as the application of the idea is concerned.

Each of the first three lessons should not be done more than twice a day each, preferably morning and evening. Nor should they be attempted for more than a minute or so, unless that entails a sense of hurry. A comfortable sense of leisure is essential.

Lesson 2

'I have given everything I see in this room [on this street, from this window, in this place] all the meaning that it has for me.'

The exercises with this idea are the same as those for the first one. Begin with the things that are near you, and apply the idea to whatever your glance rests on. Then increase the range outward. Turn your head so that you include whatever is on either side. If possible, turn around and apply the idea to what was behind you. Remain as indiscriminate as possible in selecting subjects for its application, do not concentrate on anything in particular, and do not attempt to include everything you see in a given area, or you will introduce strain.

Merely glance easily and fairly quickly around you, trying to avoid selection by size, brightness, colour, material, or relative importance to you. Take the subjects simply as you see them. Try to apply the exercise with equal ease to a body or a button, a fly or a floor, an arm or an apple. The sole criterion for applying the idea to anything is merely that your eyes have lighted on it. Make no attempt to include anything particular, but be sure that nothing is specifically excluded.

Lesson 3

'I do not understand anything I see in this room [on this street, from this window, in this place].'

Apply this idea in the same way as the previous ones, without making distinctions of any kind. Whatever you see becomes a proper subject for applying the idea. Be sure that you do not question the suitability of anything for application of the idea. These are not exercises in judgement. Anything is suitable if you see it. Some of the things you see may have emotionally charged meaning for you. Try to lay such feelings aside, and merely use these things exactly as you would anything else.

The point of the exercises is to help you clear your mind of all past associations, to see things exactly as they appear to you now, and to realize how little you really understand about them. It is therefore essential that you keep a perfectly open mind, unhampered by judgement, in selecting the things to which the idea for the day is to be applied. For this purpose one thing is like another; equally suitable and therefore equally useful.

Lesson 4

'These thoughts do not mean anything. They are like the things I see in this room [on this street, from this window, in this place].'

Unlike the preceding ones, these exercises do not begin with the idea for the day. In these practice periods, begin with noting the thoughts that are crossing your mind for about a minute. Then apply the idea to them. If you are already aware of unhappy thoughts, use them as subjects for the idea. Do not, however, select only the thoughts you think are 'bad'. You will find, if you train yourself to look at your thoughts, that they represent such a mixture that, in a sense, none of them can be called 'good' or 'bad'. This is why they do not mean anything.

In selecting the subjects for the application of today's idea, the usual specificity is required. Do not be afraid to use 'good' thoughts as well as 'bad'. None of them represents your real thoughts, which are being covered up by them. The 'good' ones are but shadows of what lies beyond, and shadows make sight difficult. The 'bad' ones are blocks to sight, and make seeing impossible. You do not want either.

This is a major exercise, and will be repeated from time to time in somewhat different form. The aim here is to train you in the first steps towards the goal of separating the meaningless from the meaningful. It is a first attempt in the long-range purpose of learning to see the meaningless as outside you, and the meaningful within. It is also the beginning of training your mind to recognize what is the same and what is different.

In using your thoughts for application of the idea for today, identify each thought by the central figure or event it contains; for example:

'This thought about—does not mean anything. It is like the things I see in this room [on this street, and so on].'

You can also use the idea for a particular thought that you recognize as harmful. This practice is useful, but is not a substitute for the more random procedures to be followed for the exercises. Do not, however, examine your mind for more than a minute or so. You are too inexperienced as yet to avoid a tendency to become pointlessly preoccupied.

Further, since these exercises are the first of their kind, you may find the suspension of judgement in connection with thoughts particularly difficult. Do not repeat these exercises more than three or four times during the day. We will return to them later.

Lesson 5

'I am never upset for the reason I think.'

This idea, like the preceding one, can be used with any person, situation or event you think is causing you pain. Apply it specifically to whatever you believe is the cause of your upset, using the description of the feeling in whatever term seems accurate to you. The upset may seem to be fear, worry, depression, anxiety, anger, hatred, jealousy or any number of forms, all of which will be perceived as different. This is not true. However, until you learn that form does not matter, each form becomes a proper subject for the exercises for the day. Applying the same idea to each of them separately is the first step in ultimately recognizing they are all the same.

When using the idea for today for a specific perceived cause of an upset in any form, use both the name of the form in which you see the upset, and the cause which you ascribe to it. For example:

'I am not angry at—for the reason I think.'
'I am not afraid of—for the reason I think.'

But again, this should not be substituted for practice periods in which you first search your mind for 'sources' of upset in which you believe, and forms of upset which you think result.

In these exercises, more than in the preceding ones, you may find it hard to be indiscriminate, and to avoid giving greater weight to some subjects than to others. It might help to precede the exercises with the statement:

'*There are no small upsets. They are all equally disturbing to my peace of mind.*'

Then examine your mind for whatever is distressing you, regardless of how much or how little you think it is doing so.

You may also find yourself less willing to apply today's idea to some perceived sources of upset than to others. If this occurs, think first of this:

'*I cannot keep this form of upset and let the others go. For the purposes of these exercises, then, I will regard them all as the same.*'

Then search your mind for no more than a minute or so, and try to identify a number of different forms of upset that are disturbing you, regardless of the relative importance you may give them. Apply the idea for today to each of them, using the name of both the source of the upset as you perceive it, and of the feeling as you experience it. Further examples are:

'*I am not worried about—for the reason I think.*'
'*I am not depressed about—for the reason I think.*'

Three or four times during the day is enough.

Lesson 6

'I am upset because I see something that is not there.'

The exercises with this idea are very similar to the preceding ones. Again, it is necessary to name both the form of upset (anger, fear, worry, depression and so on) and the perceived source very specifically for any application of the idea. For example:

'*I am angry at—because I see something that is not there.*'
'*I am worried about—because I see something that is not there.*'

Today's idea is useful for application to anything that seems to upset you, and can profitably be used throughout the day for that purpose.

However, the three or four practice periods which are required should be preceded by a minute or so of mind searching, as before, and the application of the idea to each upsetting thought uncovered in the search.

Again, if you resist applying the idea to some upsetting thoughts more than to others, remind yourself of the two cautions stated in the previous lesson:

'There are no small upsets. They are all equally disturbing to my peace of mind.'

and

'I cannot keep this form of upset and let the others go. For the purposes of these exercises, then, I will regard them all as the same.'

Lesson 7

'I see only the past.'

This idea is particularly difficult to believe at first. Yet it is the rationale for all of the preceding ones.

It is the reason why nothing that you see means anything.

It is the reason why you have given everything you see all the meaning that it has for you.

It is the reason why you do not understand anything you see.

It is the reason why your thoughts do not mean anything, and why they are like the things you see.

It is the reason why you are never upset for the reason you think.

It is the reason why you are upset because you see something that is not there.

Old ideas about time are very difficult to change, because everything you believe is rooted in time, and depends on your not learning these new ideas about it. Yet that is precisely why you need new ideas about time. This first time idea is not really so strange as it may sound at first.

Look at a cup, for example. Do you see a cup, or are you merely reviewing your past experiences of picking up a cup, being thirsty, drinking from a cup, feeling the rim of a cup against your lips, having breakfast and so on? Are not your aesthetic reactions to the cup, too, based on past experiences? How else would you know whether or not this kind of cup will break if you drop it? What do you know about this cup except what you learned in the past? You would have no idea what this cup is, except for your past learning. Do you, then, really see it?

Look about you. This is equally true of whatever you look at. Acknowledge this by applying the idea for today indiscriminately to whatever catches your eye. For example:

'I see only the past in this pencil.'
'I see only the past in this shoe.'
'I see only the past in this hand.'
'I see only the past in that body.'
'I see only the past in that face.'

Do not linger over any one thing in particular, but remember to omit nothing specifically. Glance briefly at each subject, and then move on to the next. Three or four practice periods, each to last a minute or so, will be enough.

The Multi-Dimensional Personality

JANE ROBERTS
The Nature of Personal Reality

Jane Roberts was a poet and novelist who, to her surprise, began to enter into altered states of consciousness. Through these states another persona, who called himself Seth, channelled some of the most sophisticated and intelligent psychological insights of the century. People who might otherwise have avoided any material tainted by the idea of mediumship or channelling, found themselves caught by the brilliant perspectives Seth brought to bear on the nature of human reality.

The Seth books have been extremely influential. Many pioneers in holistic medicine and psychology, such as Deepak Chopra, recommend the Seth books as essential texts. They are the key source for many of the self-help books which promote the idea that people create their personal and social reality out of powerful unconscious attitudes. Roberts was also the first writer to clearly explain what is called 'cellular memory', the idea that all the body cells contain their own memory of life's events and that psychology is not limited to the brain.

Your feeling-tones are your emotional attitudes towards yourself and life in general, and these generally govern the large areas of experience.

They give the overall emotional coloration that characterizes what happens to you. Period. *You* are what happens to you. Your emotional feelings are often transitory, but beneath there are certain qualities of feeling uniquely your own, that are like deep musical chords. While your day-to-day feelings may rise or fall, these characteristic feeling-tones lie beneath.

Sometimes they rise to the surface, but in great long rhythms. You cannot call these negative or positive. They are instead tones of your being. They represent the most inner portion of your experience. This does not mean that they are hidden from you, or are meant to be. It simply means that they represent the core from which you form your experience.

If you have become afraid of emotion or the expression of feeling, or if you have been taught that the inner self is no more than a repository of uncivilized impulses, then you may have the habit of denying this deep rhythm. You may try to operate as if it did not exist, or even try to refute it. But it represents your deepest, most creative impulses; to fight against it is like trying to swim upstream against a strong current.

Now you may take your break.

These feeling-tones, then, pervade your being.

They are the form your spirit takes when combined with flesh. From them, from their core, your flesh arises.

Everything that you experience has consciousness, and each consciousness is endowed with its own feeling-tone. There is great cooperation involved in the formation of the earth as you think of it, and so the individual living structures of the planet rise up from the feeling-tone within each atom and molecule.

Your flesh springs about you in response to these inner chords of your being, and the trees, rocks, seas and mountains spring up as the body of the earth from the deep inner chords within the atoms and molecules, which are also living. Because of the creative cooperation that exists, the miracle of physical materialization is performed so smoothly and automatically that consciously you are not aware of your part in it.

The feeling-tone then is the motion and fibre – the timber – the portion of your energy devoted to your physical experience. Now it flows into what you are as a physical being and materializes you in the world of seasons, space, flesh, and time. Its source, however, is quite independent of the world that you know.

Once you learn to get the feeling of your own inner tone, then you are aware of its power, strength and durability, and you can to some extent ride with it into deeper realities of experience.

The incredible emotional richness and variety and splendour of physical experience is the material reflection of this inner feeling-tone. It pervades the events in your life, the overall inner direction, the quality of perception. It fills up and illuminates the individual aspects of your life, and largely determines the persuasive subjective climate in which you dwell.

It is the essence of yourself. Its sweeps are broad in range, however. It does not determine, for example, specific events. It paints the colours in the large 'landscape' of your experience. It is the *feeling* of yourself, inexhaustible.

In other terms it represents the expression of yourself in pure energy, from which your individuality rises, the You of you, unmistakably given identity that is never duplicated.

This energy comes from the core of BEING (in capital letters), from All That Is (with our usual capitals), and represents the source of never-ending vitality. It is Being, Being in You. As such, all of the energy and power of Being is focused and reflected through you in the direction of your three-dimensional existence.

You may take your break.

While your feeling-tone is uniquely yours, still it is expressed in a certain fashion that is shared by all consciousnesses focused in physical reality. So in those terms you spring from the earth as all the other creatures and natural living structures. You are, while physical, a portion of nature, therefore, not apart from it.

Trees and rocks possess their own consciousness, and also share a gestalt consciousness, even as the living portions of your body. The cells and organs have their own awarenesses, and a gestalt one. So the race of man also has individual consciousness and a gestalt or mass consciousness, of which you individually are hardly aware.

The mass race consciousness, in its terms, possesses an identity. You are a portion of that identity while still being unique, individual and independent. You are confined only to the extent that you have chosen physical reality, and so placed yourself within its context of experience. While physical, you follow physical laws, or assumptions. These form the framework for corporeal expression.

Within this framework you have full freedom to create your experience, your personal life in all of its aspects, the living picture of the world. Your personal life, and to some extent your individual living experience, help create the world as it is known in your time. [. . .]

You breathe, grow, and perform multitudinous delicate and precise activities constantly, without being consciously aware of how you carry out such manipulations. You live without consciously knowing how you maintain this miracle of physical awareness in the world of flesh and time.

The seemingly unconscious portions of yourself draw atoms and molecules from the air to form your image. Your lips move, your tongue speaks your name. Does the name belong to the atoms and molecules within your lips or tongue? The atoms and molecules move constantly, forming into cells, tissues and organs. How can the name the tongue speaks belong to them?

They do not read or write, yet they speak complicated syllables that communicate to other beings such as yourself anything from a simple feeling to the most complicated information. How do they do this?

The atoms and molecules of the tongue do not know the syntax of the language they speak. When you begin a sentence you do not have the slightest conscious idea, often, of how you will finish it, yet you take it on faith that the words will make sense, and your meaning will flow out effortlessly.

All of this happens because the inner portions of your being operate spontaneously, joyfully, freely; all of this occurs because your inner self believes in you, often even while you do not believe in it. These unconscious portions of your being operate amazingly well, frequently despite the greatest misunderstanding on your part of their nature and function, and in the face of strong interference from you because of your beliefs.

Each person experiences a unique reality, different from any other individual's. This reality springs outward from the inner landscape of thoughts, feelings, expectations and beliefs. If you believe that the inner self works against you rather than for you, then you hamper its functioning – or rather, you force it to behave in a certain way because of your beliefs.

The conscious mind is meant to make clear judgements about your position in physical reality. Often false beliefs will prevent it from making these, for the egotistically held ideas will cloud its clear vision.
[. . .]

Your beliefs can be like fences that surround you.

You must first recognize the existence of such barriers – you must see them or you will not even realize that you are not free, simply because you will not see beyond the fences. They will represent the boundaries of your experience.

There is one belief, however, that destroys artificial barriers to perception, an expanding belief that automatically pierces false and inhibiting ideas.

The Self Is Not Limited.

That statement is a statement of fact. It exists regardless of your belief or disbelief in it. Following this concept is another:

There Are No Boundaries or Separations of the Self.

Those that you experience are the result of false beliefs. Following this is the idea that I have already mentioned:

You Make Your Own Reality.

To understand yourself and what you are, you can learn to experience yourself directly apart from your beliefs about yourself. What I would like each reader to do is to sit quietly. Close your eyes. Try to sense within yourself the deep feeling-tones that I mentioned earlier. This is not difficult to do.

Your knowledge of their existence will help you recognize their deep rhythms within you. Each individual will sense these tones in his or her own way, so do not worry about how they should feel. Simply tell yourself that they exist, that they are composed of the great energies of your being made flesh.

Then let yourself experience. If you are used to terms like meditation, try to forget the term during this procedure. Do not use any name. Free yourself from concepts, and experience the being of yourself and the motion of your own vitality. Do not question, 'Is this right? Am I doing it correctly? Am I feeling what I should feel?' This is the book's first exercise for you. You are not to use other people's criteria. There are no standards but your own feelings.

No particular time limit is recommended. This should be an enjoyable experience. Accept whatever happens as uniquely your own. The exercise will put you in touch with yourself. It will return you to yourself. Whenever you are nervous or upset, take a few moments to sense this feeling-tone within you, and you will find yourself centred in your own being, secure.

When you have tried this exercise several times, then feel these deep rhythms go out from you in all directions, as indeed they do. Electromagnetically they radiate out through your physical being; and in ways that I hope to explain later, they form the environment that you know even as they form your physical image.

I told you that the self was not limited, yet surely you think that your self stops where your skin meets space, that you are inside your skin. Period. Yet your environment is an extension of your self. It is the body of your experience, coalesced in physical form. The inner self forms the objects that you know as surely and automatically as it forms your finger or your eye.

Your environment is the physical picture of your thoughts, emotions and beliefs made visible. Since your thoughts, emotions and beliefs move through space and time, you therefore affect physical conditions separate from you.

Consider the spectacular framework of your body just from the physical standpoint. You perceive it as solid, as you perceive all other physical matter; yet the more matter is explored the more obvious it becomes that within it energy takes on specific shape (in the form of organs, cells, molecules, atoms, electrons), each less physical than the last, each combining in mysterious gestalt to form matter.

The atoms within your body spin. There is constant commotion and activity. The flesh that seemed so solid turns out to be composed of swiftly moving particles – often orbiting each other – in which great exchanges of energy continually occur.

The stuff, the space outside of your body, is composed of the same elements, but in different proportions. There is a constant physical interchange between the structure you call your body and the space outside it; chemical interactions, basic exchanges without which life as you know it would be impossible.

To hold your breath is to die. Breath, which represents the most intimate and most necessary of your physical sensations, must flow out from what you are, passing into the world that seems to be not you. Physically, portions of you leave your body constantly and intermix with the elements. You know what happens when adrenalin

373

is released through the bloodstream. It stirs you up and prepares you for action. But in other ways the adrenalin does not just stay in your body. It is cast into the air and it affects the atmosphere, though it is transformed.

Any of your emotions liberate hormones, but these also leave you as your breath leaves you; and in that respect you can say that you release chemicals into the air that then affect it.

Physical storms, then, are caused by such interactions. I am telling you that you form your own reality once again, and this includes the physical weather – which is the result, *en masse*, of your individual reactions.

I will elaborate much more specifically on this particular point later in the book. You are in physical existence to learn and understand that your energy, translated into feelings, thoughts and emotions, causes *all* experience. *There are no exceptions.*

References

New Science

Science as Mysticism
FRITJOF CAPRA *The Tao of Physics*
1 F. Hoyle, *Frontiers of Astronomy* (Heinemann, London, 1970), 304.
2 Quoted in M. Capek, *The Philosophical Impact of Contemporary Physics* (D. Van Nostrand, Princeton, New Jersey, 1961), 319.

A Quantum Model of Consciousness
DANAH ZOHAR *The Quantum Self*
1 David Bohm, *Quantum Theory*, 169.
2 'Imagine that the "vacuum" in which we live is analogous to a "weak *superconductor*" . . .' *The Quantum Universe*, 151. Also, 'A Theory of the vacuum', 7.
3 I. N. Marshall, *Excitations of a Bose-Einstein Condensate*.
4 Pierre Teilhard de Chardin, *The Phenomenon of Man*.
5 John B. Cobb, in David Ray Griffin, *Process Theology: An Introductory Exposition*, 1976.
6 Pierre Teilhard de Chardin, *The Phenomenon of Man*.
7 C. G. Jung, *Memories, Dreams, Reflections*, 236–7.
8 Stephen Hawking, *A Brief History of Time*, 175.

Psychology

Orgasm and Body Armour
WILLIAM REICH *The Function of the Orgasm*
1 Cf. Reich, *Psychischer Kontakt und vegetative Strömung*, 1934; and *Orgasmusreflex, Muskelhaltung und Körperausdruck*, Sexpol Verlag, 1937.

Gaia – The Living Earth

The Politics of Ecology
JONATHON PORRITT *Seeing Green*
1 Elgin, *Voluntary Simplicity*, 160.
2 R. H. Tawney, *The Acquisitive Society* (Penguin, Harmondsworth, 1921).
3 Brown, *Building a Sustainable Society*, 349.
4 Tom Bender, 'Why We Need to Get Poor Quick', *Futurist*, August 1977.
5 Skolimowski, *Economics Today: What Do We Need?*, 15.
6 Simple Living Collective of San Francisco, *Taking Charge* (Bantam, New York, 1977).
7 Barry Commoner, *The Closing Circle* (Alfred A. Knopf, New York, 1971), 292.
8 Erik Dammann, *The Future in Our Hands* (Pergamon Press, Oxford, 1979), 167.
9 Fritjof Capra, *The Turning Point*, 18.

Buddhist Ecology
E. F. SCHUMACHER *Small is Beautiful*
1 Richard B. Gregg, *A Philosophy of Indian Economic Development* (Navaji-van Publishing House, Ahmedabad, 1958).

Beyond the Information Age
HAZEL HENDERSON *Paradigms in Progress*
1 *Business Week*, 3 June 1991.
2 Eric K. Drexler, *Energies of Creation* (Doubleday, New York, 1986).
3 *Business Week*, 'Creating Chips an Atom at a Time', 29 July 1991, 54.
4 Ilya Prigogine, *From Being to Becoming* (H. H. Freeman, San Francisco, 1980).

Feminism and the Goddess

Feminism and Witchcraft
STARHAWK *The Spiral Dance*
1 Herb Goldberg, *The Hazards of Being Male* (Signet, New York, 1977), 4.
2 Goldberg, 39.

Women's Psychology
MARION WOODMAN *The Pregnant Virgin*
1 John Keats, Letter to George and Georgiana Keats (21 April 1819), quoted in David Perkins, ed., *English Romantic Writers* (Harcourt Brace Jovanovich, New York, 1967), 1225.

2 Thomas H. Johnson, ed., *The Complete Poems of Emily Dickinson* (Little, Brown and Company, Boston, 1960), number 508, 247.

3 The term *puer aeternus* (Latin, 'eternal youth') refers to the type of man who remains too long in adolescent psychology, generally associated with a strong unconscious attachment to the mother (actual or symbolic). His female counterpart is the *puella aeterna*, an 'eternal girl' with a corresponding attachment to the father world.

Gyn/Ecology

MARY DALY *Gyn/Ecology – The Metaethics of Radical Feminism*

1 Conversation with Jane Caputi, Boston, May 1977.

2 See Robert Graves, *The Greek Myths* (Penguin Books, Baltimore, MD.), I, 24 o-m.

3 Virginia Woolf, *Three Guineas* (Harcourt Brace, New York, 1938), 36.

Mystic and Esoteric Religion

The Mystic Experience

WILLIAM JAMES *The Varieties of Religious Experience*

1 Newman's *Securus judicat orbis terrarum* is another instance.

2 'Mesopotamia' is the stock comic instance. An excellent old German lady, who had done some travelling in her day, used to describe to me her *Sehnsucht* that she might yet visit 'Philadelphia', whose wondrous name had always haunted her imagination. Of John Foster it is said that single words (as *chalcedony*), or the names of ancient heroes, had a mighty fascination over him. At any time the word *hermit* was enough to transport him. The words *woods* and *forests* would produce the most powerful emotion. *Foster's Life*, by RYLAND, New York, 1846, p. 3.

3 'The Two Voices'. In a letter to Mr B. P. Blood, Tennyson reports of himself as follows:

I have never had any revelations through anæsthetics, but a kind of waking trance – this for lack of a better word – I have frequently had, quite up from boyhood, when I have been all alone. This has come upon me through repeating my own name to myself silently, till all at once, as it were out of the intensity of the consciousness of individuality, individuality itself seemed to dissolve and fade away into boundless being, and this not a confused state but the clearest, the surest of the surest, utterly beyond words – where death was an almost laughable impossibility – the loss of personality (if so it were) seeming no extinction, but the only true life. I am ashamed of my feeble description. Have I not said the state is utterly beyond words?

Professor Tyndall, in a letter, recalls Tennyson saying of this condition: 'By God Almighty! there is no delusion in the matter! It is no nebulous ecstasy, but a state of transcendent wonder, associated with absolute clearness of mind.' *Memoirs of Alfred Tennyson*, ii. 473.

4 *The Lancet*, 6 and 13 July, 1895, reprinted as the Cavendish Lecture, on Dreamy Mental States, London, Baillière, 1895. See, for example, BERNARD-LEROY: *L'Illusion de fausse reconnaissance*, Paris, 1898.

5 Charles Kingsley's *Life*, i. 55, quoted by INGE: Christian Mysticism, London, 1899, p. 341.

Gnostic Christianity
ELAINE PAGELS *The Gnostic Gospels*

1 John 14:5–6.

2 Irenaeus, AH 3.11.7. For discussion, see E. Pagels, *The Johanine Gospel in Gnostic Exegesis* (Nashville, 1973).

3 *Dialogue of the Saviour* 142. 16–19, in NHL 237.

4 *Gospel of Thomas* 38.4–10, in NHL 121.

5 F. Wise, 'Gnosticism and Early Monasticism in Egypt', in *Gnosis: Festschrift für Hans Jonas* (Göttingen, 1978), 431–40.

6 B. Layton, ed., *The Rediscovery of Gnosticism*.

7 Irenaeus, AH 4.11.2

8 *Ibid.*, 4.11.2.

9 Justin Martyr, *Dialogue with Trypho*, 4.

10 Gospel of Philip 71.35–7.4, in NHL 143.

11 Irenaeus, AH 1.11.1.

12 *Ibid.*, 1.12.3.

13 *Ibid.*, 1.12.3.

14 *Ibid.*, 1.12.4.

15 *Ibid.*, 1.30.6.

The Book of Changes
RICHARD WILHELM *The I Ching*

1 [Second half of fifth century BC]

2 [551–479 BC]

3 *Lun Yü*, IX, 16. [This book comprises conversations of Confucius and his disciples.]

4 [Here, as throughout the book, Wilhelm uses the German word *Sinn* ('meaning') in capitals (*SINN*) for the Chinese word *tao*. The reasons that led Wilhelm to choose *SINN* to represent *tao* (see p. XIV of the introduction to his translation of Lao-tse: *Tao Te King: Das Buch des Alten von Sinn und Leben*, 3rd edn., Düsseldorf and Cologne, 1952) have no relation to the

English word 'meaning'. Therefore in the English rendering, 'tao' has been used wherever *SINN* occurs.]

5 [Known as *t'ai chi t'u*, 'the supreme ultimate'. See R. Wilhelm, *A Short History of Chinese Civilization*, tr. by J. Joshua (London, 1929), p. 249.]

6 Cf. the noteworthy discussions of Liang Ch'i-ch'ao in the Chinese journal *The Endeavor*, 15 and 22 July, 1923, also the English essay by B. Schindler, 'The Development of the Chinese Conceptions of Supreme Beings', *Asia Major*, Hirth Anniversary Volume (Probsthain, London, n.d.), pp. 298–366.

7 Cf. the extremely important discussions of Hu Shih in *The Development of the Logical Method in Ancient China* (2nd edn., Paragon, New York, 1963), and the even more detailed discussion in the first volume of his history of philosophy [*Chung-kuo che-hsüeh-shih ta-kang*; not available in translation].

Modern Prophesy

The Evolution of Human Consciousness

PIERRE TEILHARD DE CHARDIN *The Phenomenon of Man*

1 The same 'common sense' which has again and again been corrected beyond all question by physics.

Permissions

Every effort has been made to trace or contact all copyright holders. The publishers would be pleased to rectify any omissions brought to their notice at the earliest opportunity.

MARGO ANAND: from *The Art of Sexual Ecstasy* (Jeremy P. Tarcher, 1989/ The Aquarian Press, 1990), © Margo Anand (a.k.a. M. E. Naslednikov) 1989; ANONYMOUS: from *A Course in Miracles* (Routledge & Kegan Paul, Inc. in association with Methuen, Inc., 1975/Arkana, 1985), © 1975, 1999, reprinted by permission of the Foundation for *A Course in Miracles*, 1275 Tennanah Lake Road, Roscoe, NY 12776-5905; ROBERTO ASSAGIOLI: from *Psychosynthesis: A Manual of Principles and Techniques* (Hobbs, Dorman & Company, 1965/Viking, 1971), © 1965 by Psychosynthesis Research Foundation; SRI AUROBINDO: from *The Life Divine* (Sri Aurobindo International, 1955), reprinted by permission of the Sri Aurobindo Ashram Trust; ALICE BAILEY: from *Esoteric Healing. Volume IV: A Treatise on the Seven Rays* (Lucis Press, 1953), © 1953 by Lucis Trust, reprinted by permission of the Lucis Trust; ITZHAK BENTOV: from *Stalking the Wild Pendulum: On the Mechanics of Consciousness* (Destiny Books, an imprint of Inner Traditions International, Rochester, VT 05767, 1988), © 1977 Itzhak Bentov, © 1988 Mirtala Bentov, reprinted by permission of the publisher; DAVID BOHM: from *Wholeness and the Implicate Order* (Routledge & Kegan Paul, 1980), © David Bohm, 1980, reprinted by permission of the publisher; THE BOSTON WOMEN'S HEALTH COLLECTIVE: from *Our Bodies Ourselves* (Penguin, 1978), © The Boston Women's Health Collective, Inc., 1971, 1973, 1976, new material for British edition copyright © Angela Phillips and Jill Rakusen; EDWARD ESPE BROWN: 'Baking Bread' from *Tassajara Bread Book* (Shambhala Publications, 1970), © 1970 by the Chief Priest, Zen Center, San Francisco; FRITJOF CAPRA: from *The Tao of Physics* (Wildwood House, 1975/Flamingo, 1983), © Fritjof Capra 1975, 1983, 1991; CARLOS CASTANEDA: from *The Teachings of Don Juan: A Yaqui Way of Knowledge*. Thirtieth Anniversary Edition (University of California Press, 1968/Penguin, 1970), © 1968 The Regents of the University of California, © renewed 1996 Carlos Castaneda, reprinted by permission of the University of California Press; PIERRE TEILHARD DE CHARDIN:

Index

Numbers in italics indicate figures; those in bold indicate authors of chapters.